Post Wa

tasc *at* NEW ISLAND publications to date

For Richer, For Poorer
An Investigation of the Irish Pension System
edited by Jim Stewart, tasc at New Island, 2005

An Outburst of Frankness
Community Arts in Ireland – A Reader
edited by Sandy Fitzgerald, tasc at New Island, 2004

Selling Out? Privatisation in Ireland
by Paul Sweeney,
tasc at New Island, 2004

After the Ball
by Fintan O'Toole,
tasc at New Island, 2003

POST WASHINGTON

Why America Can't Rule the World

Tony Kinsella

&

Fintan O'Toole

POST WASHINGTON
First published 2005
by tasc at New Island
an imprint of New Island
2 Brookside
Dundrum Road
Dublin 14

www.newisland.ie

The authors have asserted their moral rights.

ISBN 1 904301 86 X

British Library Cataloguing in Publication Data.
A CIP catalogue record for this book is available
from the British Library.

Typeset by New Island
Cover and layout design by Public Communications Centre
Printed in the UK by CPD, Ebbw Vale, Wales

CONTENTS

We dedicate this book to the Clares: our partners Clare Doyle and Clare Connell, without whose support, encouragement and tolerance it would never have seen the light of day. The next generation: Rory and Ciarán Oliver; Sam and Fionn O'Toole, who will have to help make sense of our Post Washington world, also deserve a special mention.

Many people have helped make *Post Washington* possible: Paula Clancy and all at tasc; Edwin Higel, Deirdre Nolan and the professionals of New Island. Special thanks are due to Professor John Belchem of the University of Liverpool and his wife Mary. (*Post Washington* was conceived on the banks of the Mersey in 2002 when we responded to John's invitation to lecture at the University's Centre of Irish Studies.) Ralph and Gay Murphy, Walter Borton and Ann Jones offered encouragement, support and criticism; Caroline Swain the final proofreading. They, and many others, deserve our heartfelt thanks.

The arguments, and any errors, are ours – and ours alone.

Tony Kinsella and Fintan O'Toole
May 2005

Superman and the Krypton Factor

'While the storm clouds gather far across the sea,
Let us swear allegiance to a land that's free,
Let us all be grateful for a land so fair,
As we raise our voices in a solemn prayer.'
— Irving Berlin, 'God Bless America'

'The attitudes of Superman to current social problems...reflect
the strong-arm totalitarian methods of the immature and barbaric
mind...Superman is ruthlessly efficient in carrying on a one-man
crusade against crooks and anti-social forces [without] appeal to
the process of law. Justice is represented as an affair of personal
strength alone ... [He] seems to embody a mounting impatience
with the laborious processes of civilised life and a restless
eagerness to embrace violent solutions.'
— Marshall McLuhan, *The Mechanical Bride*[1]

At the heart of the world lies a unique country, the
United States of America. A country that blends influences and peoples from every corner of the globe. A
state that is not only the most militarily powerful in the
world, but the most militarily powerful the world has
ever known. A recently constructed nation whose
stories and images are now interwoven with the
cultures of every other country in the world. A land
whose glamour creates a glint in the eyes of people who
will never be able to go there, whose allure attracts

millions of legal and illegal migrants every year. It is therefore a nation that has a duty to lead the world into a brighter tomorrow, one modelled closely, or exclusively, on its achievements. The rest of our world has somehow lost its way, and in extreme cases must be redeemed through the use of a stern but just application of American force. The US, and the US alone, has the courage and the ability to deploy such force. Our future thus lies in a US Imperium, a Pax Americana.

These assumptions have their roots in reality. The US *is* a unique, and in many respects a wonderful, country. It is the largest military, economic and cultural power in history, it exercises an influence on the world's destiny that is hugely disproportionate to the size of its population and we have inherited an ad hoc system of global management which depends, largely by default, on Washington. Whether or not this is a desirable state of affairs is normally presented as a question of choice.

Our central argument is that it is not a question of choice. We argue that the United States of America is incapable of maintaining its dominant position in the world.

Economic development and innovation have always been, and are likely to remain, the primary motors of social and political change. Today's US economy is extraordinarily fragile in a number of important ways. There are three very distinct branches of US business. One is made up of world-beating corporations developing and selling products across the globe. Another is largely composed of hollowed-out corporations where long-term success has been sacrificed to maximise short-term profit. The third sector is made up of defence-dependent, almost nationalised, industries with the US government as their primary client. By looking only at the first sector, it is easy to assume that the US economy is invincible. When the other two come into the picture, a much more unstable and insecure system becomes visible.

US agriculture can be described as a disaster waiting to happen in terms of its over-concentration, its industrialised, high-volume/low-margin structure and its dependence both on public subsidies and on an ever-narrowing range of plant and animal varieties.

The US has become a less open, less socially mobile society, with an ever-widening gap between a rich elite and the rest of society. While the US can boast some of the best hospitals and universities in the world, access to them is ever more dependent on family wealth. For many, the American Dream is moving from attainable reality to tantalising myth. Soon the very dream itself may become impossible.

As a stand-alone nation the US cannot afford the armed forces it has, much less the ones it is currently seeking to develop. Nor can it sustain its level of public and private debt. Inexorably, at a certain point, reality must intrude. In the harsh light of that reality, the dream of a Pax Americana will evaporate.

Without undertaking substantial and fundamental reform the US cannot continue to either maintain its standards of living or its armed forces. The organisation of US politics, the focus of the US media and the US Constitution all combine to inhibit debate about the necessity of such reforms, never mind allowing for any consideration of their content.

The US system cannot continue. At the moment it seems incapable of even recognising the need for change. Sooner or later, without serious structural reform, it will collapse into crisis. The policies of the George W. Bush administration are bringing such a collapse ever nearer. This breakdown may be dramatic. More probably, it will be incremental. We argue that it is now inevitable.

Our world order with Washington at its centre is therefore unsustainable.

From Siegfried to Superman

Myths are an important part of life. Personal, family, national and even international myths all help to shape our view of the world. Although we recognise some myths for what they are, we continue to draw comfort from them.

3

Stories that once had an immediate function slowly enter the realm of mythology and become essentially harmless. New Yorkers can daydream about the Wild West, Londoners about Arthur's Camelot and Dubliners about Fionn MacCumhail and his band of warriors. Indeed, since whatever kernel of truth that once lay at the heart of these myths has long vanished under layers of romantic embellishment, it is just as easy, and perhaps just as harmless, for the Dubliner to be a Wild West outlaw and the New Yorker to be a Celtic warrior. Myths become dangerous when they approach the frontier of knowledge. Once myth and knowledge become confused, almost anything can be justified.

Myth-making had a long, and often vicious, vogue in Europe. As Prussia built the German Empire during the nineteenth century, a sense of Germanness became essential. The emerging German state was careful to construct it, plunging back into half-remembered popular legends of Siegfried to 'prove' a continuum between the past and the present. The French Second Empire then excavated Vercingetorix, Victorian Britain dug up Camelot, Belgium found Ambiorix and the new Italian state claimed the Roman Empire. An Italian deputy speaking in the first Italian Parliament pointed out: 'We have made Italy, now we have to make Italians.'[2] These reinvigorated myths validated the national existence and distinguished each nation from its neighbour.

Myths have the added advantage of discharging us from any responsibility. Reality is something we should examine, seek to influence and alter, whereas myths cannot be questioned – they come to us whole. Details can perhaps be altered, but the essence is presented on a take-it-or-leave-it basis.

If we cannot question something, then we cannot learn from it. In the cradle of democracy of ancient Athens, Socrates argued that questions should be used to establish people's beliefs and values. Argument could then be developed by presenting counter-examples, leading to a deeper understanding. If we

4

accept myth rather than reality, then we cannot explore the arguments and cannot analyse the information, deepen our knowledge and emerge with a reasoned decision. Without a reasonable grasp of reality, we cannot expand our understanding. If we cannot expand our understanding, we risk repeating past mistakes – 'those who cannot remember the past are condemned to repeat it'[3] – and those who cannot forget the national myths that once sustained their hopes are trapped within them.

Romantic nationalism and its facile myths provided one of the explosive elements which were to collectively plunge Europe into two world wars within half a century, killing over 60 million people. The two world wars resulted in more than a million war deaths a year between 1900 and 1945 – over two people per minute were killed every minute for 45 years. That's the expensive price tag for competitive nationalist mythologies. It would be reassuring to believe that such expensive mistakes belong in our collective past, that we citizens of the twenty-first century – children of television, radio and the Internet – are not likely to once again become prisoners of poisonous myths.

Until quite recently there were grounds for such optimism. The Cold War, which had dominated our planet for almost half a century and threatened it with nuclear destruction, had come to a peaceful end. The once-warring nations of Europe were slowly, painfully and tediously creating a new polity, the European Union, within which their national myths and tensions could play out peacefully and prosperously and, at worst, be bored into extinction by the routine business of getting on with the governance of an extremely diverse continent.

On the world stage, almost 200 sovereign nation-states were finding common ground to address global issues of trade, justice, sustainable development, human rights, the environment, health and myriad other issues. Our species's first real attempt at global order, the United Nations, was exchanging the ill-fitting dentures

5

of the Cold War for real teeth – milk teeth perhaps, but teeth all the same.

Yet the optimism that followed the end of the Cold War was short lived. The resurgence of appalling political barbarism in Yugoslavia, Rwanda, the Congo and Chechnya presented a challenge that the global order could not meet. People in developed countries had a new experience – televised mass murder, live and in colour, reported via satellite in real time. The gap between what we knew and what we could affect seemed larger than at any time in history. Collective responses were pitifully inadequate and collective processes were discredited. So when another episode of mass murder was played out live on our screens on 11 September 2001, the resort to unilateral violence was almost automatic. Yet that response itself was saturated in a sense of futility.

The ability even of the US, the world's great, charismatic and indefatigable power, to shape the world to its desires was shown to be at best severely limited. The myths of romantic nationalism – the clash of civilisations, god's chosen people against the evildoers, progress against barbarism – were mobilised and restored to a central place in world politics. McLuhan's description of Superman, the great American mythic hero – its Siegfried or King Arthur – at the head of this chapter, written in the early 1950s, could be taken with a few minor changes as a description of the posture of the Bush administration over Iraq. But even Superman could not take a country apart and put it back together again in line with instructions from Washington. US twenty-first-century myths proved to be no more useful than their counterparts had been in early twentieth-century Europe.

One of the differences between the US and most of the rest of the developed world is that the US is less disillusioned. The sense of destiny is more intact. Most of the emerging nation-states of the nineteenth century conceived of themselves as being uniquely chosen. They argued for their own distinctiveness on the basis not just of ethnic or linguistic differences, but of a great mission that had been given to them by god or fate or history. They had a special destiny – to save Christianity, to raise up the savages, to hold on to an inherited purity, to enlighten the world and so on. For most, that aura of destiny was scoured away by the viciousness of twentieth-century history. They came to understand, usually through the agency of shame, that they were no better than common humanity after all. The disgrace of atrocity (in the case of Germany, Italy and Japan), the disgrace of Empire (Britain, France) the collapse of millenarian communism (Russia) and/or the experience of defeat (France, Germany, Italy, Japan) brought a rude awakening from the dreams of national destiny.

America is exceptional. It shared the mood of the nineteenth century. Manifest Destiny – a phrase used by leaders and politicians in the 1840s to explain continental expansion by the US – revitalised a sense of 'mission' or national vocation for Americans. The people of the US were told that it was their mission to extend the 'boundaries of freedom' to others by imparting their idealism and belief in democratic institutions to those who were capable of self-government. It excluded those people who were perceived as being incapable of self-government, such as Native American people and those of non-European origin. Instead of being worn down by bitter experience, this sense of destiny was hugely reinforced in the twentieth century by victory in the two world wars.

It ought to have come to an end in the paddy fields and city streets of Vietnam, where the US experienced the two things that had disillusioned much of the rest of the world – defeat and shame, the realisation that you are not chosen by god to be invincible and the even more painful awareness that you are capable of savagery and degradation. But even though Vietnam still looms large in American public life, it has not been a powerful enough force to defuse Manifest Destiny once and for all.

There are three obvious reasons for this. One is that for a powerful faction of US culture, including those who are currently in power, Vietnam is seen not as an external defeat but as an internal one. America was laid low not by the Viet Cong, but by the enemy within – the corrupt, pot-smoking children of the Sixties who sapped the nation's morale and who must be punished for their apostasy. A second is that the US's sense of a special destiny is constantly reinforced from without – much of the rest of the world has the habit of continually looking to America for salvation. A third is that American culture was, and still is, shaped by a religious mindset in which god's special plan for each individual is easily converted into a collective sense of sacred fate.

A key aspect of this notion of destiny and of America's most persistent and cherished myth is its sense of its own essential innocence. In its collective imagination, the US is by definition a force for good, on the side of light against darkness, of truth against lies, of civility against barbarism. Yet even as its adventure in Iraq was beginning to unravel, detailed evidence of the capacity of ordinary Americans to commit atrocities in uniform was emerging. The unit in Iraq that most stirred patriotic pride was the 101st Airborne. While it was struggling with insurgency in Iraq in October 2003, the *Toledo Blade* newspaper published a detailed investigation into the activities of an elite group within the 101st Airborne during the Vietnam War. It discovered that an army inquiry conducted in 1974 had concluded that at least 18 Tiger Force soldiers committed war crimes in 1967, but nothing was ever publicly disclosed, no charges were filed and the documents had remained classified.

The statements of witnesses before the inquiry were a matter-of-fact account of the descent into extreme cruelty of kids who had started out as normal young Americans. Typical was the statement of James R. Barnett:

> Our entire element then moved out from there with the two women and the baby, and we went about 200 to 300 metres and stopped at another hooch. Myself, [Sgt. Harold] Trout and three others then took the two women and the child inside…I saw that Trout and the woman went down into the bunker inside the building. After about five

minutes or a little longer Trout appeared from the hooch
by himself and mentioned something to the effect that 'this
was pretty good stuff'. In other words he was insinuating
that he had screwed her. After another couple of hours
Trout came out of the hooch again and told me that I was
going to have to kill that woman...I asked Trout at this
point if he was sure that this was what he wanted to do and
he replied 'Grease her.' The term 'greasing' was one of
Trout's favourite expressions...I took my M-16 rifle and
pointed it at her and then shot her in the chest. She fell over
and I turned around and saw that Trout was behind me
and had seen the whole thing. We left her lying there and
joined the rest of the element.
Why did you shoot that woman, Mr Barnett?
Because I was told by Trout to do it and I carried out what
he told me.[4]

The publication of these statements and the un-
controverted evidence of war crimes by US soldiers
ought to have caused at least some debate in the context
of a new US war in Asia, especially since there was an
increasing number of reports of US troops killing
civilians in Iraq. But the conjunction of myth and reality
was perhaps too sharp to be assimilated into American
domestic discourse. It was as if the unbesmirched
valour of the 101st Airborne was the hard fact and the
documents emerging from the archives were the mythic
fantasies. The very idea that something could be learned
from the degradation of America's finest values in the
conduct of war was almost literally unthinkable.

At the beginning of our twenty-first century, we
must now examine where myth ends and reality
begins. How do we organise our world? How do we
decide whether our accepted norms are sustainable –
or even reliable? Are we chugging along on essentially
the right road, or shuffling steadily towards disaster?

At the centre of any such examination of our world
stands one dominant entity – the United States of America. Myth and reality meet, mingle and occasionally
collide in that amazing country, as it is seen by its
citizens, by its friends and by its enemies.

What is the United States of America? Can we
distinguish American myth from global reality? How
does such a distinction inform us?

American Myth and Global Reality

We all know the United States of America – or at least
we feel we do. Every foreign visitor to the US is struck
by a powerful feeling of déja vu. We have all seen the
Manhattan skyline, the road signs, the Washington
monument, the police cars, the taxis and the clothes
thousands, if not millions, of times on our televisions
and in our cinemas. We have read the books and
magazines and increasingly visited the websites. The
US is partly 'home' to us all, even if we have never set
foot in the country.

That in itself is a powerful mark of the centrality of
the US to our world. Other sights and landmarks may
be familiar – red double-decker buses in London, the
Eiffel Tower in Paris, the pyramids outside Cairo – but
they are icons of abroad, not emblems of 'home'.

English, but primarily the US variant of it, has
become a universal language as none before. A Parisian
travels to Minsk to meet his Belorussian bride. Not only
do they communicate in English, but it seems perfectly
normal that they should do so.

This book is being typed on a computer manufactured
by a US company, using software designed by another
US company. This is 'Dog Bites Man', common news. It
would be unusual to report anything different.

We have witnessed the US reach out, almost alone,
project an army halfway round the world and physically conquer a country of 24 million people roughly
the size of France in less than a month. The surprises of
the 2003 Iraq War come not from the US victory, but
from the degree of resistance offered to both the invasion and the subsequent occupation. That we are
surprised at the resistance speaks volumes for the place
the US occupies in our mental tables of world power.

Instinctively we see the US as the biggest, wealthiest, most dynamic and most powerful nation in the world, therefore it must lie at the heart of any world order. But is the US the biggest, the wealthiest and the most powerful? Well, it is and it isn't.

At 9.4 million square kilometres the US is the fourth-largest country in the world, after Russia, Canada and China. With a population of around 280 million, it comes third behind China and India – fourth if you count the European Union as a single entity. Such figures are interesting but not overly informative. Greenland may well be the globe's biggest island, but only a fraction of it is habitable.[5]

In terms of gross domestic product (GDP) per capita, the US comes third once again, behind Luxembourg and Norway, and is one of 17 countries with a GDP per capita over $25,000.[6] In other words, while the US definitely plays in the Premier League, it is really only one of the teams in that league, albeit an important one. The US has just under 5 per cent of the global population, but just over 25 per cent of the world's wealth and it accounts for 23.1 per cent of world imports and 16.3 per cent of world exports.[7]

When it comes to military power, the comparisons are as clear, and confusing, as the following tables show.[8]

Table 1.1: Defence Headline Figure Comparisons

Country	Defence Budget 2002 (€, bn)	Troops	Tanks	Combat Aircraft
France	37.4	281,872	1,960	430
Germany	30.6	338,000	2,800	369
UK	46.2	248,526	616	366
US	349	1,365,800	7,900	2,835

Table 1.2: US–EU Defence Comparisons

Polity	Defence Budget 2002 (€, bn)	Troops	Tanks	Combat Aircraft
EU	180.7	1,977,461	13,367	3,099
US	349	1,365,800	7,900	2,835

These are crude general figures, offered to paint a general picture rather than a description of the operational effectiveness of different services and weapons.

At $396 billion, the US military budget for 2003 was more than six times larger than that of Russia, the second-largest spender, and is more than the combined spending of the next 25 nations.[9] The projected US expenditure on national defence for 2005 amounts to $500 billion.[10] The $48 billion increase in US defence spending for 2003 was in itself greater than the defence budget of most other nation-states.

So what does all that tell us? In marketing terms, the US has two major selling points. Firstly, it spends more on its military than any other nation. Secondly, what can broadly be described as its culture, particularly its business culture, serves as a semi-universal model, or benchmark. This culture has become a benchmark because others believe in its success. Should that belief be seriously shaken, the US's power status would come to depend uniquely on its military spending. Interestingly, that was the status of the USSR – before it collapsed.

Not Just Another Empire

We are reassured by familiarity and unsettled by the novel. Many are comforted by seeing US power, and the influence that goes with it, as simply a successor to earlier empires such as the British, or more fancifully, the Roman. US power is different and without precedent in human history. It is global in a way no other power has ever been. It is virtual in that it hardly possesses any external territories. All earlier empires were physical, regional or specialised.

The early empires of the eastern Mediterranean and Middle East that flourished following the discovery of agriculture (Assyrian, Babylonian, Hittite, Persian and Egyptian) were all regional powers, significant or dominant players in one corner of the world. So was the Roman Empire. At its zenith it stretched from the Irish to the Caspian Seas, but it coexisted with the Indian Gupta and the Chinese Han Empires. While there is evidence of trade and other exchanges between those empires, they not only posed no threat to each other, they were physically and technologically incapable of posing such a threat. The Roman Legions could not physically be deployed to China. Even if Rome had shipped its legions halfway around the world to China, they would have been confronted by an army their technological equal.

The Meso-American civilisations (Olmec and Zapotec) and the Andean precursors of the Inca civilisation were also regional, incapable of posing a commercial or military threat to their Roman, Indian or Chinese contemporaries.

In short, all human political history involves what were either regional powers or powers with particular strengths (the Russian Empire had an enormous army but no real navy, while the British Empire was primarily a naval power with a small army). Europe's late nineteenth-century empires were all more or less evenly matched militarily, as the stalemate and carnage of World War One were to demonstrate.

US Power and US Destiny

For some in the US the unprecedented power of their country in cultural-economic and military terms represents a unique opportunity to establish a global order, a Pax Americana, which will allow the entire planet to develop and flourish as the US has. Some see this as an expression of divine will, others as a development of human history and still others as a fortuitous accident. Whatever the reasons for the dominant position of the US today, there is widespread agreement across many associated with the current US administration that this opportunity should be seized.

In *The End of History and the Last Man*, the US academic Francis Fukuyama, a leading intellectual apologist for the US neoconservative right, argues that 'liberal democracy may constitute the end point of mankind's ideological evolution.' He goes on to argue that 'modern natural science makes possible the limitless accumulation of wealth...All countries undergoing economic modernisation must increasingly resemble one another.'[11] The implicit statement is that liberal democracy and the free market economy represent the ultimate form of human development and that the US is the model other countries will come to resemble more and more.

This intellectual argument is as valid as any other, but takes on an air of quiet threat when expressed in official policy. In *The National Security Strategy of the United States of America*, President George W. Bush writes of 'a single sustainable model for national success: freedom, democracy, and free enterprise.' He concludes his introduction with 'Today, humanity holds in its hands the opportunity to further freedom's triumph over all these foes. The United States welcomes our responsibility to lead in this great mission.'[12]

Myth or Reality?

For many, the US model represents an ever brighter future, one to be emulated if not copied. The US encapsulates and exudes modernity. It is our future and our goal.

If this is our reality, then the question becomes one of how best to work with, or under, the US. One of the best-known advocates of this approach is the UK Prime

Minister, Tony Blair. For others the very same model represents a threat to be resisted by every possible means. Perhaps reality lies somewhere between, and astride, these two positions?

If the preponderance of US power is largely, or even partly, myth, then the question for the rest of the world becomes different: how can we seek to organise our world without primarily depending on US power?

Our contention is that US power, though devastatingly real, is partly mythical and significantly fragile.

2

Jingle All the Way

'And a ceaseless voice in my heart that said, I want, I want, I want, oh, I want.'
— Saul Bellow, *Henderson the Rain King*

'Oh Lord, won't you buy me a Mercedes Benz?
My friends all drive Porsches, I must make amends.
Worked hard all my lifetime, no help from my friends,
So Lord, won't you buy me a Mercedes Benz?'
— Janis Joplin, 'Mercedes Benz'

Asked to name the top visitor attraction in the US, most people would probably hazard a guess at Disneyland, the Empire State Building, Niagara Falls or Yosemite National Park. It is in fact an ugly 32-hectare sprawl of concrete, steel and glass off Interstate 35 in the profoundly unfashionable city of Bloomington, Minnesota. It is a vast shopping complex called the Mall of America, and it attracts over 40 million visitors, mostly Americans, every year. Amongst shoppers, the Mall is the holy of holies, the only place in the world where you can find Bloomingdale's, Macy's, Nordstrom and Sears under one roof. Along with another 520 or so stores and 60 restaurants, they stretch over 6.5 kilometres of store frontage, occupying 400,000 square metres of retail bliss. Its 12,000 staff will sell you everything from condoms to Chryslers, from porcelain teacups to custom-made teddy bears. In this place alone, $1.7 billion is spent every year.

The great mall is to the US what the Great Wall was to China – a symbol of national power. It features in Hollywood movies like Arnold Schwarzenegger's *Jingle All the Way*. Its aura is such that enough Americans want to be married there to justify its very own Chapel of Love, where every year a local radio station organises the simultaneous exchange of vows by 92 couples, the figure commemorating the holy year of 1992 when the Mall opened for business. That a collection of shops should have acquired such glamour is a mark of the passion generated by America's long affair with con-sumption, for in a sense the entire Mall is a Chapel of Love, consecrated to the worship of Stuff.

American consumption matters greatly to the rest of the world, since the feeding of this appetite for goods generates economic activity around the globe. The conspicuous abundance of America is one of its great attractions for migrants. A big suburban supermarket in New Jersey or California, its shelves groaning with the produce not just of a continent, but of a planet, is an awe-inspiring spectacle. The infinite quantity and variety of things to buy displays not just material wealth, but a sense that here is the magnetic centre of the world, the irresistible force that attracts to itself everything that anyone could possibly need or want. To see that force in action is to believe in American power.

At the centre of the world's image of the power and status of the US lies our sense of that country as the most successful, innovative and competitive economy on the planet. There is a lot of truth behind that image, but not as much as one might imagine and nothing like as much as there once was.

The US *is* the world's biggest economy. It generates vast wealth, consumes massive resources and creates products that global consumers want to buy. Its workers are incredibly hard working and productive and its companies lead the field in many areas, using brilliantly skilled researchers, developing innovative production and management techniques and making marketing almost an art form. Nothing seems more obvious in today's world than the status of the US as an economic, as well as military and political, superpower.

More than anything it is the dynamism of the US economy that validates American claims to world leadership. Critics of the use of US power inevitably come up against the undeniable reality that this is a country that works, and a country on which the rest of the world depends. In their daily lives, ordinary people in Europe and Asia have learned to pray for the US economy. They have become used to the simple truth that their own prosperity depends on the continuing success of the wealth-creating powerhouses of Seattle and Palo Alto, Wall Street and The Loop and the wealth-consuming malls of America. They know that the US drives the world. What they usually do not know, however, is that the world also drives the US.

The US Trade Deficit

'Annual Income twenty pounds, annual expenditure nineteen nineteen six, result happiness. Annual income twenty pounds, annual expenditure twenty pounds nought and six, result misery.'

– Charles Dickens, *David Copperfield* (1850)

The US economy depends on the rest of the world even more than the rest of the world depends on the US. The US is not just the world's richest economy, it is also the world's biggest debtor. To feed its vast appetite for consumption, it borrows. By every important economic measure, it takes more from other countries than they take from it, and the scale of the imbalance has become so dramatic that even organisations like the International Monetary Fund (IMF), which generally repeats US economic orthodoxy, are finding it necessary to use strong language. At the start of 2004, the IMF warned that the United States' net financial obligations to the rest of the world could be equal to 40 per cent of its total economy within a few years — 'an unprecedented level of external debt for a large industrial country' according to the IMF, and one that had now become a serious threat to the world economy.[1]

The US trade deficit is running at a record level of just under $500 billion, a figure which requires a daily net inflow of foreign capital into the US of $1.5 billion if US markets and the dollar are not to collapse.[2] The US borrows almost $50 billion a month from the rest of the world to pay for its imports and fund its federal deficit.

For a long time now, the US has been importing more than it exports, as the insatiable demand of US consumers for everything from Japanese electronics to Nike runners made in Vietnamese sweatshops outstrips the capacity of US industry to sell its products overseas. Even during the 1990s and the longest and strongest business expansion ever known, the American trade and current account deficits were high and rising. Private spending on consumer goods and business spending on capital programmes with a high import content meant that import growth was extremely high, with a rise of 10.6 per cent a year from early 1991 to mid-2000.[3]

The factors influencing these deficits include high consumption relative to income; a record-low personal savings rate; a huge boom in capital spending and investments in new enterprises and companies involved in the New Technology bubble; almost insatiable demands for imports, both by consumers and businesses, to support business activity and consumption; a super-strong dollar that made imports very cheap; tight labour markets; and large bilateral trade imbalances globally, particularly with Japan and China, but also Canada and Germany.

Around half of those imports are goods and services produced by foreign subsidiaries of US companies, then exported to the US.[4] In a globalised economy, the balance of trade figures may not in themselves be all that vital or informative. If General Motors is adjusting its prices on trades with Vauxhall in the UK, Opel in Germany, Saab in Sweden and Daewoo in Korea, then the impact on import-export statistics may not give a really accurate reflection of the health of either General Motors or the larger US economy. What is striking, however, is the alarming pattern of increase in the deficit. The 2003 trade deficit of $489.4 billion was 17.1 per cent larger than the previous record shortfall of $418 billion posted in 2002. Even more strikingly, the deficit for 2004 is likely to have risen to over $600 million, even though a weaker dollar should have depressed imports.

The Federal Deficit

The problem is exacerbated by rising levels of public debt. In 1950, after the expense of World War Two, US public debt stood at $257 billion. Even by 1970 it was just $389 billion and by 1980 it had reached $930 billion. Then a foot went on the accelerator: by 1990 the debt stood at $3.2 trillion and by 2000 it was $5.7 trillion. At the end of 2003, it had reached almost $7 trillion. That's a 13-digit number: $6,951,808,546,861. Simply paying the interest on the debt cost the US government $32.6 billion in the fiscal year 2004. In itself this level of public debt – over 60 per cent of GDP – might be sustainable, but the rates of growth in the debt are not. The Congressional Budget Office estimates that by 2008 the debt will be $9.7 trillion and that by 2015 it will stand at $12.7 trillion. Sooner or later, the brakes will have to be applied.[5]

Instead of tackling the rise in the federal deficit, however, the Bush administration has added to the problem with its two main policy platforms: foreign wars and domestic tax cuts. In his first three years in office, George W. Bush managed to turn a projected $5.6 trillion surplus into a $4 trillion deficit, an almost $10 trillion reverse. While the Iraq invasion alone was costing an average of $5.8 billion a month, Bush was spending money without raising it. In his first three years alone, President Bush cut $3.12 trillion in tax revenue. Revenue from individual income taxes in 2004 as a percentage of GDP was the lowest since 1951.

The Financial Times reported in May 2003 that the Bush administration had buried a US Treasury report which predicted that US deficits would rise to 10 times the current US national debt, or the equivalent of four years' US economic output or 94 per cent of all US household assets. Alan Greenspan, chairman of the US Federal Reserve, voiced concern over what he called Washington's 'deafening' silence about the financial disaster the US federal government was racing towards. Addressing the budget deficit could require a 66 per cent across-the-board increase in US federal income tax.[6] On 3 November 2004, the US Treasury announced a borrowing requirement of $147 billion for the first quarter of 2005. This is a new all-time record, but one that is likely to be eclipsed later in 2005.[7]

These growing deficits cannot be domestically funded, as US citizens hold historically low levels of personal savings. If the nation is in hock, its citizens are even more so.

A Mountain of Personal Debt

Most countries operate budget deficits as the state borrows money to invest in infrastructure or to maintain levels of state services in times of economic downturn. Usually, in developed economies, a significant proportion of this national debt is funded by the country's own citizens. People save money through pension funds, life insurance schemes, unit trusts, etc. The managers of these funds normally place a significant percentage of their funds in 'blue chip' government bonds. The security of these bonds tends to compensate for their relatively low return on investment.

This traditional approach is no longer valid in the

US. Personal savings are at an all-time low. The US personal savings rate was down to 0.2 per cent of disposable personal income in September 2004, from a rate of around 7.7 per cent as recently as 1992.[8] As we have seen, consumer spending in the malls and car lots funds both the US and the global economies. Observers might nervously welcome a decision by US consumers to simply spend their savings, but they are alarmed by the reality that US consumers have borrowed, many to the hilt, to fund their consumption. The US economy spent its way out of the dotcom collapse through $2 trillion worth of consumer debt. The typical US household now holds eight credit cards with an average debit balance of $7,500 on each.[9]

This has important implications for US households and for the whole structure of US society, something we will look at in greater detail in Chapter 3. It also has major implications for US economic and fiscal policy, as this personal borrowing has been contracted on the basis of historically low interest rates. Should the Federal Reserve decide to consistently or significantly raise US interest rates, a considerable percentage of US consumer debt might quickly become worthless. Individuals operating on extremely tight budgets could find themselves incapable of repaying their borrowings.

US credit institutions are aware of this threat and are increasingly employing a practice known as 'universal default'. This means that the credit card issuer monitors not only their client's performance on the card, but also their payments of utility bills, car loans and other repayments. A delayed payment on one debt can trigger an instant rise in the card interest rate from an existing rate of 9.2 per cent to 18 per cent, and in some instances to as high as 28 per cent.[10]

The World Owns More of the US than the US Owns of the World

At the start of the 1990s, it was quite right to assume that the US owned more of the outside world than the outside world owned of the US. In 1990, the value of all foreign assets owned by Americans exceeded the value of all US assets held by foreigners by $500 billion. But by the end of 1998, this position had been dramatically reversed. The value of all US assets held by foreigners exceeded the value of all foreign assets held by Americans by more than $1.5 trillion.[11]

At the end of 2002, a year when the net inflow of foreign direct investment to the US sank to its lowest level since 1992, the value of foreign investments in the United States still exceeded the value of US investments abroad by $2,387.2 billion. This was an increase of $407.3 billion from the previous year, even though the fall in the value of the dollar had significantly raised the dollar value of US investments abroad. US acquisitions of assets abroad in 2002 amounted to $179.0 billion, while foreign acquisitions of assets in the US in 2002 were $707 billion – over three and a half times greater.[12]

US-owned assets abroad were worth $6,189.2 billion, whereas foreign-owned assets in the US were worth $8,576.4 billion. During 2002, liabilities to unaffiliated foreigners reported by US non-banking concerns increased by $71.1 billion to $870.3 billion, reflecting US corporate borrowing, mostly from Western Europe and the Caribbean. US currency held by foreigners increased by $21.5 billion to $297.1 billion. Holdings of US Treasury securities by private foreigners and international financial institutions increased by $114.6 billion to $503.6 billion.

In 2002, the amount of money US non-banking firms borrowed from foreigners ($72.1 billion) was more than twice as large as the new loans they made and deposits they placed abroad ($31.9 billion). US banks as a whole were admittedly in credit, owed $1.46 trillion by foreigners as against liabilities to foreigners of $1.41 trillion. Overall, though, US companies were still borrowing more from abroad than foreigners were borrowing from the US.

All of this means that by the end of 2002, US net liabilities to the rest of the world rose to an amount

($2.6 trillion) that equalled 24.9 per cent of US gross domestic product (GDP).[13] Even the foreign reserves of the US government itself are in deficit compared with the rest of the world. At the end of 2002, the US government's international reserves totalled just $158.6 billion. By contrast, the dollar reserves that foreign governments and official institutions held as investments in US financial assets totalled $1.13 trillion.

It was these large inflows of foreign money that helped to fuel the long US consumer boom of the 1990s. From 1992 to 2002, foreign holdings of US credit instruments increased threefold as foreign investors supplied over 14 per cent of the total increase in funds borrowed in US credit markets.

Global Confidence

Together, these imbalances create a huge dependency in the US economy, making it extremely vulnerable to the perceptions and decisions of foreign investors. As the Congressional Trade Deficit Review Commission put it in 2000:

> Every year that the United States has a current account deficit, the negative net international investment position will grow. And every year, the United States will have to pay profits, interest, rents, and dividends on a growing scale to foreign owners of these assets. Some are concerned that these growing payments may limit the future US standard of living. Furthermore, some are concerned that foreigners may not be willing to continue to provide capital to the United States to finance future trade deficits or, in the extreme, that they may not be willing to keep their current investments in the United States.

In a paper prepared for the Trade Deficit Review Commission, the economist Allen Sinai pointed out:

> So long as the deficits can be financed from outside the US, either through direct or indirect investments, or both, and there are adequate flows-of-funds from the lending and investments of other countries into the US, there need be no problem. But, no one can be sure what levels of asset and

debt holdings will cause satiation for lenders and investors and whether the investors, individuals, financial institutions, corporations and governments might, for a variety of reasons, withdraw funds and move them elsewhere. In such a situation, the dollar very likely would decline, perhaps sharply, contributing to substantially higher inflation, lower expected real returns after adjustments for exchange rates, rises of interest rates, reductions in the availability of credit and financing, a slowdown in economic activity, and perhaps even a recession.[14]

The key phrase here is 'so long as the deficits can be financed from outside the US'. Essentially, the US depends on foreign investment to keep its high levels of consumption afloat. Without the constant inward flow of money, the cycle of spending and investment that makes the US economy so dynamic would be unsustainable, and that inflow itself depends in large part on the ability of Americans to borrow money. The cycle works like this: American consumers use their credit cards to buy foreign imports. The sale of these goods puts dollars into the hands of the foreign companies who leave much of the money in the US because they get high returns by lending it to Americans. Americans borrow the money to fund more consumption.

Up to a point, everyone is happy, but the scale of the borrowing by consumers and government agencies is phenomenal. In the second quarter of 2003, net new borrowing by all domestic non-financial sectors of the American economy (households, federal, state and local governments and businesses) rose to $2.52 trillion while their outstanding credit market debt reached $21.6 trillion, and a whopping 42 per cent of this money came from foreigners.

This makes for a pretty fundamental vulnerability. As Jane D'Arista puts it, 'In the future, the foreign investment that has sustained the US economy may very well falter if American households and businesses reach the point where they can no longer afford to borrow in order to buy the imports that put dollars into the hands of foreign investors.'[15]

The funding of the US federal deficit depends on foreign governments, companies and individuals holding some of their reserves in US dollars, US Treasury bonds and so on. Traditionally 15 per cent of US Treasury paper was held by foreign governments (usually central banks). Today's figure is 40 per cent.[16]

There are signs, so far small ones, that foreign investors are beginning to question the wisdom of holding quite so much of their wealth, or their country's reserves, in dollars or US bonds. Some Saudi investors, who collectively have about $1 trillion deposited in the US, are beginning to move funds to Europe and into euros.[17] OECD figures for 2003, released in June 2004, showed that China had supplanted the US as the world's first destination for foreign investment. France was second.[18]

On 9 September 2004, the US Treasury held one of its routine sales of treasury bonds. Usually slightly more than half the bonds offered for sale on such occasions are bought by foreign investors, particularly the Chinese and Japanese central banks which collectively hold some $1.3 trillion in reserves. Yet on 9 September 2004 there were no Chinese or Japanese buyers. Sadakichi Robbins, the head of global fixed-income trading at Bank Julius Baer, described the market reaction: 'Thoughts of panic flickered out there...a doomsday scenario.' The 9 September flicker of panic followed the returns which showed that during August 2004 foreign private investors sold $2 billion more of US stocks than they bought, while sales of foreign-owned US government bonds outstripped purchases by $4 billion.[19]

The 9 September experience was not repeated at the following treasury bond sale, but everyone had understood the warning – in the words of C. Fred Bergsten, director of the Washington-based Institute for International Economics, 'A run for the exits could happen any day, that's for sure.'[20] Stephen Lewis of Monument Securities put it more sanguinely: 'The truth is that the US fiscal and monetary excesses, which have been essential to keeping the global economy afloat in recent years, are no longer tolerated in foreign exchange markets. The status quo is not an option. The only question is how the pain of adjustment will be apportioned?'[21]

Bush's Washington: 'Lunatics in Charge of the Asylum'

George W. Bush and his Republican-dominated Congress are aware of the disastrous situation of their nation's finances, yet they continue to display a curious and intriguing mixture of blind confidence that things will get better and a range of policies seemingly designed to make them worse.

There is no easy solution to the US trade deficit, but active policies designed to reduce US consumption of imported oil would not hurt. Yet this administration seems determined to maintain one of the most oil-thirsty societies on the planet, complete with tax-efficient but fuel-guzzling SUVs and an ageing industrial infrastructure.

The first Bush administration bears direct responsibility for the burgeoning federal deficit. It inherited a federal budget that was in surplus and has transformed it into a record deficit. The non-partisan Congressional Budget Office reported in March 2004 that the federal budget deficit now stems entirely from tax cuts and spending increases rather than from the lingering effects of the economic slowdown.[22]

Bush's sweeping cuts in US taxation will add almost $2 billion to the US deficit over the coming years, particularly if, as seems likely, the White House seeks to convert these 'temporary measures' into permanent ones. This tax-cutting drive is rooted in the theory of supply-side economics first embraced by the Reagan administrations. Under this theory, cutting the amount people pay in taxes leaves them with more money to spend. This additional spending fuels economic development and over time increases the state's tax take. The theory was largely discredited in the Reagan years, and as most of the current tax cuts will go to the top 1 per cent of US society, little additional expenditure is likely. The first President Bush famously dismissed supply-side theory as 'voodoo economics'.[23]

If the White House is not prepared to raise taxation levels, its choices become distinctly limited, given that the US central bank, the Federal Reserve, is independent of the government, an independence fiercely defended by its chairman, the formidable Alan Greenspan. Bush's domestic policy choices are restricted by his political ideology to two possible approaches. One is to significantly cut federal expenditure. The other is to shift major elements of federal expenditure to states, cities and counties or to private citizens. From the statements and actions of the Bush administrations and their acolytes, it looks as if the White House plans to achieve both.

The US federal government spent approximately $2.2 trillion in the US fiscal year 2003. $860 billion of this was what is termed 'discretionary spending', where the government can exercise a degree of choice as to whether it wants to spend that money or not. The balance went on 'mandatory spending', where the government is obliged by law to spend those amounts.[24] As 49.5 per cent of the discretionary spending, or $425 billion, went on defence[25] – an area where the Bush White House intends to spend ever more – the prime target for expenditure reduction (and for responsibility and expenditure transfer) has to be mandatory spending.

The Republican Right understands that any frontal attack on federal social spending programmes, Medicare, Medicaid and Social Security, would be unpopular and difficult to impose on Congress. The goal, as announced by Grover S. Norquist of Americans for Tax Reform, is to reduce federal revenues to a point where such programmes collapse for want of funding.

When asked if it was dangerous to announce the agenda so clearly, he replied, 'No. I think the smart guys on the left have known for a long time that they are in trouble – and that we're going to dig out their whole structure of programs and power.'[26]

The Financial Times described the same approach in scathing terms:

> The lunatics are now in charge of the asylum...Proposing to slash federal spending, particularly on social programs, is a tricky electoral proposition, but a fiscal crisis offers the tantalizing prospect of forcing such cuts through the back door. For them [extreme Republicans] undermining the multilateral international order is not enough; long-held views on income distribution also require radical revision.[27]

President Bush's Republican majorities in both houses of Congress plan to achieve what *The New York Times* called 'a fiscal train wreck.'[28] The US government would then be able to cease funding a range of increasingly expensive mandatory programmes, probably seeking to transfer more responsibility to the 50 states and myriad local authorities across the country, as well as making private citizens pay more for their health care and retirement provisions.

There are at least two major problems with implementing such an approach, although as a high-risk strategy it has its attractions. The primary attraction is that in the decade 2010–2020 some 76 million US baby boomers are scheduled to retire, adding trillions of dollars to mandatory federal Social Security and Medicare costs. If those who aspire to be in government in 10 years' time could dodge that particular bullet, their lives would be that much easier. One major problem is that it is already too late for most of these 76 million about-to-retire US citizens to make serious private provision for their retirement. Therefore, it would be attractive to shift the burden away from the federal government and onto the 50 states. This is where the second problem arises. The states are broke as well.

State Funding Crisis

The 50 states of the US are facing what the executive director of the National Governors' Association, Ray Scheppach, described as the worst funding crisis since statistical records began in 1812.[29] The states are cumulatively facing a budget shortfall of $100 billion, and 49 out of 50 of them are legally obliged to maintain balanced budgets.[30] The stock market collapse, growing unemployment and business failures have eaten into state tax revenues. Most states had trimmed their taxes and expenditure during the 1990s boom and have used reserve funds to tide them over 2001 and 2002. Now, with falling income, rising costs and exhausted reserves, state legislatures are facing major challenges.

States are cutting services and raising taxes where they can. In many states new taxes or tax increases are subject to approval by referendum. The states' share of Medicaid expenses is rising and Washington wants to shift more of the burden to the states.

At the core of this lies neoconservative ideology. If some states wish to maintain minimal social programmes after a bankrupt Washington withdraws, they are free to do so. Such states will of course have to adopt massive tax increases. Market forces will then come into play, as they did in US cities in the 1960s and 1970s. The wealthy can move to states with lower taxes and less services, leaving their poorer fellow citizens to flounder in the failing states next door.

Ten to 20 years of pain may be required to produce a fiscally sound government in the US, but that sacrifice will also produce a nation effectively weaned from what many on the right of the Republican Party see as state dependence. This amounts to a harsh reiteration of a traditionally held view in such circles that if people are poor, it must be their own fault. Commenting on unemployed people in the US whose lifetime quota of welfare benefits have run out, Melissa Pardue of Washington's conservative Heritage Foundation praised the Clinton-era welfare reforms: 'The people who continue to be affected [by the recession] are not working. People who choose not to get a job are not going to see more income. It's all the more reason to give greater incentives to looking for work.'[31] As their poverty is their fault, they, rather than society at large, should suffer the consequences of their actions, or inaction.

'Cry For Us Argentina'

For most of us, six- and seven-figure sums are like dinosaurs – we know they're big but since we've never seen them we do not quite know how big. We need those diagrams that put a picture of a Tyrannosaurus Rex beside one of a human. So it is with national budget deficits and balances of payments expressed in millions, billions and trillions. The simple fact is that the US, as a stand-alone nation-state, is not just broke, it's bankrupt. If it were a company, its management would be guilty of illegal trading.

The White House seems quite content to watch, even trigger, a decline in the value of the dollar. Alan Greenspan stated at a conference in Frankfurt in November 2004 that 'Given the size of the US current account deficit, a diminished appetite for adding to dollar balances must occur at some point. International investors will eventually adjust their accumulation of dollar assets or, alternatively, seek higher dollar returns to offset concentration risk, elevating the cost of financing the US current account deficit and rendering it increasingly less tenable.'[32] He had earlier predicted that there was a 75 per cent chance of a dollar crisis within the next five years.[33]

In theory, a declining dollar should make US exports more attractive and imports more expensive, thus cutting the US trade deficit. Quite apart from the fact that such a situation would not reduce the federal deficit, there are three major areas of doubt as to whether a declining dollar will really help the US economy, even in the short term.

The first is that Beijing doggedly keeps the value of its Renminbi currency pegged to the dollar, so Chinese exports will not become more expensive in the US. Secondly, as half the US trade deficit is made up of goods and services supplied by foreign subsidiaries of US corporations, any fall in such sales will adversely affect corporate balance sheets and the US stock market. Thirdly, as the dollar becomes less attractive to foreign investors, the Federal Reserve will be obliged to raise US interest rates to offer a higher return to those same investors. A rise in interest rates will cripple US households.

A number of highly respected US commentators have expressed their growing concern at the state of their nation's finances. Robert Rubin, the former Treasury secretary, together with Peter Orszag of the Brookings Institution and Allan Sinai of Decision Economics, presented a paper to the American Economic Association in January 2004. The paper stated that official US projections that the deficit will decline over time are not based on 'credible assumptions.' They went on to warn:

> Substantial ongoing deficits may severely and adversely affect expectations and confidence, which in turn can generate a self-reinforcing negative cycle among the underlying fiscal deficit, financial markets, and the real economy...The potential costs and fallout from such fiscal and financial disarray provide perhaps the strongest motivation for avoiding substantial, ongoing budget deficits.

Professor Paul Krugman of Princeton University added:

> Argentina retained the confidence of international investors almost to the end of the 1990's. Analysts shrugged off its large budget and trade deficits; business-friendly, free-market policies would, they insisted, allow the country to grow out of all that. But when confidence collapsed, that optimism proved foolish. Argentina, once a showpiece for the new world order, quickly became a byword for economic catastrophe...Do Cry for us Argentina.[34]

Alan Greenspan argues that such concerns are based on outdated concepts of international finance: 'History suggests that the odds are favorable that current imbalances will be defused with little disruption.' In January 2004 he pointed out to a British Treasury conference that new financial instruments had allowed the international system to digest the hundreds of billions lost when the telecoms' bubble burst: 'Unlike in previous periods of large financial distress, no major institution defaulted ...' These new approaches for hedging risk had created 'far more flexible, efficient, and hence resilient financial systems than existed just a quarter-century ago.' Since investors have become less tied to their home markets, this 'has enabled the United States to incur and finance a much larger current account deficit than would have been feasible in earlier decades.'[35]

What both sides of this argument would seem to agree on is that the solution to the US's financial problems lies within a global framework. If the crisis evoked by former Treasury Secretary Rubin materialises, institutions such as the IMF will have a key role to play in any rescue operation. If Alan Greenspan is proved right, then we are already living in a new global economic system, one where the US is just another player, albeit an important one.

If this is our reality, then our global systems will need serious overhaul, involving the replacement of the US dollar as our international reserve currency. In such a scenario the proposal of John Maynard Keynes to the 1944 Bretton Woods conference for the creation of an International Clearing Union using its own virtual currency to balance trade fluctuations may finally come to be recognised as the imaginative and equitable proposal that it is.[36]

Whatever the solution, it has to be global and multilateral – the direct opposite of the unilateral policies of the current US administration. Instead of protecting the prosperity of ordinary Americans and US businesses, that administration is making them ever more vulnerable.

The whole system depends on Mr and Mrs Average American being well off enough to be able to service their debts and buy more stuff. The working assumption — and it has worked for most of the last 150 years — is that the ordinary American is able to live the good life, with ever greater levels of prosperity creating an ever deeper hunger for consumer goods. In this sense, the power of the US is generated at least as much by the shopping malls as by the military. Hitting middle America in its pockets is just as much an assault on the heartland as attacking it with bombs and terror.

The essence of middle America is the American Dream – the belief that anybody, and by extension everybody, can make it to the top. But the American Dream is deeply troubled, and the US government is making it more uneasy all the time.

3

The Pre-Rich: Class and Poverty in Today's US

'We are nearer today to the ideal of the abolition of poverty and fear from the lives of men and women than ever before in any land.'

– Herbert Hoover, October 1928

The cover of an anthology by the Danish poet Piet Hein carries a cartoon of a portly, balding, middle-aged Copenhagen businessman peering into a small pond. The reflection he sees is that of a tall Viking warrior. What would a similar US drawing depict? A reflected image drawn in equal parts from the Wild West and the West Wing? At the heart of the American Dream is a vision of independence, self-reliance and a rough-and-ready republican equality where every man and woman is, or can be, as good, as successful and as rich as they are capable of being.

In the US, there is still an active Horatio Alger Society, dedicated to preserving and furthering the ideals of the nineteenth-century popular novelist who invented the 'rags-to-riches' story. Its aim, it says, is 'to encourage the spirit of Strive and Succeed that for half of a century guided Alger's undaunted heroes – lads whose struggles epitomized the great American Dream and inspired hero ideals in countless millions of young Americans.' Each year it presents a 'Horatio Alger Award' to Americans who 'demonstrate individual initiative and a commitment to excellence as exemplified by remarkable achievements accomplished through honesty, hard work, self-reliance, and perseverance.'[1] It thus keeps alive the lesson taught by Alger in hundreds of best-selling stories – that in America, anyone, however destitute and disadvantaged, can achieve wealth and success through honesty, industry and resilience.

This settler-pioneer-individualist dream, though, is not just American. Its glamour is felt around the world. It exercised a strong influence on the 20 million-odd European migrants who sailed for the US in the nineteenth and early twentieth centuries, drawn not just by the prospect of wealth but by the desire to live their lives beyond the reach of feudal tyrannies and prejudices. And it continues to attract millions of people from Latin America, Asia, Africa and Europe, including, and perhaps especially, the illegal and undocumented migrants whose prospects are in reality bleak.

The dream exercises its power by sometimes coming true. The US is in some respects a genuinely open society. Some poor immigrants do make fortunes. The first generation of each new wave is prepared to suffer, work incredibly long hours, run almost any risk, dig tunnels, build skyscrapers, mine ore, lay tracks, smelt steel or work all hours in small diners and shops in the knowledge that their children can aspire to a better life. Historically, the vast majority have bettered themselves and built the cities, schools, hospitals and institutions which helped offer their children and grandchildren those better lives. Those who failed have been forgotten, but enough succeeded to validate the dream. Their gratitude fuels a strong sense of patriotism.

Myth, however, plays a significant part in the self-image of the US middle class. In a *Time* magazine 2000 survey, 19 per cent of respondents said they were in the top 1 per cent of earners and a further 20 per cent expected to enter the top 1 per cent one day. In the words of David Brooks, author of *Bobos in Paradise: The New Upper Class and How They Got There* (Simon & Schuster 2000), 'None of us is really poor; we're just pre-rich.'[2] The power of this self-image of the US as a nation of pre-rich people cannot be underestimated. It may be delusional, but it is a mighty delusion. If you imagine that wealth is just around the corner, you do not resent those who are already rich. You do not want to beat them, but join them.

Because of the preponderance of US film and television production, the images that US society projects to itself are also the same images the US projects worldwide. Two themes recur in these projected images: the attainability of success and a laid-back, relaxed society where what you do and what you achieve are far more important than where you come from. There is no formal aristocracy. A bright kid from a relatively poor and unhappy background, like Bill Clinton, can become president.

In contrast, European societies are often perceived as being more formal, more hidebound and more class ridden. Even if you yourself are extraordinarily successful, old European money, the aristocrat-based upper class, will freeze you out, perhaps eventually allowing your grandchildren access to the upper echelons of society if their parents have managed to attend the right schools and learned which fork to use for what dish.

Social images and current realities are often at odds, however. While snobbish distinctions between 'old' and 'new' money continue to exist in golf and country clubs on both sides of the Atlantic, they are largely irrelevant to the broader shape of social reality.

The US today is a more class-divided society than any of its European counterparts. US class divisions, like most European ones, are based on money. Realistic opportunities for ordinary people to advance themselves are considerably smaller in the US than in Europe, and considerably more influenced by where they were born and how much money their parents have.

In overall terms, the US is the seventh most developed country in the world, according to the 2003 UNDP's Human Development Index. This puts it behind Norway, Iceland, Sweden, Australia, the Netherlands and Belgium, but still pretty high in the league of decent places to live. However, in the UNDP's Human Poverty Index (HPI-2), which measures poverty and inequality, the US is seventeenth – worst of all the developed OECD economies.

Table 3.1: HPI-2 Ranks for 17 Selected OECD Countries

Rank	Country
1	Sweden
2	Norway
3	Finland
4	Netherlands
5	Denmark
6	Germany
7	Luxembourg
8	France
9	Spain
10	Japan
11	Italy
12	Canada
13	Belgium
14	Australia
15	UK
16	Ireland
17	US

Disparities in wealth are socially and politically less important than mobility between different social groups. In our post-industrial societies it is almost meaningless to talk of a working class in nineteenth-century terms. Industrial workers can expect to earn enough to live in a society where their children are not obliged to become industrial workers. Twenty-first-century society can be divided into three social sectors: a rich elite, an underclass and a large, if multilayered, middle class.

The level of mobility between those classes is a vital yardstick for measuring social and economic success – and stability. Do the wealthy lose their privileges if they lose their wealth? How easy is it for those in the under-class to move up the social ladder? Does the middle class have a reasonable measure of security, coupled with reasonable hope that their children may do better? Are all groups reflected in that society's institutions and preoccupations?

According to a 2004 survey, one-third of all US res-idents no longer believe in the American Dream. Some have lost faith because they worked hard all their lives only to face desperate poverty in their old age; others question the very dream itself.[3]

In the US now, the level of social disparity and social immobility is little short of grotesque. The US is the most unequal society in terms of wealth distribution in the industrialised world. That does not bode well for US society. More importantly, for any realistic measure-ment of US power, it does not bode well for an economy which depends so strongly on the ability of ordinary people to keep borrowing money and consuming goods.

If the overall US economy is in trouble, it naturally follows that the opportunities for individual success in today's US are limited. That in itself is enough to weaken the American Dream. The active commitment to and pursuit of policies that prevent its realisation fundamentally undermines it.

The Very Wealthy

Wealth is relative. Which of us does not remember our first pay packet? It might not have been very much, but it was a hell of a lot more than we'd ever had before, and nearly all of it was disposable. Most of us felt rich that day – many of us felt richer that day than we ever have since. So one definition of wealth is its relation to how wealthy other people in your community are. That entails another relative definition. What's your community? Is it your family? Your town? Your country?

Wealth is also relative to consumption. Let us assume that the proportion of miserly Scrooges is constant across the human race. As people have more wealth, they consume more – up to a certain point. The wealth-consumption relationship holds true across the middle class. When you earn more money, you buy a bigger house or car, take better holidays, eat out more often and at better restaurants, replace the bottle of Bulgarian Chardonnay with a Meursault and the chain store clothes with an Armani suit.

As you ascend the wealth ladder, however, this tight relationship between wealth and consumption begins to loosen and it eventually disappears. When you have the perfect house in the best neighbourhood, the three holiday homes, the servants and the cars, there comes a point where you are less and less likely to add another one. At the high end of the wealth ladder, additional wealth triggers less and less additional consumption. If you earn $5,000 an hour (just over $10 million a year) and you get a 50 per cent rise, you are very unlikely to spend 50 per cent more. On the other hand, if you earn close to the US minimum wage of $5.15 an hour and get a raise to $7.50, the probability is that you will spend pretty much all of your extra money. In other words, if you want people to keep consuming, it makes sense to give more money to the relatively poor than to the relatively rich. In fact, the opposite has been happening in the US.

Some would have us believe that while there are

more wealthy people in the US today than there were 20 years ago, they are not really all that much more wealthy. Alan Greenspan, the chairman of the US Federal Reserve (central bank), argued in 1998 that although top earnings had risen, they had not risen that much when compared to overall earnings.[4] Greenspan had US census figures to support his argument.

There is a problem with those figures, however. Like all statistics, it depends on how you count. If two friends are having a drink after work and one earns $90,000 a year, the other $110,000, saying that their average income is $100,000 gives you a reasonable picture. However, if somebody earning $1.2 million joins them, the average income for the three drinkers has become $460,000, which is meaningless.

US income statistics are often divided into ten 10 per cent categories or deciles. Alan Greenspan used deciles to show that the income of the top 10 per cent of US families had not moved that far ahead of the other 90 per cent. So all is well.

Well, not quite. In 1998 the top 10 per cent of US income tax payers started at $81,000, but most of the gains accruing to that top 10 per cent went to the top 1 per cent. The income bracket for the top 1 per cent started at $230,000. If you look more closely, the pyramid narrows. Sixty per cent of the gains accruing to the top 1 per cent of taxpayers went to the top 0.1 per cent – incomes beginning at $790,000 – and almost half that additional income went to the top 0.01 per cent, 13,000 taxpayers with an income of at least $3.6 million and an average income of $17 million.[5] So although the top 10 per cent did a little better than the rest, the top 1 per cent did a whole lot better. According to the Congressional Budget Office, 49 per cent of US taxes on investment income were paid by the top 1 per cent of taxpayers.[6]

The average annual salary in the US (in 1998 inflation-adjusted dollars) increased from $32,522 in 1970 to $35,864 in 1999, or by just over 10 per cent. Over the same period *Fortune* magazine calculated that the average real income (salaries, bonuses and stock options) of corporate CEOs went from $1.3 million to $37.5 million, or an increase of 2,785 per cent. In 1970 CEOs were paid 39 times the average wage, but by 1999 they were being paid over 1,000 times more.[7] This is a fundamental change. Cornell University economist Robert Frank commented: 'It's possible to become a wealthy person just by what you earn for doing your job. That was not very often possible 25 years ago.'[8] A Congressional Budget Office study found that in the period 1979–1997, the after-tax incomes of the top 1 per cent of families rose 157 per cent, whereas middle-income families saw their incomes rise by 10 per cent over the same period.[9]

The richest 1 per cent of the US population owns 38 per cent of that nation's wealth.[10] New York University economist Edward N. Wolff noted that the number of millionaire households in the US had almost doubled to 4.8 million from the early 1980s to the late 1990s. In 1995, out of the 130 million US families filing income tax returns, 1.3 million reported an income in excess of $200,000. By 2001, 3 million families were reporting such an income.[11]

The Very Poor

At the other end of the social spectrum, in the poorest 20 per cent of the (official) US population, the reverse image is startlingly clear. The official poverty line for an adult aged 18 to 64 was $9,214 in 2001. According to the US Census Bureau, 32.9 million US residents, or 11.7 per cent of the population, were under this poverty line, as were 16.3 per cent of children under 18. Children account for 35.7 per cent of the poor but only 25.6 per cent of the overall population; 18.2 per cent of children under six were poor. The poverty rates for non-Hispanic whites and people between 18 and 64 were increasing.[12] The US Department of Agriculture (DOA) described 31 million US residents as being 'food insecure' (not being sure where their next meal was coming from). Over 9 million of those were categorised as experiencing real hunger, which the DOA describes as an 'uneasy or painful sensation caused by lack of food due to lack of resources to obtain food.' Demand for emergency food assistance rose by almost 20 per cent across 25 major US cities in 2002. There are now more US residents living in poverty than there were in 1965.[13]

The average severity of poverty also increased – the 'depth of poverty' measurement. The average amount by which those who are officially classified as poor fell short of that threshold was $2,707 per poor person, which represents the largest 'per-person poverty gap' ever recorded in the US.[14] Almost 18 million US residents aged 18 to 64 thus found themselves with an annual average income of $6,507 in 2001. In 2002, New York City soup kitchens refused meals to 84,000 hungry children because they had run out of food, a 218 per cent increase over 2000. New York food banks and soup kitchens were feeding 1 million hungry New Yorkers every day in 2002.[15]

This in a country where over 40 million residents have no health insurance and a further 29 million are estimated to be under-insured.[16] The problem is getting steadily worse – between 2001 and 2002, the number of people with no health insurance rose by 2.4 million to 43.6 million. An estimated 15.2 per cent of the population had no health insurance coverage during all of 2002, up from 14.6 per cent in 2001.[17] Almost 11 million US children under 18 have no health insurance at all[18] and 900,000 additional US children are expected to lose their health insurance in the next three years.[19] This is a question of political choice, not of resources – the US, one of the richest countries in today's world, spent almost 14 per cent of its GDP on health care in 2002. By contrast, the World Health Organization described France's health care system as 'the best in the world when it looked at access to healthcare, efficiency and effectiveness' that same year. In 2002, France spent 9.9

per cent of its GDP on health care, providing the best service in the world to its 59 million inhabitants – 10 million less than the 69 million US inhabitants that have either no health cover or inadequate cover.[20] There are 322 physicians per 100,000 people in the European Union, whereas the comparable US figure is 279.[21]

Around 15 per cent of the US population, many of them working poor, are now trapped in the nightmare situation where if anything goes wrong, they find themselves on a one-way trip to destitution. The case of 63-year-old Chicago nurse Rose Shaffer illustrates this reality. In October 2000 Ms Shaffer collapsed on a Chicago street, the victim of a heart attack. An ambulance took her to the nearest hospital, South Suburban, a Lutheran-run charity chain, Advocate Health Care, rather than the further away public Cook County Hospital. At Cook she would have been treated for free. At Advocate she was a non-insured patient. As a non-insured patient she was charged the full whack of $6,000 a day for her three-day stay (health insurance companies negotiate discounts for their policy holders, while uninsured patients on average pay 139 per cent more for hospital care). Ms Shaffer could not pay, and the Advocate Health Care charity, as obliged by federal law, handed her dossier to a debt-collection agency who very actively pursued her until she was forced into bankruptcy. She is working long hours, seven days a week, at a nursing agency to save her last asset, her house.[22]

It is not surprising that under these conditions, the US, in spite of having many of the best medical schools and hospitals in the world, is getting sicker. While treatments for common conditions have got ever better, the number of people without access to those treatments has risen. The budgetary crises in the individual states have led to cuts in basic health programmes. Efforts to combat diseases such as tuberculosis and asthma are grossly under-funded. A lack of community-based services for the mentally ill has meant that thousands have been left on the streets or in jail. Some states, such as Kentucky, are cutting back severely on health care for the elderly. Others, like Texas, are cutting preventive health care for children.

The results are predictable. A quarter of infants in Texas are not vaccinated. Over a tenth of the entire population of Mississippi has diabetes. The same proportion of the population of Maine has asthma. And while there were just three states where people had an average of more than six days a month where they were ill in 1993–1995, by 1999–2001, there were 14.[23]

Life expectancy in the US is lower than in Canada, Japan and most Western European countries. Male life expectancy in the US is lower than in Costa Rica. The Swedish infant mortality rate is half that of the US,[24] while Libya, Mauritius and the Seychelles have lower infant mortality rates than the city of Detroit.[25]

The absence of any national US health insurance system has become a major headache for US businesses. US businesses have to shoulder large costs, sometimes open-ended ones, to insure their employees. This can be a factor when it comes to decisions about locating new investment. At General Motors' plants in the US, the cost of employee health care is now greater than the cost of steel. Health care is becoming a jobs issue.[26]

Housing is also a critical concern for those on low incomes. While housing costs account for 37 per cent of the average family budget,[27] 7.2 million of the poorest US families spend more than half of their incomes on housing.[28] Almost 20 per cent of homeless people in the US are employed in full- or part-time jobs.[29] The 2004 US federal budget cut or abolished several key social housing measures, such as the Hope IV programme.[30]

Right through the 1990s the 20 million poorest US families suffered from a shortage of affordable housing. California cut social housing programmes from $578 million in 2000–2001 to $11 million for 2002–2003. Connecticut has cut rental assistance programmes to $11 million. North Carolina cut its State Housing Trust Fund from $9 million to $3 million in 2002. Ohio housing programmes will have been cut by 25 per cent in just over a year. The US Conference of Mayors and the National League of Cities have called for a National Housing Trust Fund, yet US Secretary of Housing and Urban Development (HUD), Mel Martinez, has dismissed the affordable housing crisis as 'a local problem that does not require a significant Federal response.'[31] In 1998 the US National Coalition for the Homeless estimated that an employee needed to be earning $8.99 an hour to be able to afford a one-bedroom rented apartment. That same year the US Economic Policy Institute calculated that 30 per cent of the US workforce was receiving $8 an hour or less.[32]

One of the distinctive aspects of the US, indeed, is precisely the extent to which poverty and welfare are not synonymous. In most other developed societies, the poor are generally the unemployed, the sick and the disabled. Their poverty is directly related to their exclusion from the workforce. But in the US, people who work grindingly hard are nevertheless trapped in poverty. The reality is most starkly obvious in one of the country's great retail institutions, the Wal-Mart chain of discount stores. While its owners, the five Walton children, were valued at $20.5 billion each in the *Forbes* rich list for 2003, making them the richest single family on Earth, Wal-Mart pays its workers so poorly that personnel managers hand out information to new recruits on how to obtain government food stamps.[33]

A joint study by the Annie E. Casey, Ford and Rockefeller Foundations, published in October 2004, showed that 9.2 million working families in the US were barely able to survive financially. It reveals that one in five workers are in occupations where the median wage is less than $8.84 an hour – the poverty-level wage for a family of four. Salaries are simply too low. As the study puts it, 'Consider the motel housekeeper, the retail clerk at the hardware store or the coffee shop cook, if they have children, chances are good that their families are living on an income too low to provide for their basic needs.'[34]

US journalist Barbara Ehrenreich worked in low-paid jobs as a waitress, nursing home assistant, home cleaner and sales assistant in Florida, Maine and Minnesota during 1998–1999. Her experiences are recounted in her 2001 book *Nickel and Dimed*. She found that working in jobs paying in or around the federal minimum wage of $5.15 an hour, she needed one full-time and one part-time job to be able to afford the rent on the most basic of homes, such as a trailer or mobile home in a caravan park. For the standard family of two adults and two children, this meant that the adults had to hold at least three jobs between them, working a minimum of 12 hours a day each. The time left for family life, social development, help with school work, etc. when commuting, shopping and all other time demands were factored in was minimal indeed.

Ehrenreich concluded: 'Something is wrong, very wrong, when a single person in good health, a person who in addition possesses a working car, can barely support herself by the sweat of her brow. You do not need a degree in economics to see that wages are too low and rents too high.'[35]

And Those in the Middle?

While the American Dream may be of little interest to the already wealthy and seems little more than a distant mirage for those at the bottom, it is the very stuff of middle-class aspirations. We define the middle class as those some steps above the federal poverty line and below the highest 10 per cent tax bracket, people earning between $20,000 and $90,000 a year.

The stark reality is that the earning power of middle US has been gradually eroded over the last 20 years. The mathematics are relatively simple, as Professor Paul Krugman points out: 'If the rich get more, that leaves less for everyone else.'[36]

Restaurant and budget hotel managers earn just over $20,000 a year.[37] Airline pilots in low-cost operators such as American Eagle (American Airlines), Delta Connection (Delta Airlines) or Continental Express (Continental Airlines) start at $13,000– $16,000 a year. A senior pilot with several years' experience at those airlines can reach $40,000 a year.[38] The average teacher's pay is $41,351.[39] A New York telecoms technician could expect to earn $50,000 a year in 2002.[40] A full-time therapist working with impaired children in a California hospital and his wife, who worked as a supply teacher, jointly earned $48,444 in 1996.[41]

Median incomes rose by 10 per cent in the 20 years up to 1997, but median household money income actually declined 1.1 per cent in real terms from 2001 to $42,409 in 2002[42], and for many in the middle income brackets real wages actually fell in inflation-adjusted dollars over the same period. Their relative wealth and sense of security were also damaged. From 1980 to 1995, 39 million US employees lost their jobs in corporate downsizing exercises.[43] In the US, health insurance goes with the job and most pension schemes are tied to the employer, so losing your job, even if you quickly get another one, may impact negatively on your health cover and your retirement planning.

Three realities have fuelled the US booms of the last 20 years – working women, personal debt and the great US tradition of immigration.

The US has generated the world's largest service sector. Fourteen million jobs have been created in US shopping malls, hospitals and health care centres. Most of them have been taken up by women. Nearly half of all US families are now two-income families.[44] Employees in the US are working longer hours – averaging 50 hours a week – and have the least amount of paid holidays of workers anywhere in the developed world.[45]

Much of the boom these jobs were created to serve has been fuelled by personal debt. By the end of 2001, mortgage originations (new mortgages or refinancing of existing mortgages) in the US were over $2 trillion. Sixty per cent of that, or $1.2 trillion, was refinancing, i.e.

raising equity on property rather than borrowing to purchase a property.[46] The proportion of income consumed by debt servicing for those on incomes under $50,000 reached 22 per cent in 1998.[47]

The US middle class has been running faster and faster – more of them have entered the labour market and they work longer and longer hours – in order to stand still. They depend almost entirely on their earnings and borrowings to fund their lifestyles. For them, the generally held view of the US as a nation of stockholders is largely mythical. According to CCH Incorporated, a tax analysis firm based in Riverwoods, Illinois, in 2000 only 14 per cent of those with earnings under $20,000 reported any stock income and just 20 per cent of those with earnings between $20,000 and $75,000 had some stock income, but 87 per cent of taxpayers with incomes in excess of $200,000 reported income from stocks and bonds.[48] According to the New York Stock Exchange, in 1998, 33.8 million of the US's 84 million shareholders directly held stocks. In other words, 60 per cent of shares in the US were held in pension funds, retirement accounts or mutual equity funds.[49] The myth of a share-dealing middle-class stakeholder economy in the US is just that – a myth.

Efficiency and Mobility

So earnings in the US vary more extremely than they do in other market economies, but, neoconservatives will argue, so what? By freeing up the labour market and creating easy access to jobs, however low skilled or low paid they may be, the US makes it easier for people to get a foot on the bottom rung of the social ladder. Once on that ladder, the hard-working succeed, driven to some extent by the extra income incentives available higher up. Any attempt to limit those incentives, much less to effect any redistribution of wealth, inevitably leads to the old Soviet situation where 'the State pretends to pay us and we pretend to work.'

All the evidence points in the other direction. Social mobility in the US today is lower than in comparable European market economies. A major study comparing the US labour market with seven major European economies, including three Nordic countries where the labour market is highly regulated, found that the US had the lowest numbers of workers moving from the bottom 20 per cent of the labour force into the next 20 per cent, the lowest rate moving into the top 60 per cent and the highest share of workers unable to maintain full-time employment.[50]

A recent OECD study showed that those in full-time employment in Britain, Italy and Germany had more rapid growth in their earnings than their US counterparts. Conversely, US workers were much more likely to see their earnings decline. The OECD also found that the US did not have higher labour mobility than its more regulated European counterparts.[51]

The Strange Afterlife of Horatio Alger

Given these realities, why does the Horatio Alger myth persist? Because in a very real sense the US has become several different countries. Different people inhabit these countries and there is often little social or cultural interaction between them. Race and ethnic considerations still play a role in settlement patterns, but wealth plays a greater one.

At the top end of the social spectrum, the really wealthy have all but seceded from the US. Their wealth allows them to live almost completely independently of any public provision. They inhabit their extensive private properties, educate their children in private schools and universities which are among the best in the world, organise their own private health insurance which pays for them to be treated in world-beating private hospitals and clinics and travel in private aircraft which often fly between privately owned airfields.

The ultimate expression of this separation has been

the growth of private gated communities called Home Owner Associations (HOAs). Here whole communities can effectively secede from their counties and states. Residents set conditions for would-be purchasers: how many children a family can have and what minimum ages they must have, whether domestic pets are allowed, and if so, what kind, right down to the type and weight of dogs allowed. Private security firms seal some HOAs from the outside world, admission is by invitation and intruders can be shot. Some of these HOAs now have populations numbering up to 50,000. Up to 7 million households now live in such communities in the US[52]; the figure in 1996 was under 3 million.[53] US architect Neal Payton writes, 'Gated communities are anathema to civic life. What they do is isolate individual neighborhoods from each other and from the public realm.' Almost 40 per cent of new homes in California are behind walls.[54]

Much of middle-class America also leads a separate life, separated not just from those poorer, but also from those richer. Manhattan is a rare exception where somebody earning a much better than average salary (over $100,000 a year) is constantly confronted with goods and properties that are far beyond even their most optimistic purchasing projections.

David Brooks sums up US middle-class reality in the following terms:

> But if you are a middle-class person in most of America, you are not brought into incessant contact with things you cannot afford. There are not Lexus dealerships on every corner. There are no snooty restaurants with water sommeliers to help you sort though the bottled eau selections. You can afford most of the things at Wal-Mart or Kohl's and the occasional meal at the Macaroni Grill. Moreover, it would be socially unacceptable for you to pull up to church in a Jaguar or to hire a caterer for your dinner party anyway. So you are not plagued by a nagging feeling of doing without.[55]

The US middle class, with significant state and

federal aid, became homeowners in the 1945–1965 period. At the beginning of that period, 45 per cent of US households owned homes, while by the end that figure had risen to 65 per cent. However, despite a 30 per cent increase in the US population since the mid-1970s, new housing starts fell by 40 per cent from 1975 to 2000. In much of urban California today, less than 40 per cent of households qualify for a home loan. Many middle-class buyers are being excluded from the US housing market.[56]

At the bottom end of the scale, the segregation becomes more stark. The US National Housing Conference reports that one in seven households faces the choice between spending more than 50 per cent of their income on housing or living in substandard locations.[57]

At the bottom of the working heap, at or close to the federal minimum wage, workers can expect a maximum gross income of around $1,200 a month. This is useful when it is additional family income (a working spouse), but creates its own problems as a living wage. When waitressing in Florida, Barbara Ehrenreich found that she could rent a one-room 'efficiency' apartment, basically a shack behind a mobile home, for $500 a month 50 kilometres from where she worked. She had to pay a deposit and her first month's rent in advance – $1,000 – and she could only afford that because she had given herself a $1,300 float to begin with. Saving up $1,000 out of a $1,200 monthly income is almost impossible.

She described the living conditions of her co-workers. One was sharing a room in what she describes as a 'flophouse' for $600 a month. One pregnant 20-year-old lived with her mother. One shared a $700-a-month one-person trailer. One couple without a car were paying $60 a night for a cheap hotel room (75 per cent of their monthly income), while another lived in a van parked behind a local shopping centre and 'rented' the hotel couple's shower in the mornings.[58]

If you live in a HOA you're not likely to bump into a waitress living in a van, nor to shop at Wal-Mart. If you spend 75 per cent of your joint income on a cheap hotel room, you're not likely to do all that much shopping anywhere.

In today's America, great wealth, middle-class comfort and struggling poverty are less and less likely to bump into each other. Each group, and most likely the subgroups within them, draw most of their social measurements from within their own peer group. This segregation threatens both the state and its economy. Naturally, those with more money, education and free time have a greater impact on political debate and government policies. If the parameters of that debate are largely defined within a specific income group, then the debate's conclusions logically reflect that group's preoccupations.

Education and Social Ascension

The less fortunate may draw some hope from the American Dream – that however difficult their lives are, their children can hope for better. Education has provided the doorway to success and upward social mobility for many a poor family.

Education is a vital development tool for the economy and for society as a whole. Universal primary education was established in the nineteenth century for political and economic reasons. Industrial economies needed a more educated workforce, and people with education were more likely to succeed in identifying market opportunities. Education was also vital for the development of democratic societies.

Thomas Jefferson, one of the founders of the US and its third president, wrote, 'I know of no safe depository of the ultimate powers of society but the people themselves; and if we think them not enlightened enough to exercise their control with a wholesome discretion, the remedy is not to take it from them, but to inform their discretion by education.'[59] Fifty years later, the British Conservative politician and Prime Minister Benjamin Disraeli put it more succinctly: 'Upon the education of the people of this country the fate of this country depends.'[60]

Countries around the world introduced universal primary education and even made it compulsory. This was followed by the provision of almost universal second-level education and eventually by providing access to third-level education for an ever larger swathe of society. In some countries access to third-level education is free, while others provide public support for students from less well-off backgrounds, usually through some mixture of grants and low-interest long-term student loans.

In 1944 the US government made funds available to war veterans (the GI Bill) to give them access to third-level education. For many working-class families this allowed their first-ever member to attend college and to purchase their own home. The GI Bill was dubbed 'the magic carpet to the middle class' and has been described as one of the most revolutionary pieces of legislation in American history.[61] The baby boomers' parents incarnated the American Dream, moving socially upwards through educational and professional achievement.

Two related trends are undermining the role of education as a motor for social advancement in today's US. One is the increasing withdrawal of the very wealthy from the public education system. The second is the reduction of public funding for education as local authorities and states struggle to balance their budgets.

Eleven per cent of US school students are educated in private schools such as Andover and Exeter (the UK figure is 7 per cent). In third-level education that figure doubles — 22 per cent of students attend private universities or colleges. These world-class institutions include the east coast Ivy League (Harvard, Yale, Cornell, Princeton), Stanford in California, Rice in Texas, Chicago University and Northwestern in Illinois, Emory in Georgia and Duke in North Carolina. The world-famous Massachusetts Institute of Technology (MIT) and Caltech are also private. Annual attendance at these institutions can cost up to $40,000.[62]

According to the OECD, the US spends about 1.4 per

cent of its GDP on third-level education. This compares to 0.7 per cent in the UK and approximately 1 per cent each in France and Germany. However, 92 per cent of that 1.4 per cent is spent on private universities and colleges.[63] So while the US spends about 40 per cent more than France on its third-level education, only 8 per cent of that spending goes to the public universities and colleges.

The average tuition cost at a private university was $18,273 and just over $4,000 at state-supported ones. Maintenance and living costs are extra and estimated to run around $10,000 a year in smaller towns and cities.[64] The main federal mechanism to support low-income students, the Pell grant, covered 80 per cent of the cost of a four-year course at a public university in 1965, but by 2000 it was covering just under 40 per cent.[65] Tuition fees at US public universities rose by 13 per cent in 2003 and by a further 10.5 per cent in 2004.[66]

US Department of Education statistics show that 15.9 per cent of those under 25 had left high school without any diploma in 2000. Their average earnings would be approximately $16,000 a year, while those with Master's degrees could expect to average $50,000. More startlingly, 51.2 per cent of high school drop-outs were either unemployed or described as being 'not in labour force'.[67] In a system where personal wealth is a determinant for educational access, the children of those who have not done well in education have little chance of attending the better schools and colleges.

This does not just threaten the American Dream of social mobility, it seriously degrades the skills of future American workers and thus the economic potential of the US. If a small number of world-beating US universities still lead the world in cutting-edge research, the story one step down the ladder is very different. China produced 325,000 engineering graduates in 2004, five times as many as the US (where the numbers of graduating engineers have been declining since the 1980s). The Chinese government invested $60 billion in research and development in 2003, and while the US figure was $282 billion, lower Chinese costs meant that there were 1.3 million Chinese researchers beavering away compared to 743,000 in the US.[68]

The percentage of US students graduating with Bachelor's degrees in science and engineering is less than half the comparable percentage in China and Japan. The annual Intel-sponsored international science competition attracts some 50,000 US high school students compared to 6 million Chinese entrants.[69] As *The New York Times*'s columnist Thomas Friedman put it, 'In China, Bill Gates is Britney Spears, in America Britney Spears is Britney Spears...The Chinese and the Indians are not racing us to the bottom. They are racing us to the top.'[70]

An international comparison of science scores by school students at the end of secondary school (1994–1995) across 21 countries ranked the US fifteenth, ahead of Italy, Hungary, Lithuania, Cyprus and South Africa, but behind Sweden, the Netherlands, Iceland, Norway, Canada, New Zealand, Australia, Switzerland, Austria, Slovenia, Denmark, Germany, France, the Czech Republic and Russia.[71] A survey of 556 seniors at 55 of the most prestigious universities in the US found that 40 per cent of them did not know when the US Civil War had taken place.[72]

Public educational funding in the US is a local responsibility. Federal funding accounted for 5 per cent in 1970, and this had fallen to around 4 per cent by 1999. In 1970, local authorities contributed over 50 per cent and the states made up the rest. That balance has reversed over the last 30 years, with states covering just over 50 per cent by 1999.[73]

Public funding for education across the US has been under pressure for some time, and this has been exacerbated by the current crisis in state and local taxation and income. A reporter described the library at a Philadelphia elementary school in the following terms: 'Chairs and tables are old, mismatched or broken. There isn't a computer in sight.' She went on to point out that the books in the library were so out of date that they did not mention the last five US presidents.[74]

Corvallis, Oregon has shut three of the city's 15 schools and cut kindergarten provision to half a day as part of the $2.3 million cuts this city of 52,000 is forced to make in its $30 million budget.[75] In Tulsa, Oklahoma the city is running crash courses to train mothers and grandparents as volunteer substitute teachers. School principals in Tucson, Arizona are asking parents to bring in toilet paper and sponges for schools and they are bartering any surplus for other supplies.[76]

Oklahoma cut school financing by $158 million, or 8 per cent, in 2002 and may have to shed 5,000 of the state's 44,000 teachers. The Alabama Association of School Boards expected to see 'the worst budget for public education in 30 years.' Oregon has cut $418 million from its $5.2 billion school budget and expects to cut a further $95 million, primarily by cutting 15 days from the school year, with another 28 days of schooling earmarked to go. In Portland, that means students will no longer study the metric system in arithmetic, electricity in science or Oregon's history. The 15-day cut in the school year would mean teachers would earn up to $5,000 a year less at the top end of their pay scale (experienced teachers with Master's degrees can earn up to $56,700 in Oregon).[77] Some Colorado school districts have gone to a four-day school week to cut costs. In California, preventive lay-off notices have gone out to 25,000 teachers.[78]

Corporate sponsorship and advertising is playing an ever increasing role in US public schools. The ZapMe! Corporation provides schools with a free computer lab and access to pre-selected websites which the school must use four hours per day. The ZapMe! system has constantly scrolling advertisements on the screen and the company collects information on students' browsing habits for sale to other companies. Channel One provides free educational television to 8 million students in 12,000 schools across the US. However, only

20 per cent of the daily twelve-minute broadcast is devoted to economic, cultural, social or political issues. The other 80 per cent is made up of advertising, sports, weather and Channel One promotions.[79]

Soft drinks companies such as Coca-Cola and PepsiCo have operated schemes whereby schools take part of the revenues from drink vending machines installed in school premises. According to the Centers for Disease Control and Prevention, such machines provide revenue to 98 per cent of high schools, 74 per cent of middle schools and 43 per cent of elementary schools. The products carried in these vending machines are advertised on Channel One. Interestingly, the rate of obesity amongst US school students has risen from 5 per cent to 15 per cent over the last 30 years.[80]

Universities are also suffering. Nebraska has ended aid to 1,000 university students and cut 401 jobs in state colleges. The University of Iowa has increased tuition fees by 18 per cent, the University of Georgia has operated a hiring freeze for more than a year and the state of Oklahoma has asked the University of Oklahoma to return money it was already granted.[81]

Twenty-six of the 50 US states cut their education budgets in 2002 and private endowments to the better-off private universities fell by 6 per cent. Every state increased its tuition fees, some by as much as 20 per cent. Not surprisingly, requests for aid have also boomed, doubling in Ohio, tripling in California and recording a fivefold increase in Massachusetts. Increases in requests in New York state are up 50 per cent, 39 per cent in Michigan and 30 per cent in Maine.[82]

University of Virginia law professor James Ryan wrote in *The Washington Post* that 'Children in this country are exposed to vastly different and unequal educational opportunities simply by accident of birth and place of residence. The impact of these inequalities is profound. Originally intended to be a social equalizer, public schools more often than not perpetuate the inequalities that exist in our society.'[83]

The New York Times went further. In an editorial it noted that the federal government had spent $10 on university education for wealthy students for every $1 it had spent on poorer ones over the last decade. The editorial recognised that the profound problems in American education also threaten the whole notion of a society based on opportunity for all: 'About 25 percent of high-achieving, poor students fail to enrol in college at all. If this pattern continues to play out, the dream of upward mobility through education will splutter and die.'[84]

Labour and Migration

In its traditional boom periods, US economic growth has always been driven by an influx of new labour. Most immigrants are willing to take the worst-paid jobs. They boost the output of their host economy through their labour and boost its production through their consumption. In the nineteenth and early twentieth centuries, this was supplied by the flood of mainly European immigrants.

A similar influx of new labour occurred during the 1990s, with up to 13.5 million new people arriving in the US, according to one study, coming predominantly from Latin America and Asia. This migratory wave exceeds that of the 'Great Wave' at the end of the nineteenth century and represents the highest number of immigrants in US history. 2.8 million of these migrants filled a gap in the 25–34 age range of the labour force. Few of them were elderly and there were significantly more men than women. Twenty-seven per cent were graduates and they are over-represented in science, engineering and IT, while being under-represented in teaching. Two-thirds of them are estimated to be in the US illegally, working in low-paid service and industrial jobs such as meat packing.[85]

If these findings are roughly accurate, the US economic motor received yet another low-cost labour boost, but other figures suggest that the longer-term economic effects of this may differ considerably from earlier waves of immigration. Technology and global development may be ironing out the kinks in how migrants spend their income.

The 'Great Wave' US immigrants washed into the US to build a new life, either with their families or to found families in their new country. As they built houses, bought food and furniture and sent their children to school, they funded the development of the US economy. By contrast, some, perhaps many, of today's Latin American immigrants in the US may not be considering settling there. Technology such as satellite broadcasting and cheaper phone calls and market developments like cheaper airfares make it easier for them to remain in contact with their countries of origin. The gradual improvement in Latin American economies and the provision of better services there may tempt them to return home rather than settle in the US. Their illegal, or dubious, status in the US also makes it more difficult for them to install families and send their children to school.

Jorge Pinto of Pace University, New York and former executive director of the World Bank commented: 'People think emigrants come to stay. Many are always with their eye to go back. Whenever they feel they have capital or critical mass they buy the property.' Salvadorans living in the US have been returning to El Salvador since the mid-1990s. Eighty-six per cent of some middle-class housing developments in San Salvador have been bought by Salvadorans working in the US.[86]

The incentive to send money home rather than spend it in the US is growing. While Mexican public health provision may be rudimentary, if the migrant worker can supply some dollars to their family, the health care they can obtain far outstrips anything available to an illegal worker in the US. In 2002, over $24 billion was transferred from the US to Latin America in the form of emigrants' remittances. El Salvador received $2 billion, 33 times the amount it received in official US aid, while

$1.6 billion went to Colombia. The Mexican government has offered to match 'migra-dollar' funding for local development projects such as schools, infrastructure and business. Remittances have increased since September 11th while US foreign investment has tailed off.

Latin American leaders from President Fox of Mexico to San Salvador's Mayor, Hector Silva, are pressing the US to give migrant workers a better deal. As the economy crumbled in Argentina, it was estimated that Latin America lost $25 billion in foreign investment between 1999 and 2001, but emigrants' remittances provided almost twice that amount. Latin American diplomats in the US have traditionally kept their distance from their illegal countrymen, but no longer. In November 2002, Luis Alberto Moreno, the Colombian ambassador to the US, joined in a vigil outside the White House demanding temporary work permits for Colombian immigrants in the US.[87]

If a substantial portion of this new immigrant wave is not planning to settle in the US, preferring instead to either work seasonally or for a period of years to finance a farm or business in their country of origin, then the boost to the US economy from their consumption may be a great deal less than that generated by similar waves of new cheap labour in the past.

Waking from the Dream

The American Dream of ever increasing wealth and social mobility is in trouble. The disparities between rich and poor, indeed between rich and the middle class, are greater than in many comparable market economies, and greater than they have been in the US since the 1920s.

The US spends more on its health care and third-level education than comparable countries, but this spending is concentrated on the better off. This concentration of health expenditure has become a factor mitigating against job creation in the US, while the concentration of educational expenditure is depriving US companies of a vital tranche of engineering and science graduates.

The US middle class is working longer hours than it has for many decades, and is working longer hours with fewer holidays than its counterparts in other countries. It is becoming harder and harder for the less well off to enter or finish third-level education.

The current wave of cheap migrant labour is not settling in the US to anything like the same degree its predecessors did. Much of the wealth they generate will be spent in San Salvador, Santiago or São Paolo rather than in Syracuse or San Francisco.

Together, all of these factors call the sustainability of an economy that depends on the capacity of ordinary Americans to keep borrowing and buying into serious doubt. There are already suggestions that the US economy may be approaching the point of debt saturation, with consumers borrowing not to buy more stuff, but to pay off old debts. It now takes $6 of extra debt to generate $1 of growth in the US economy.[88] By impoverishing its underclass and putting its middle class under ever increasing pressure, the US is creating a real danger that the cycle of consumption and borrowing that attracts foreign money and keeps the nation from bankruptcy will slowly grind to a halt.

The absence of action, even interest, in many of these semi-invisible issues is adding to the critical challenges US industry faces – and it has more than enough of those already.

4

From Fordism to Fantasy:
The Hollowing of American Industry

The greatest boosters of American economic might are its enemies. For a certain kind of vulgar Marxist, generic leftist and would-be anti-imperialist radical, the might of American capital is a given. It is unified and co-ordinated. The president and the Congress, whoever they may be, are its puppets and the military is its enforcer. It wants to rule the world and it is getting its wish.

In fact, American capital is not one single thing. There are three very different branches of US industry. One is made up of world-class transnational corporations developing and selling products across the globe. Another is largely composed of hollowed-out corporations where long-term success has been sacrificed to maximise short-term profit. Some of these corporations have migrated into the third sector, the defence and aerospace military-industrial complex. These are virtually nationalised industries, as their primary client is the US government.

The world-beating corporations need a stable framework of global agreements and governments. The other categories, the virtual shells and those dependent on tax dollars, require an ever more unilateralist US government. This is their story.

From 1870 onwards the US supplanted the UK as the world's leading economy.[1] In the early 1900s Henry Ford created Fordism, efficient mass production and marketing on a scale hitherto unknown. Fordism was the coming of age of the Industrial Revolution, the development of mass production and consumption. It established methods of industrial production, distribution and marketing which were to revolutionise the world and allow the US to become Roosevelt's 'Arsenal of Democracy',[2] turning out millions of weapons, aircraft, vehicles and tools during World War Two.

This Fordist model inspired industrial and economic development worldwide, spawning global corporations and management techniques. Fordist-inspired industrial production drove the US, and world, economies well into the last quarter of the twentieth century.

Henry Ford rejected the established business logic that the road to higher profits lay through paying the lowest wages possible and pricing the finished goods as high as the market could bear. Instead he paid high wages and stressed low pricing to create, or capture, a market.

Ford helped to create the great American consumer. In 1914 he offered workers $5 a day, more than double the going rate, and cut the working day from nine to eight hours. These conditions produced a motivated Ford workforce and a market for Ford products. This was not philanthropy. Workers were potential consumers, and to consume they had to have money. In later life Henry Ford was to argue against further automation in his factories on the grounds that 'robots don't buy motor cars'.[3]

The other side of this process was the use of mass production techniques to make cars so cheap that his own workers and their equivalents in other industries could afford them. The price of a Model T fell from $950 in 1908 to $290 by 1927. As a result, Ford sold 17 million cars between 1908 and 1927 – more cars than the rest of the world's automobile industry produced over the same period.

Ford's calculation was based on the creation of a virtuous circle. Well-paid workers with reasonable working hours would have both the money to buy what had previously been luxury products and the leisure time to enjoy them. The mass market thus created would lower unit costs, bringing the price down and allowing even more workers to buy them. More demand meant more workers with more money to spend, and the whole process renewed itself ever more vigorously.

Life and economies are never that simple, of course, and the journey towards a consumer paradise was interrupted by crises and wars, but the Fordist model did describe the essential dynamism of the American industrial economy. The combination of ingenuity, hard work, reasonable products and a social framework revalidated the American Dream. Everybody could make it, if not to the top, then at least several steps up the ladder. The guy on the Ford production line could retrace on a more modest scale Henry Ford's own journey from Dearborn farm boy to mega-rich tycoon.

US corporations such as Ford did not rely on the stock market for their capital. Their high profit levels came from the innovation of their founders and managers in a rapidly growing economy. 'Growth was driven by floods of innovative immigrants entre-preneurially combining cheap land and labour to exploit continental-scale market opportunities.'[4]

The traditional role of the stock market was to allow the founders of successful corporations to realise their capital by selling some of their corporations to the public.

The Wall Street crash and ensuing Depression which spread from the US to the world was essentially caused by the failure of the self-regulating and self-governing systems in the US banking sector. Laissez-faire capital-ism failed to police itself and imploded. A vital aspect of the New Deal inaugurated by Franklin Delano Roosevelt's election as president was the reform and regulation of the banking sector through the

Glass-Steagall Act of 1933. In 1934 the Securities and Exchange Commission (SEC) was established to regulate margin trading in stocks and to ensure that corporations published accurate annual accounts. Other legislation tightly regulated power utilities and other vital sectors.

US corporate legislation regulated the role of the emerging chief executive officers (CEOs), who effectively ran corporations they did not own. Most corporations had been built and run by their founder/owners. Now more professionals were being hired to discharge this role. Regulation established the CEO's first duty as one of running their corporation successfully. Dividends and responsibilities to shareholders came second.

The US economy grew by 3 per cent on average each year from World War Two up to the late 1970s, largely through corporations investing considerable amounts of their own profits into growing their companies. Federal defence spending contributed in certain key economic sectors and more generally in promoting research and development in leading-edge sciences and technologies.

Private Investors and Institutional Shareholders

One by-product of this growth and profit was a complete reversal of US share-owning patterns. In 1945, 93 per cent of US shares were owned by individuals, but by 1997 that had fallen to 43 per cent.[5] Private and institutional shareholders have very different interests and demands.

The private investor bought shares in Ford, Boeing or IBM primarily as a method of saving for retirement. The return on the investment was higher than the interest offered by financial institutions on savings and the arrangement benefited both parties. The private investor thus selected the shares he or she invested in not only carefully, but also with a view to their long-term yield. In effect, the investor was buying part of the company, and part of the reason for that purchase was the company's long-term performance.

The institutional investor is more likely to buy shares as a product, with a view to making a profit in a relatively short period of time. The underlying performance of the corporation becomes less important than its stock market image. Shares became a commodity in their own right. The 1990s high-tech boom accelerated the process of seeking short-term gains on share dealings. Shares in the Internet company Yahoo! were held for an average of eight days and Amazon's for seven, but shares in Coca-Cola were generally held for 26 months.[6]

As institutional investment grew, so did pressures to remove many of the constraints on share-dealing and financial services introduced after the Wall Street crash. Deregulation became the political catch-cry of the shareholder value revolution. Piece by piece, the network of checks and balances was dismantled. The Glass-Steagall Act was repealed in 1998.

In many ways that vote of the US Congress lowered the curtain on Fordism. The priorities of US corporate management had changed, the share price replaced profit and loss as the measuring tool for corporate performance, the shareholders became more important than the corporation and CEOs were now being largely paid in options on their corporations' shares. The higher the share price, the happier the shareholders were – and the richer the CEO became.

The overall value of executive stock options in the US in 2000 was $600 billion, which Will Hutton describes as 'one of the greatest wealth transfers recorded in world history'.[7] It was an ideologically and politically driven recipe for corporate change on a staggering scale, but it is not the best recipe for real corporate success.

Shareholder Value and Hollow Companies

General Electric Co. (GE), one of the largest and most diversified corporations in the world, was founded by another great figure from the heroic age of US capitalism, Thomas Alva Edison (1847–1931). Edison, another US rags-to-riches entrepreneur, is credited with the invention of the electric light bulb, the phonograph and the precursor of the electronic valve, amongst others. At his death he held over 1,000 patents.

GE's highest-profile products are its domestic white goods under the GE and Hotpoint brands, but these account for a fraction of its turnover. It is involved in media and broadcasting through NBC, CNBC, MSNBC and NBC Universal. It manufactures electricity-generating plant, aero engines and a host of other industrial products. A significant percentage of its industrial sales are to the US Department of Defense. Around half the company's activities are now in financial services (GE Financial Services).

The modern GE story is closely bound up with that of its flamboyant CEO, Jack Welch, who came to epitomise the new US management style during his 20 years at the head of GE from 1981. Under his leadership, GE turned in annual earnings increases of 14 per cent, fully meeting Welch's commitment to maximising shareholder value and thereby becoming one of the darlings of Wall Street.[8] For comparative purposes it is worth noting that a very attractive return on railway investments at the height of the 1834–1837 boom in England was 9.5 per cent.[9]

During Welch's tenure, GE did not create startling new products, nor sell hundreds of thousands of additional washing machines or jet engines. The move from manufacturing into financial services was a significant corporate development, as were some GE acquisitions, but the main earnings contributions came from paring costs, closing plants, shedding workers and cutting back savagely on research and development. GE shed 100,000 employees under Welch.

Welch accumulated a personal fortune estimated at $1 billion and was being paid over $17 million in salary, bonuses and stock options in 2000. The cash element of his retirement package is a $60,000-a-year consultancy retainer, but the non-cash elements are much more significant. GE undertook to give him 'continued lifetime access to company facilities and services comparable to those which are currently made available to him by the company.'[10]

GE's earning performance during 1981 to 2001 is neither repeatable nor sustainable. Doubtless some further efficiency savings can be made, but finally somebody has to make and sell the washing machines and jet engines and vet the financial service products. In short, GE cannot shed another 100,000 staff and continue to exist in its present form. A Wall Street trader who deals in GE stock commented that 'the G.E. that Jack Welch constructed wasn't going to produce the profit growth that this company has always forecast.'[11]

Boeing illustrates the shift in corporate management priorities from growing and developing a top-notch company to maximising current shareholder income. Boeing's research and development has also shrunk to a point where its ability to design and build radically new aircraft – the skill that made Boeing the world's leading aircraft manufacturer in the past – is now questionable.

Boeing pioneered the development of single-wing all metal aircraft, designing and building heavy bomber aircraft for the US Army, including the B-17 Flying Fortress (1935) and the B-29 Super Fortress (1942). Boeing evolved in Seattle, Washington to benefit from the local aluminium industry, which in turn had grown up because of the availability of cheap electricity from New Deal hydroelectric projects such as those on the Columbia River. Boeing later designed and built the B-52 and helped in the B-1 bomber programme. It went on to design and build a hugely successful range of jet passenger aircraft – the 707, 727, 737, 747, 757, 767 and 777.

Boeing's best-known airliner is the 747 jumbo jet, which was first mooted in the 1960s. Boeing's gamble was that the future of passenger airline traffic lay in moving large numbers of passengers relatively cheaply in a single aircraft. Boeing management bet the company's future on the 747 – this while Europe was betting on air travel continuing to be a luxury market and was building the Anglo-French Concorde.

Boeing had its own cash reserves, most of its shareholders were small and loyal and Boeing had a good working relationship with a network of regional banks in the US north-west. Boeing also had a large pre-production order from Pan Am for its revolutionary aircraft. Pan Am had the necessary mass and guaranteed profitability in a regulated environment to place and finance the order. The US Civil Aeronautics Board (CAB) regulated the airline industry to guarantee profitability for airlines and to fund aircraft development and technical innovation.

Twelve thousand five hundred Boeing engineers worked on the 747 for almost 10 years. The project had cost Boeing almost $2 billion when the first jumbo jet was delivered to Pan Am in 1970, but it was not until 1978 that Boeing received orders for 83 747s. Over the next decade or so, Boeing was to realise a $20 billion return on its $2 billion investment. The project time span had been 20 years.[12]

Political changes mean that Boeing cannot repeat the 747 gamble of building a revolutionary aircraft. Banking deregulation slashed the number of regional banks. It is estimated that the number of banks in the US declined by 50 per cent from 1980 to 2000. This made once-off profits for banks and brokering houses but concentrated major banking decisions in fewer headquarters. The banks themselves had to nurture their share price quotations.[13] No single bank or small group of large banks could afford to finance a $2 billion industrial gamble for 20 years. Wall Street would not accept it and the banks' share prices would suffer. Neither would Wall Street investors contemplate making such an investment themselves.

The almost total airline deregulation which took place following the abolition of the US Civil Aeronautics Board in 1978 has produced cheaper fares for passengers on some routes at a cost of paring airline margins to the bone and provoking a range of mergers and bankruptcies. Airlines in the US no longer have either the scale of Pan Am nor the financial security to plan aircraft acquisition years, if not decades, ahead. Airlines must also carefully monitor their share price performance.

In 1987, a small group of fund managers were persuaded by T. Boone Pickens of the US Shareholders' Association to mount a raid on Boeing. Boeing's shares were trading at $7 against an estimated asset value of $75. Wall Street was worried by stories that Boeing was considering the development of a replacement for the 747.[14] The raid was defeated, but Boeing management got the message. Plans for new aircraft were shelved, research and development budgets slashed and almost 50,000 workers laid off. The share price climbed to $60. Phil Condit, the then Boeing CEO (who in 1996 held $9.8 million worth of Boeing stock options),[15] said that Boeing's priorities were no longer building 'an airplane that went further than somebody else's. Now we are going into a value-based environment where the unit cost, return on investment, shareholder return are the measures by which you'll be judged. That's a big shift.'[16]

The shift proved problematic when in October 1997 Boeing's low-cost just-in-time (JIT) parts ordering and delivery system broke down. The purpose of such systems is to cut costs by the final manufacturer not having to hold stocks of vital parts. Instead, suppliers deliver them JIT. The Boeing plants stopped production for lack of parts at a cost of $2.6 billion to the company.[17]

Boeing toyed with, then abandoned the idea of building its Sonic Cruiser, an airliner that would fly just below the speed of sound. In 2002 it announced that it was moving its headquarters from Seattle to Chicago. Its research and development programmes have been so drastically cut that apart from its military projects, Boeing has only one new passenger aircraft in the pipeline.[18]

The Boeing 747 replacement, the A-380, designed

and built by Europe's Airbus Industrie at Toulouse, France, rolled out in early 2005. Development costs are budgeted at €12 billion. Meantime, Boeing has announced its plans to build the world's biggest aircraft – the Pelican military transport. Aeronautical engineers claim that it will be able to fly 14,000 tons of cargo (17 main battle tanks) more than 16,000 kilometres. The Pelican will be designed to fly at an altitude of six metres over water using the buoyant aerodynamic wing-in-ground effect to provide its maximum economic range.[19]

Boeing's switch from competitive airliner design to federally funded military contracts is illustrated by its impressive list of government projects. Boeing designed and built parts of the Atlas and Saturn moon rockets, the MX Inter-Continental Ballistic Missile (ICBM) and the Air-Launched Cruise Missile (ALCM). Boeing bought the helicopter maker Vertol in 1960 (Chinook CH-47D transport helicopter) and its only US competitor in civil airliner construction, McDonnell Douglas, in 1997. McDonnell Douglas is the major manufacturer of current fighter aircraft, including the F-15 Eagle and the F-18. Boeing also developed the (recently cancelled) RAH-66 Comanche helicopter, the revolutionary (and controversial) V-22 Osprey and the C-17 military transport aircraft.

If Boeing cannot afford to design and develop new products, its share of the civil airliner market must inevitably shrink. Already Airbus is slightly ahead in sales, and Brazil's Embraer is nipping at its heels.[20] In the longer term, Boeing will either have to abandon civil airliner construction or watch its share price tumble. Once a world leader, Boeing has been hobbled by ideologically driven political decisions and is increasingly dependent on the US government for its business. According to *The Washington Post*, Boeing needs 'a staggering $1 billion per week, and it can no longer rely on its struggling commercial aircraft business to supply most of that figure.'[21] In the name of private property rights, Boeing has become a state-dependent enterprise.

Fantasy Replaces Fordism

Our economies change continuously. New products and services develop and consumer tastes and preferences evolve. Whatever the changes, certain basics remain immutable. Companies must make profits to survive. They must have goods and services to sell, and they must sell those goods and services for more than it costs to produce them.

There have been a number of spectacular US corporate collapses in recent years, collapses so spectacular that Enron and WorldCom have become familiar names. Some of these collapses have involved fraudulent practices. Since corporate management is probably neither more virtuous nor more venal than any other group of people, there is nothing particularly striking about that.

However, two elements of these corporate failures are striking. Firstly, political cronyism played a role in changing regulatory provisions to favour certain companies and sectors. Cronyism is not in itself abnormal, but what stood out was how extraordinarily blatant the cronies were. Secondly, in the intertwining of business and politics, fantasy became a key management tool. In politics, reality is being redefined to suit ideology or faith. In business, when reality became uncomfortable, rather than change its practices, management simply invented a new reality. Companies that were losing money, and which had no real hope of making money, lied to themselves, their shareholders, their clients, their employees and to the world in general. Management came, fatally, to believe its own propaganda and successfully sold that propaganda to investors.

Enron and Energy Deregulation

Enron was a successful, profitable pipeline company. Every year in the US, 25 billion hectolitres of oil and trillions of cubic metres of natural gas move through over 3 million kilometres of local, state and interstate pipelines. Enron was 'the Kings of the American pipeline business', owning more pipeline than any other company and transporting 17.5 per cent of all the gas consumed in the US.[22] One former Houston Natural Gas executive said of pipelines, 'All they do is make money. It's boring, but it's dependable.'

Enron was owned by Ken Lay, a Texas Republican and an active supporter of both Bush presidents. He lobbied hard for deregulation of energy utilities and the pipeline business. Among his targets were the New Deal Public Utility Holding Company and the Federal Power and Communications Acts, which capped prices and profits for companies in the sector. Government approval was required for bond issues. There could be no offshore or off-book company holdings and, most significantly, such companies could not make any political donations at all.[23] President Bush, Sr. approved electricity and telecoms deregulation before he left office in 1992, including removing the Uniform System of Accounts which was obligatory in the power sector.

Governor George W. Bush undertook similar deregulation in Texas. The market was now open to Enron, and it could design its own accountancy systems. The electricity industry expressed its gratitude by directly contributing $6.5 million to the Bush 2000 campaign and $2.4 million to Gore. Overall the industry was to spend $19 million on the presidential elections in 2000.[24]

Enron began its transformation from a pipeline to a trading company in the early 1990s. Ken Lay brought on a whole new management generation headed by former McKinsey consultant Jeff Skilling, with Andy Fastow as chief financial officer and a whiz-kid specialist in electronic trading, Louise Kitchen. By the end of the decade, EnronOnline was up and running.

EnronOnline launched in November 1999 and quickly became the biggest e-commerce site the Internet had ever seen. It was based in Enron's 40-storey, $300 million Houston tower which had four trading floors, each capable of holding 500 highly computerised trading desks. Enron's European HQ in London cost another $100 million.

In the first five months of 2000, EnronOnline did 110,000 transactions worth over $45 billion. Enron knew about gas, electricity and related commodities, so EnronOnline started trading them, and lots of other things as well – coal, refined products, bandwidth, paper, plastics, clean air credits... Enron was trading over 800 different products. EnronOnline became the market setter. Wall Street commodity traders always had one computer screen tuned to the Enron site.

Enron's IT platform was impressive, the best. It could assess the risk, process and account the trade instantly. Its traders were the best and almost every trade was balanced with a hedge. As a supplier and a consumer, Enron could read the market. Enron began to make the market.

Skilling told *The Financial Times* in June 2000: 'We believe that markets are the best way to order an industrial enterprise. You are going to see the disintegration of the business systems we have all grown up with.'

There was one wrinkle in all this hyper-growth, this dawning of the perfect market. The trading generated no profits for Enron. It was the market maker, trading hedges, and it needed cash to back all those trades. Enron did not have the money so it had to borrow it, but Enron was already heavily indebted. In the first six months of 2000, Enron borrowed $3.4 billion to finance its operations. It had a negative cash flow from those operations of $547 million during that same period, and by the end of June 2000 it was paying $2 million a day in interest.

Enron needed fresh money, but if it borrowed more its credit rating might slip, and the costs of servicing the borrowing would rise, adding to the losses. Some new source of money was needed, one that would not affect the company's credit rating.

Chief financial officer Andy Fastow was to show a particular genius at 'creative accounting'. Creative accounting often involves bending rules, and if you bend them far enough, they break. Fastow was to boast that his financial engineering 'could strip out any risk'.

At the end of 1999 his peers recognised his genius. *Chief Financial Officer Magazine* named him as one of their CFOs of the Year and gave him its CFO Excellence Award for Capital Structure for helping make Enron into a 'master of creative financing'. Enron paid Fastow over $11 million a year between 1998 and 2001 for his creative genius.

Fastow's idea was simplicity itself. He would create offshore companies where high-cost or high-risk Enron investments would be parked. These companies, and there were many of them, including four known as the Raptors, would 'buy' any acquisitions that Enron preferred not to have on its books. With a touch of a keyboard, Enron's balance sheet would look better, its credit ratings and stock price would improve and the company and its executives would prosper.

Since Enron owned the companies 'buying' its embarrassing acquisitions, the deals could be quick and the price fixed to suit Enron. This intricate network of offshore companies needed financing, and the financing was arranged against Enron stock. The better the Raptors and their siblings made the Enron balance sheet, the higher the Enron stock went. At the beginning of 2000, Enron's stock stood at $43 and on 23 August 2000 it peaked at $90 per share. Enron pledged $1 billion of its stock to finance Fastow's offshore empire, and since Fastow owned part or most of the empire, he made an additional $45 million on the deals.

There were two problems with all this creative financing. One was that is was based on nothing more than massaging the Enron stock price upwards to levels that bore no resemblance whatsoever to the company's real performance. To quote *Time* magazine, it was all 'smoke and mirrors'.[25]

The second problem was that much of it was, as Enron's own legal department warned, illegal. An Enron attorney e-mailed his superiors on 1 September 2000, saying: 'We have discovered that a majority of the investments being introduced into the Raptor Structure are bad ones. This is disconcerting – it might lead one to believe that the financial books at Enron are being "cooked" in order to eliminate a drag on earnings.' Enron's accountants and auditors, the now-defunct Arthur Andersen practice, did not seem to have a problem. It handled all the accounting for the Raptor deals – and charged Enron $1.3 million for its services.[26]

The Enron house of cards collapsed, with Arthur Andersen imploding in its wake. The stench of corruption wafted across corporate America and into the Rose Garden of the White House. Enron filed for bankruptcy in December 2001. The investigations, arrests and seizures continue. Shareholders, including mutual funds across the US, lost $67 billion. Twelve thousand six hundred Enron staff were laid off immediately. The Enron pension scheme – called a 401(k) in the US, where pension schemes are tied to the employer – was stuffed with now worthless Enron shares. Former Enron employees who had paid into the 401(k) scheme for years were left with no pension provision at all, and this in a state (Texas) and a country (the US) which has no effective social welfare safety net.[27]

Fantasy evaporated in the harsh light of reality, and took the profitable remains of Enron's Fordist pipeline business with it.

WorldCom and Telecoms Deregulation

Telecommunications was once a highly regulated sector in the US, with restrictions not vastly different from those applied to power utilities. Telecom corporations benefited from deregulation of their industry by President Bush, Sr. just before he left office. The industry was not ungrateful. The telecoms start-up Global Crossing paid President Bush, Sr. in stock options for a lecture to its board. When Global Crossing went public, those options were worth $13 million.[28] Global Crossing recorded a $25.5 billion bankruptcy on 2 January 2002.[29]

The best-known telecoms fiasco is WorldCom.

WorldCom perpetrated what *Time* magazine called 'the most sweeping bookkeeping deception in history.' *Time* went on to describe the WorldCom scam in the following terms: 'Unlike Enron which fooled investors with esoteric and highly creative accounting tricks, WorldCom cooked its books with a scheme even an Accounting 101 student could have devised.'[30] WorldCom simply recorded $3.8 billion in business expenses as investment in capital assets. Electricity bills became energy investments, and $3.8 billion in expenditure became a positive element on the balance sheet. Twenty thousand jobs have gone at WorldCom and WorldCom's 401(k) pension scheme is worthless. WorldCom losses amount to over $150 billion and it has debts of $32 billion. Arthur Andersen were WorldCom's accountants, consultants and auditors.

In post-war Iraq, the Pentagon was to award a $45 million deal without a tendering process to build a mobile telecoms system to MCI, the survivor of the WorldCom fiasco.[31] The US-led Coalition Provisional Authority acted to close the GSM mobile system which Batelco (Bahrain Telecommunications Company) opened in Baghdad in July 2003, leaving MCI with a monopoly. MCI has no experience of operating mobile phone services.[32]

Tyco – Greed is Good

The Tyco Group was promoted as proof of the modern version of the American Dream – or 'greed is good'. Dennis Kozlowski, the son of a Newark, New Jersey detective, joined what was to become the Tyco Group in 1975. By 1992 he was its CEO. In less than 10 years he transformed it from a $3 billion-a-year group into a $38.5 billion-a-year conglomerate with a huge range of products and services. Under his reign, Tyco multiplied its profits by 40 and its stock price twelvefold.[33]

The group was described as 'hyper-efficient' by *Business Week* in May 2001, where Kozlowski was featured standing in front of his corporate helicopter. He told the magazine that his ambition was 'to build another General Electric'.[34]

Kozlowski's strategy was to have his in-house team of merchant bankers seek out and purchase solid companies with low market quotations as cheaply as possible. Once purchased, these companies were rapidly slimmed down to become profit machines for Tyco, or simply asset-stripped. Tyco got a taste for offshore holdings in 1997 and then went offshore big time. Tyco was avoiding, or evading, up to $500 million a year in taxes.

Tyco was built on credit, on new deals replacing old, and the group was carrying $26 billion in debts when the market began to slow. Following the Enron collapse, accounts were more carefully scrutinised, and Wall Street's faith-based optimism started to crumble. Tyco's share price slid from $60 to $7. Up to $80 billion of investors' money had become worth less than $10 billion overnight – and worse was to come.[35] Behind his simple working-class-boy-done-well image, Dennis Kozlowski may have helped himself to up to $135 million from the firm's coffers. He was arrested on 3 June 2002, the day after he resigned as Tyco CEO. According to a 2002 study by *The Financial Times*, US corporate insiders from the top 25 bankrupt companies took $3.3 billion in stock sales, bonuses and other compensation even as their firms were spiralling into insolvency.[36]

Fraudulent management practices added to Tyco's problems, but the roots of the disaster lay in its expectations of never-ending credit-financed deals. No deal needed to make even a paper profit, as it would soon be superseded by the next, even bigger, deal. This is the classic stock market bubble described by Nobel prize-winning economist Joseph Stiglitz as having

> echoes of tulip mania – What were these seeds of destruction? The first was the boom itself: it was a classic bubble, asset prices unrelated to underlying values, of a kind familiar to capitalism over the centuries. Bubbles are based on a certain irrational exuberance, and perhaps not since the days of tulip bulb mania had the irrationality of the market been more in evidence...[37]

Finance Capitalism

We still think of business in terms of making goods and selling services, yet today's reality is that we have moved beyond that into what can be termed 'finance capitalism'. More money – much more – is made from moving and trading money than is made from making cars, extracting ores, growing food, cutting hair or dry cleaning clothes. And money is global, moving electronically from Tokyo to Taipei to Cairo to Frankfurt to London to New York and back to Tokyo via the Cayman Islands in minutes, 24 hours a day, seven days a week, 365 days a year.

This is finance capitalism — 'making money from trading stocks, bonds, currencies and other forms of securities as well as lending money to companies, governments, and consumers rather than manufacturing products and selling them at prices determined by unfettered markets.'[38] Adam Smith (1723–1790), often seen as the great apologist for free enterprise, believed that most capitalists would prefer to make money than things, and so it can be argued that finance capitalism is a logical evolution of capitalism.

Finance capitalism deals in intangibles, the values of currencies and stocks, rather than physical goods. Valuing intangibles is essentially a question of political decisions made by individual analysts and traders. The value of the intangible should bear some relationship to a reality, and not just be the result of speculation, much less fraud. Therefore, there is a requirement for transparency and oversight. In short, an element of regulation is required to ensure the effective working of the market, yet deregulation retains almost mystical – not to stay fantasy – values for US neoconservatives.

The radical changes in US corporate behaviour came about as a result of distinct political choices made by the US executive and Congress to deregulate whole sections of the US economy. This deregulation drive flows from a mixture of the traditional US definitions of freedom and from a concerted campaign by neoconservatives whose ideological thought can be summed up as follows: 'the public interest is simply the sum of all private interests. Public intervention is an unwarranted interference in the sacred duty of a corporate management to its shareholders.'[39]

Alan Greenspan, chairman of the US Federal Reserve (central bank), makes the argument for a regulatory role for state or international authorities: 'Modern market forces must be coupled with advanced financial regulatory systems, a sophisticated legal architecture and a culture supportive of the rule of law.'[40]

Although the regulatory pendulum has swung slightly back in the US, it remains considerably more lax than its European counterparts, and more lax than it was in the US even 20 years ago. This regulatory weakness threatens the very system itself – 'Only capitalists can kill capitalism, but the system cannot stand much more abuse of the type we have witnessed recently...Enron, WorldCom, Global Crossing, Tyco and their CEOs.'[41]

Global Reality versus Fantasia Americana

In all of these scandals, the intertwining of business and politics has helped to create disaster. Ironically, however, the over-arching political agenda of the neoconservatives threatens US companies from the opposite angle – it directly contradicts the long-term interests of those successful global transnational corporations (TNCs).

On the one side, US neoconservatives and their nationalist allies take an essentially hostile approach to the international community and are viscerally opposed to the very concept of international law. John R. Bolton, former Under Secretary at the US State Department, argues this position quite clearly: 'It is a big mistake for us to grant any validity to international law, even when it may seem in our short-term interest to do so — because, over the long term, the goal of those who think that international law really means anything are those who want to constrict the US.'[42]

On the other side, however, the giants of US business are now global entities, and their profitability is crucial to the entire US system. In the 1990s, US corporate profits from activities outside the US grew at twice the rate for activities within the US. In 2000, US exports amounted to $1.1 trillion, while in the same year sales by foreign affiliates of US corporations amounted to $2.9 trillion.[43]

The developed economies are becoming so interdependent that the very idea that the US can go it alone is patently absurd. BMW makes vehicles in the US, for sale in the US, with the profits returning to Munich. Ford similarly makes vehicles in Germany, and their profits head for Detroit. Dell makes computers in Ireland out of components which arrive from all over the world. To describe BMW simply as a German company or Ford as simply an American company is as meaningless as calling Dell an Irish company.

Thus, when the Bush administration started to treat France and Germany as hostile nations in the run-up to the Iraq War, its stance was a direct denial of the economic realities of the nation it governs. US TNCs invest around the world, but Europe is still the primary destination for US money. During 1994 to 2002, US investment in the Netherlands was twice the US investment in Mexico and 10 times more than US investment in China.[44] In 2000, the total output of US corporate affiliates outside the US amounted to just over $600 billion, with 55 per cent of that output coming from Europe. At over $300 billion, US corporate assets in Germany are greater than total US corporate assets in Latin America. Conversely, just over two-thirds of foreign assets held in the US, or $3.3 trillion, are held by European firms.[45]

Neoconservatives like to point out that trade with Europe makes up a minority of US business dealings with the outside world, but as a measure of economic interdependence, trade is often misleading. In 1989, total trade between the US and Asia amounted to $315 billion versus $188 billion for trade between the US and the EU, but combined sales by US foreign affiliates in the EU and US exports to the EU amounted to over $600 billion.[46]

A huge amount of political, diplomatic and economic effort has gone into the opening up of the Chinese market to US firms, and the 1990s saw a dramatic rise in direct US investment in the People's Republic of China (PRC), with US affiliate sales reaching $32 billion in 2000. However, this record level of sales in the PRC was still about the same as US sales in Sweden, and considerably less than the $236 billion sold in Germany or the $137.5 billion sold in France.[47]

Over the decade 1990 to 2001, the regional sources of income for foreign affiliates of US companies around the world broke down as follows in Table 4.1.[48]

Table 4.1: Regional Sources of Income for Foreign Affiliates of US Companies

Region	Percentage
Europe	50%
Asia-Pacific	19%
Latin America	11%
Canada	9%
Other	11%

Internet bandwidth gives a picture of traffic levels between different regions of the world, and thus of the extent of commercial activities. Table 4.2 illustrates Internet bandwidth traffic in 2001.[49]

Table 4.2: Internet Bandwidth Traffic, 2001

Between	Per Cent of Global Bandwidth
US and Canada – Europe	73.5%
US and Canada – Asia/Pacific	18.9%
US and Canada – Latin America	6.4%
Europe – Asia/Pacific	0.5%
US and Canada – Africa	0.35%
Europe – Africa	0.2%
Europe – Latin America	0.03%

All these figures show a global economy with a highly integrated core covering the US, Canada and Europe. This reality simply does not fit with a unilateralist approach to global problems in which global institutions like the UN are held in contempt and the US presents itself to the world as an irrational, unpredictable rogue superpower.

As we have seen, the sales by foreign affiliates of US firms and those US earnings of European affiliates in the US that are held in dollars help to fund US deficits. The US economy requires foreign capital inflows of over $1 billion per day just to operate.[50] US government policies, from selective tax cuts to environmental myopia to expensive unilateral foreign adventures, are making a bad situation worse to the point where one Nobel laureate in economics, George Akerlof, has described those policies as 'a form of looting'.[51]

Overall, the US economy is fragile and vulnerable. Should foreign confidence slip, the dollar will become steadily less attractive to foreign investors and the funding of US deficits will become ever harder to sustain. If Washington can get its head around the need to tackle this challenge in a gradual, yet determined, way, international co-operation will be vital. Should Washington continue to both deny and aggravate the situation, the US economy will crash. The ensuing economic crisis would be global both in its impact and in its solutions.

Either way, the US needs the rest of the world at least as much as the rest of the world needs the US.

5

The Military-Industrial Complex

The overall US economy, to the extent that such a single entity exists, is vulnerable in the extreme. Rising poverty, increasing wealth disparities, the absence of any health care policy and shrinking access to higher education all come together to make it more and more difficult for US consumers to sustain their levels of consumption – while denying tomorrow's businesses the educated workforce they will require. An absolutist approach to private property rights in terms of shareholders' interests has contributed to hollowing out whole swathes of US industry. It's a picture which would suggest that the US government should be committed to an industrial development policy, a partnership with business where scarce federal funds are used to boost the products and the businesses of tomorrow. Instead, the US government does the exact opposite.

Why does a US government largely led by experienced, educated and intelligent people work so very hard against the interests of the United States of America? One part of the answer is the ideological, or faith-based, beliefs which drive the neoconservatives and other ideologues within the Bush administration. The other part of the answer lies in the fact that one significant, and in political terms disproportionately influential, sector of US industry does not depend on global markets for its sales – it depends on federal dollars.

In his 1961 farewell address, President Dwight D. Eisenhower, himself a man who had commanded US forces in a global war, famously described this sector in the following terms:

> The conjunction of an immense military establishment and a huge arms industry is new in the American experience. The total influence – economic, political, and even spiritual – is felt in every city, every state house, and every office of the federal government…In the councils of government, we must guard against the acquisition of unwarranted influence, whether sought or unsought, by the military-industrial complex.[1]

Eisenhower was describing a new development. While many large general engineering groups could, and did, manufacture arms, before World War Two there were very few companies which produced only military hardware. President Eisenhower said,

> Until the latest of our world conflicts, the United States had no armaments industry. American makers of plowshares could, with time and as required, make swords as well. But now we can no longer risk emergency improvisation of national defense; we have been compelled to create a permanent armaments industry of vast proportions.

President Eisenhower's draft for his speech included the more accurate phrase 'military-industrial-congressional complex', but Eisenhower deleted 'congressional' as he felt it inappropriate for an outgoing president to criticise the Congress.[2]

This military-industrial-congressional complex is dependent on the US government for its profits and for its very survival to a degree which has led Professor Chalmers Johnson to dub the US defence sector 'state socialism'.[3] Perhaps more accurately, it is America's substitute for socialism – an ideologically acceptable method for the creation of state-subsidised industries.

The George W. Bush administrations have added a

new layer to the complex with the privatisation of war itself. A new and rapidly expanding US business sector is currently carrying out many functions previously discharged by the military. This raises serious questions of legal and political responsibility together with complex moral and ethical ones.

In 1925, President Calvin Coolidge said that 'the chief business of the American people is business',[4] which could be paraphrased today to read 'the chief business of the US government is war'.

The US Military-Industrial-Congressional Complex

The US is the world's largest military power and the world's largest arms manufacturer. It alone accounts for almost 57 per cent of global arms sales.[5]

The 2005 US Defense budget, including nuclear weapons expenditure by the Department of Energy, amounts to just over $450 billion. When military aid to foreign governments, veterans' benefits and military pensions are included, this rises to over $560 billion, more or less the size of the US federal deficit.[6] This is 15 per cent higher than what the US spent on average through the Cold War and represents a 30 per cent increase on US Defense spending since 2001. The US now accounts for over 40 per cent of global military expenditure and spends more on defence than the next 15 countries combined. The 2003 increase of $48 billion was in itself greater than the total military budget of any other single nation.[7] The seven potential 'enemy' states identified by the US in 2002 (Cuba, Iran, Iraq, Libya, North Korea, Sudan and Syria) combined, plus the Russian Federation and the People's Republic of China, collectively spent $177 billion on defence.[8]

In 2000, the Pentagon spent $133.2 billion on procurement contracts.[9] The 2004 pecking order for contractors was Lockheed Martin ($21.9 billion), Boeing ($17.3 billion), Northrop-Grumman ($11.1 billion) and

General Dynamics ($8.2 billion). In addition, the Pentagon provides around $8 billion a year in different supports and subsidies for arms exports, much of the $1.8 billion US annual military aid to Israel goes on the purchase of US weapons and the 48 Lockheed F-16s Poland will acquire in 2006 will be funded by a $3.8 billion US Treasury loan.[10]

The armed forces need weapons, private industry designs and builds those weapons and Congress votes on the budgets. Private industry needs the flow of federal dollars, so it lobbies the military and Congress. Senators and Representatives want jobs for their states and districts, so they vote in favour of 'pork barrel' contracts to benefit their constituents.

A striking example of 'pork barrel' is the Lockheed Martin C-130 Hercules transport aircraft, which is produced in Marietta, Georgia. According to the US General Accounting Office (GAO), the Air Force requested five new C-130s between 1978 and 1998. Congress voted for funds for 256 aircraft. Senator Sam Nunn of Georgia was on the Armed Services Committee and Republican House Speaker Newt Gingrich was elected from a Georgia constituency. As Congress does not usually vote on how the additional operational funds necessary for this extra equipment are to be actually deployed, much of it ends up being stored on a care-and-maintenance basis by the service involved. These costs actually lower the military capabilities of the forces by draining resources from their operational budgets.[11] In other words, vast amounts of public money are spent on weakening the armed forces.

Defence contractors are major suppliers of political campaign contributions. In 1997, the six biggest contractors received $54 billion in Pentagon contracts and made campaign contributions of $2.5 million.[12] By the 2000 elections, the four largest Pentagon contractors made $11 million in campaign contributions.[13]

Lockheed Martin and Boeing are the two biggest defence contractors. Boeing needs $1 billion a week to sustain its operations and Lockheed Martin needs $500 million a week.[14]

For 2004, the Pentagon requested $8.4 billion for the F-22 and the F-35 Joint Strike Fighter programmes – both for Lockheed Martin – with total joint programme costs estimated at $297 billion. In 2004, Boeing was earmarked for $9.7 billion for its F-18 fighter, C-17 transport aircraft, the controversial V-22 Osprey aircraft and its Comanche helicopter, with total programme costs being estimated at $202 billion.[15] In February 2004, the Pentagon cancelled the Comanche helicopter programme (having spent $8 billion on it since 1983), but the bulk of these funds was switched within the Defense budget to updating the Boeing-built Apache attack helicopter.[16]

This incestuous relationship between two branches of the US government – the presidency and Congress – and major private corporations that are largely or wholly dependent on that government for their sales and profits makes it increasingly difficult to determine where the interests of the US government end and those of its military suppliers begin. The fact that certain companies have achieved what amounts to a monopoly in certain sectors makes this relationship ever more intimate.

Lockheed Martin is a prime example. Over 80 per cent of the company's income comes from the US government, with most of the remaining 20 per cent coming from foreign arms sales funded, financed or guaranteed by that same government. Lockheed writes more computer code than Microsoft. Its systems sort mail for the US Post Office, calculate taxes, operate the census and write Social Security cheques – a $525 million programme. It has an $87 million contract to make the new Department of Homeland Security's computers talk to each other, an $18 billion programme to rebuild the US Coast Guard and will supply 6 million biometric identity cards for those working in transportation in the US.[17]

As the chief weapons procurement official of the Pentagon, Mr E.C. Aldridge, Jr. commissioned the development of Lockheed's F-22 Raptor at $258 million apiece. Mr Alridge now serves as a Lockheed board member. The traffic flows in the other direction as well. Those who have represented, worked or lobbied for Lockheed who now serve in government include the new National Security Adviser, Stephen J. Hadley, the Secretary of the Navy, the Secretary of Transportation, the director of the national nuclear weapons complex and the director of the national spy satellite agency. Former Lockheed executives serve on the US Defense Policy Board, the Defense Science Board and the Homeland Security Advisory Council. Danielle Brian of Washington's Project on Government Oversight commented that 'it's impossible to tell where government ends and Lockheed begins...The fox isn't guarding the henhouse. He lives there.'[18]

Lockheed's chief executive and former US Marine, Robert J. Stevens, whose 2003 compensation package totalled $9.5 million, described his company's position as being 'at the intersection of policy and technology... thinking through the policy dimensions of national security as well as the technological dimensions.' Mr Stevens pictures Lockheed technology offering US forces 'a picture of the battle-space, a god's-eye view.'[19]

Straightforward, old-fashioned corruption continues as well. Boeing had been granted a lease-purchase contract from the US Air Force for over 100 Boeing 767 aircraft configured as airborne tankers. This would have cost the Air Force more than if it had bought the aircraft or modernised its existing fleet, but it would have allowed Boeing to keep the 767 production line running without having to borrow additional capital, which would depress its balance sheet and share price at a cost of $20 billion to the federal government.[20] The US Congress scrapped the deal on 9 October 2004 after Air Force procurement officer Darleen A. Druyun had been convicted and sentenced to nine months' imprisonment for awarding the contract. Ms Druyun's daughter and son-in-law had been given jobs at Boeing while she was an Air Force official. She became a Boeing vice-president after she retired from the Air Force in October 2003. Several Air Force contracts with Boeing are now under review, and Boeing chief executive Philip M. Condit has resigned.[21]

This reality does not flow from accidental conjuncture, with spending on particular programmes rising while other nations come to the end of re-equipment cycles. It is a deliberate policy of the US administration, and one that has been in development for over a decade. A 1992 Department of Defense paper (often referred to as 'Cheney's Masterpiece', as it was written when Dick Cheney was Secretary of Defense under President Bush, Sr.) argued that the US must 'discourage the advanced industrial nations from challenging our leadership or even aspiring to a larger regional or global role.'[22] Although the paper was dismissed as a working draft at the time, 10 years later official US policy was to state, 'Our [US] forces will be strong enough to dissuade potential adversaries from pursuing a military build-up in hopes of surpassing, or equalling, the power of the United States.'[23]

This ambition to be the sole world power is new. While the history of the US is inextricable from the use of armed force, the relationship between political and military power has gradually shifted. For most of the nation's history, military force was a means to an end – first the creation and then the expansion of the country. Stage by stage, however, the military and the use of military force as a political tool has outgrown the state it was intended to serve. It has become more and more an end in itself, the primary tool for both foreign and domestic policies of the US government.

Nation-Building: Concord 1775 to Wounded Knee 1890

The US was a revolutionary creation, its people rebelling against British rule. Its revolutionary Continental Army and state militias, with considerable military assistance from the France of Louis XVI, helped bring the country into being during the War of Independence of 1775–1783. George Washington went on to become the first president of the country he had helped create – the United States of America.

This small country had a small army. In 1784, the US Army numbered just 80 officers and men.[24] By 1789 it had expanded to 700.[25] The army's first post-revolutionary engagement was the Battle on the Wabash on 4 November 1791 in modern-day Ohio, where it was roundly defeated by a Native American force under Chief Little Turtle. The army abandoned 630 dead and 282 wounded out of its 1,200 troops when it retreated.[26] In 1812, US armed forces numbered just under 14,000.[27]

During the Napoleonic Wars, British warships interfered with US trade, leading to a Declaration of War in June 1812. The US scored some naval successes and took Detroit. British troops burned public buildings in Washington, DC in 1814, which was the last foreign aggression on the US mainland until 11 September 2001. In December 1814, a peace treaty was signed in Ghent. However, British forces, not yet informed of the treaty, attacked the city of New Orleans (recently purchased by the US) on 8 January 1815, to be defeated by General Andrew Jackson's Southwestern Army of 6,500 men, which was also unaware that peace had been agreed.[28]

General Jackson had annexed west Florida in 1812, and went on in 1817 to attack the then Spanish possession of Florida, seeking to recapture escaped slaves living with the Seminole Indians. Spain ceded Florida to the US under the Transcontinental Treaty of 1819.[29]

As president and under the Indian Removal Act of 1830, Andrew Jackson used the US Army to round up and forcibly evict approximately 100,000 Cherokees, Chickasaws, Choctaws, Creeks and Seminoles from their lands east of the Mississippi River for resettlement in Oklahoma, despite a ruling to the contrary by the US Supreme Court. Around 25,000 people died on these forced marches, which became known as the Trail of Tears.[30] The term 'ethnic cleansing' may have come to us from the former Yugoslavia, but the practice is much older.

President James Monroe enunciated the Monroe Doctrine to the US Congress in 1823, warning that the US would not tolerate European interference anywhere on the American continents. The Doctrine was a logical consequence of the US decision to recognise the newly independent states of Latin America. The Doctrine was not, however, followed by the development of sufficient military power to enforce it.

A simmering border dispute erupted into war with Mexico on 13 May 1846 and the US Army captured Mexico City in September 1847. Mexico ceded the territory that now forms New Mexico, Utah, Nevada, Arizona, California, Texas and western Colorado to the US in the Treaty of Guadalupe Hildago in February 1848.[31]

The American Civil War (1861–1865) can be described as the first modern war. Some 2.4 million men served in the Union and Confederate armed forces. Over 600,000 were killed and a further 500,000 wounded.[32] This was the last war fought on mainland US soil. The US (Union) Army saved the Republic, established federal prerogatives and opened the way for the abolition of slavery. In 1865, the US Army numbered almost 1.1 million. That figure was reduced by 93 per cent to less than 80,000 in 1866 once the Civil War ended.[33]

Both during and following the Civil War, the US Army fought a number of wars with Native American peoples (the Indian Wars), ending with the massacre of around 200 Ogala Sioux men, women and children at Wounded Knee, South Dakota in December 1890.[34]

From 1775 until 1890, the expansion and the very existence of the US owed much to its armed forces. They had fought a civil war, the British and Spanish Empires and Mexico to create the continental United States, stretching from the Atlantic to the Pacific. They had also subdued, expelled, confined or destroyed those Native American peoples who had the misfortune to live on land desired by white settlers, often in breach of treaties signed by the US. Yet throughout all of this period, the permanent armed forces remained small and subject to political control.

Regional Power: 1890–1941

The US seized Midway Island in the Pacific as a naval base in 1867,[35] and in 1885 began its first serious naval construction programme under President Cleveland.[36] The US economy boomed after the Civil War, and by 1870 the US was challenging the UK as the world's largest economy.[37] Between 1870 and 1890, US GDP more than doubled from $76 billion to $183 billion.[38] Prior to 1884, US military spending hovered around $700 million (in 1982 dollars).

In 1895, the US intervened in a border dispute between Venezuela and British Guyana, warning the UK that Washington was now the dominant power in the Americas. London, otherwise engaged in the Boer War, accepted that the dispute be submitted to arbitration.[39] The US now had the muscle to put its 70-year-old Monroe Doctrine into effect.

In 1895, Cuba rebelled against Spanish rule. When the battleship *USS Maine* exploded and sank in mysterious circumstances at Havana in February 1898, the US Congress authorised the use of force to eject Spain from Cuba. US forces invaded Cuba and subsequently Puerto Rico. The US Navy destroyed the Spanish flotilla in the Philippines. In the Treaty of Paris (December 1899), Spain recognised Cuban independence, ceded the Pacific islands of Guam and Puerto Rico and sold the Philippines to the US for $20 million.[40] US military expenditure rose to over $4 billion in 1899 and remained above $3 billion (1982 dollars) until World War One.[41]

Theodore Roosevelt became president of the US upon the assassination of President McKinley in 1901.

Teddy Roosevelt famously spelled out his foreign policy in 1903: 'There is a homely old adage which runs: "Speak softly and carry a big stick; you will go far." If the American nation will speak softly, and yet build and keep at a pitch of the highest training a thoroughly efficient navy, the Monroe Doctrine will go far.'[42]

Under Roosevelt's presidency, the US was to engineer Panama's secession from Colombia in 1903, negotiate the lease of the Panama Canal Zone from the newly independent Panama, intervene in China[43] and broker the peace settlement of the Russo-Japanese (1904–1905) at the Portsmouth Conference in Russia's favour.[44]

The US now had sufficient military power to make the Americas the zone of influence it had proclaimed in 1823. The US developed its naval presence in the Pacific, and the construction of the Panama Canal allowed it to switch naval forces between the Atlantic and the Pacific. The US was one of eight major, and roughly equivalent, powers (the British, French, German, Russian, Ottoman, Austro-Hungarian and Japanese Empires) in the first decade of the twentieth century.

The US sought bases rather than colonies, although it was increasingly willing to impose its will on its Latin American neighbours. It had two main foreign policy priorities. It participated in the emasculation of the Chinese Empire and sought to limit the growth of the Japanese Empire to prevent the emergence of a rival power in the Pacific. The US was content to have five competing powers in Europe, as one of its main fears was the emergence of a single European power which could rival it both in the Atlantic and the Pacific. This US desire to prevent the emergence of a rival European power has been at the centre of US foreign policy for more than a century.[45]

The Russian, Austro-Hungarian and Ottoman Empires began to collapse during World War One. The Western Front confrontation between the German Empire and its French and British rivals turned into a war of attrition, with Anglo-French casualties running at 2.5 million to Germany's 1.9 million[46] and mutinies in the French Army. The threat of a German victory and the emergence of a European superpower helped persuade the US to enter World War One in 1917.[47]

US military expenditure rose from \$3.2 billion in 1916 to \$71 billion in 1919[48] and US armed forces expanded to almost 2.9 million personnel by 1918.[49] Following the war, the US either annexed or was granted trust status over several German island colonies in the Pacific (Western Samoa, the Marianas, etc.).

Following World War One and its military participation in the 1919 western intervention in the USSR, the US helped broker the Versailles Peace Conference. The US Senate rejected both the Treaty and US membership of the League of Nations and the US withdrew to its ante-bellum status of being one of now five regional powers (Britain, France, Japan and the USSR being the other four).

It shared much of the world's nervousness over the new Soviet Union, but concluded that the revolutionary USSR was too preoccupied with internal questions to pose an external threat. Britain and France were recovering, and US concerns focused increasingly on the Pacific. The Washington Naval Treaty (1923) restrained Japanese growth while maintaining US advantages.

US military spending fell back to \$5 billion a year in the 1920s[50] and the US armed forces were cut by 88 per cent to 343,000 by 1920.[51] In 1923, the US dismantled the military intelligence service it had established during the war, with Secretary Daniels saying, 'Gentlemen do not read other gentlemen's mail.'[52] The FBI retained a limited intelligence function, largely focused on Latin America.

The US continued to intervene in Latin America, but domestic concerns of the Great Depression, organised crime and Franklin D. Roosevelt's New Deal featured much more prominently on US horizons up until the outbreak of World War Two.

When Japanese naval aviation attacked Pearl Harbor on 7 December 1941 in what is probably the most famous pre-emptive strike in history, the US was a regional power ill equipped to fight a modern war. The Air Force was part of the army and lacked modern fighter aircraft, while the army itself was small and ill equipped for modern armoured warfare. The main US tank, the M3 General Grant, was out of date and US naval aviation was largely equipped with obsolete aircraft. The US did not have a foreign intelligence service and US government structures were poorly organised to process the intelligence they did receive – US naval intercepts of Japanese signals were not quickly, or adequately, processed prior to the attack on Pearl Harbor. That was all to change in four short years.

Global Power: 1945–20??

By December 1945 the US had become *the* global power, its German and Japanese rivals crushed, the USSR and France in ruins and the UK bankrupt. US forces numbered over 12 million by the end of 1945, falling to just under 1.6 million by 1947, a reduction of 87 per cent.[53] In 1939, the US Defense budget was $10 billion[54] but by 1946 it stood at just under $557 billion (inflation-adjusted dollars).[55] The US was the world's only nuclear power in 1945.

However, as the US became a global power, its military, as an extension of the presidency, expanded even though the structure of the presidency remained the same. The institution had not been designed to exercise this form of power. Gradually this extension of the presidency outgrew its parent, outgrowing US democratic political control in the process.

Threats Are Necessary

To borrow Eisenhower's words, the US had resorted to 'emergency improvisation of national defense' for World War Two. At the end of that conflict, rather than dismantling much of what it had put in place in terms of government structures and armaments industry, the US retained it to address the threat of the USSR. This threat was partly perceived in classic US foreign policy terms – the need to prevent the emergence of a single great rival power. This classic threat was amplified by the addition of an ideological fear of Soviet communism. In 1961, President Eisenhower was to describe that perception in the following terms: '... a hostile ideology – global in scope, atheistic in character, ruthless in purpose and insidious in method.'[56]

The World War Two experience left few in any doubt that the USSR would offer ferocious resistance to any attack on its territory, but many questioned whether the Soviet Union was an aggressive power outside of its 'spheres of influence' as agreed by the US and the other allies at Yalta. This was a feeling which gained currency in Europe after the death of Stalin in 1953. By the early 1970s, when the West German Chancellor Willy Brandt launched his *Ostpolitik* policy of detente with the USSR and members of the Warsaw Pact, few in Western Europe believed it likely that the USSR would attack.

In *The Sources of Soviet Conduct* (*Foreign Affairs*, July 1947), the US diplomat George Kennan argued that the USSR was a cautious power whose ideology laid down that capitalism would eventually fail because of its own contradictions. The USSR would therefore try to wait the capitalist world out, rather than frontally attack it. The piece further proposed that the Soviet Union's own weaknesses were far more serious than any on the Western side and would in time lead to its demise, and that the West's best policy was one of judicious containment. Events proved George Kennan to have been about as right as any man can hope to be on such matters, and yet, as the former senator Patrick Moynihan has written, 'The history of American foreign policy in the second half of the 20th century could be written in terms of how this message was lost.'[57]

Carl Sagan pointed out in his 1988 Gettysburg Commemorative Address that at the end of World War

Two, both the US and the USSR were invulnerable. The US had the largest economy in the world and the most effective armed forces. It was bound to the east and west by large oceans and to the north and south by weak, friendly neighbours. The USSR had the world's largest army and faced no significant military threats. Yet the US initiated a nuclear arms race, and the Soviets replied. Washington thus placed the survival of the US in the hands of the Soviet leadership, and the Soviet Politburo responded by giving the US president the final decision over the survival of the USSR.[58]

Capability and threat are different things, the one factual, the other a question of opinion. Anyone who has ever shared a restaurant table with a stranger knows that that stranger has the ability to reach across and punch you in the face. Do you feel threatened that your fellow diner might do so? In normal circumstances you do not – but that's only an opinion.

The US arrived at the opinion that the USSR posed a threat in 1945. That opinion was formed within the intelligence-armaments-military-foreign policy community and conveyed to a president and Congress who were to expend over $10 trillion between 1946 and 1989 on confrontation with the Soviet Union.

Following the collapse of the USSR, we have had much greater access to Soviet records and personalities. Apart from the ideological belief that communism would prevail and a willingness to exploit such opportunities as presented themselves, no evidence has emerged of any Soviet desire to attack the West. In fact, many questions have emerged about the reliability of several Soviet weapon systems. The missile and bomber 'gaps' identified by the US intelligence-armaments-military-foreign policy community over those 43 years have been shown to have existed largely in the minds of those who conjured them up.

While this is hindsight, it does illustrate the inherent weakness of a governing system where those charged with identifying and measuring possible threats are also those whose very jobs, and profits, depend on responding to the threats they identify.

The current US military build-up is also predicated on a threat – international terrorism. 'Terrorism' has become a neat substitute for 'communism' as a patriotic argument designed to automatically and comprehensively validate the operation of the current, and the future, military-industrial-congressional complex. Indeed, terrorism has the added advantage of being an open-ended threat that can never be defeated and that therefore seems to justify a never-ending vigilance.

The New US Military

'Transformation' is the buzz word in today's Pentagon, put into the lexicon by Donald Rumsfeld and senior aides such as Dov Zakheim and Stephen Cambone. One major aspect of 'transformation' is about making the US armed forces more effective, more lethal and less dependent on forward bases and foreign allies. If some of the projects now being initiated realise anything like their full potential, Rumsfeld's 'transformation' may change the nature of warfare as profoundly as the introduction of gunpowder to European battlefields did in the early fifteenth century. Two inter-related forces – technology and privatisation – are creating the possibility of a kind of American military power that is virtually independent of democratic structures. 'Transformation' is helping to create the final stage of the disjunction between American society as a whole and the military force that is supposed to express and enforce its collective will.

Apart from particularly sophisticated systems such as the stealth technology of the F-117 fighter-bomber and the B-2 bomber, the US armed forces and other modern forces are similarly equipped. The US, though, is more capable of projecting force around the world than any other state. There are important quantitative differences in that the US has more tanks, aircraft and aircraft carriers, but the qualitative differences are arguable. Are US F-15s, F-16s and F-18s significantly better combat aircraft than the Eurofighter or the French Rafale or even the Russian Mig-29? Is the US M1A1 Abrams tank a better armoured vehicle than the British Challenger, the French Leclerc or the German Leopard II?

Where the US leads the world is in the application of information technology to warfare. In the 1991 Gulf War, only 9 per cent of the air-dropped weapons were precision guided,[59] yet they accounted for over 60 per cent of the hits.[60] Commanders had a level of accuracy never before known in war.

By the 2003 Iraq War almost 70 per cent of air-dropped ordnance was precision guided, and it was now cheaper and more versatile. There was widespread use of joint direct attack munitions (JDAMs). In essence, a global positioning system (GPS) package is attached to a standard 'dumb' aerial bomb. Using GPS, the bomb can be dropped a considerable height and distance from its target. The JDAM packages cost around \$20,000 apiece. JDAMs turn any aircraft, from lumbering B-52s to nimble F-18s, into close support bombers. Soldiers on the ground can call in air attacks on enemy positions less than 20 metres from their own with a reasonable certainty that they will not be killed by their own bombs.

As the accuracy of the weapons is less than two metres, modern bombs can be smaller and lighter. In short, individual soldiers can now have at their disposal their very own flying artillery to destroy a tank, truck or trench without risking their lives, without having to retreat to leave the Air Force a reasonable killing ground and without having to risk large civilian casualties.

The US leads the world in unmanned aerial vehicles (UAVs). They include the RQ-4A Global Hawk, which cruises at just under 20,000 metres using an array of sensing and imaging technology to relay real-time images of the battlefield to US commanders. The RQ-1B Predator (some armed with Hellfire anti-tank missiles) is better known. It cruises at 5,000 to 8,000 metres. Both the Global Hawk and the Predator can remain on station for up to 24 hours at a time.[61] Neither the Predator nor the Global Hawk have equivalents in other forces.

The Predator has fired its missiles in Afghanistan, Iraq and perhaps most sensationally in Yemen. On Sunday, 3 November 2002, Qaed Salim Sinan al-Harethi, also known as Abu Ali, the chief suspect in the bombing of the *USS Cole* at Aden in October 2000, climbed into his car with five other people near the remote north-western Yemeni town of Marib. Mr al-Harethi was either being watched or tracked. A remotely piloted Predator fired a Hellfire missile on the direct orders of President Bush. All six people in the vehicle were killed. The Predator operator could have been in the car behind, on board a US ship, at the US Embassy in Sanaa or in Washington. A new form of warfare had been born.[62]

Two much more ambitious prototype aircraft, pilotless fighter-bombers, are already flying – the Boeing X-45A and the Northrop-Grumman X-47A Pegasus. These are formally known as unmanned combat aerial vehicles, or UCAVs. The X-45A is flat, with jagged 10-metre batwings, no tail and a bulbous nose. The two prototypes cost $256 million. The X-47A has been designed for carrier landings. Representative Curt Weldon, a Pennsylvania Republican who until recently headed up the House Sub-committee on Arms Procurement, says, 'Our intent is that within 10 years, one-third of our tactical-strike aircraft will be unmanned.' If mass produced, these UCAVs could cost as little as $20 million each, or less than one-tenth of the cost of an F-22 Raptor.[63] They would be far more manoeuvrable than any manned craft and have the enormous advantage that if shot down there would be no US casualties or prisoners.

Two unmanned ground combat vehicle prototypes have been built. The US Marines have a prototype A160 pilotless helicopter, the Hummingbird, missile-armed with a range of 4,000 kilometres. Most futuristic of all is the Organic Air Vehicle, a fully autonomous micro-craft 23 centimetres in diameter capable of landing on building ledges and using sensor packages to identify targets through gaps in foliage and camouflage. The US Defense Advanced Research Projects Agency (DARPA) calls this a 'perch and stare' capability.[64]

DARPA has launched FALCON (Force Application and Launch from the Continental US) and has invited tenders to develop two weapon systems. The first is a small launch vehicle (SLV) capable of flying at up to 10 times the speed of sound in near space. It would carry a warhead known as a common aero vehicle (CAV), which might not include any explosives as the kinetic energy of a simple titanium rod dropped from space could penetrate 30 metres of solid rock, creating an enormous shock wave. The first SLV trials are scheduled for 2006–2007.[65] The Pentagon's Defense Science Board, with strong encouragement from Donald Rumsfeld, has also proposed the development of a new generation of US nuclear weapons, including 'nuclear bunker-busters'. A former Pentagon official commented, 'Brutally, "mini-nukes" would be easier to use, and therefore more useful as a deterrent.'[66]

DARPA's second programme is for a 'reusable hypersonic cruise vehicle (HCV)...capable of taking off from a conventional military runway and striking targets 9,000 nautical miles distant in less than two hours.' SLV rockets will also give the Air Force a cheap and flexible means to launch military satellites at short notice, within weeks, days or even hours of a crisis developing.[67]

These weapons would free the US from the need for foreign allies, forward bases and negotiations for over-flight and refuelling rights. According to Lieutenant Colonel David Branham of the USAF, 'It's possible that in our lifetime we will be able to run a conflict without ever leaving the United States.'[68]

In the unfortunate event that US troops are obliged to leave the continental US, they will come equipped with weapons and integrated systems quite unlike anything known before in the history of warfare. Land Warriors technology has been part-tested by US Special Forces in Afghanistan and Iraq, and the first infantry units will be equipped from 2004. The soldier's weapon has three black tubes added. One is a camera with a powerful zoom allowing the soldier to visualise targets up to 300 metres away. The second is a thermal-imaging camera, providing vision of heat sources such as humans or motors by night and in fog, smoke or dust. The third is a laser range finder with a two-kilometre range which calculates the range, elevation, etc. of any target. The information from these three is projected onto a mini-screen attached to the helmet.

Each member of a Land Warrior team is linked to the other members by a digital network transmitting voice, data and images. The voice transmissions pick up the skull vibrations when a soldier speaks, making a whisper clearly audible to all other members of the team. Two directional helmet-mounted microphones can pick up and localise sounds out to 150 metres. The system incorporates GPS so each team member knows where their comrades are via a map projected on their screens, and if one Land Warrior inadvertently points his weapon at a comrade, an audio warning will sound in his helmet. The Land Warrior system is linked to a command net, so senior officers, air controllers and artillery units know exactly where friendly forces are in real time. Land Warriors can transmit the images and sounds they detect to anyone connected to the forces network. The whole system weighs just six kilograms.[69]

Land Warrior Mark II is already being developed by the Raytheon Corporation, which will further enhance and lighten the system and will link soldiers, vehicles and aircraft into a single system. It was tested during manoeuvres in Idaho in April 2004.[70]

This will link with the Force XXI Battle Command wireless Internet system being installed in every US Army vehicle. The US 4th Infantry Division is already fully equipped with this system, and other divisions will be in the near future. Every vehicle has a digital screen showing its position and the position of friendly and enemy forces in its vicinity. Every vehicle is linked to every other vehicle, to the command network and will soon be linked to every individual US soldier in the sector.[71]

The US Army plans to deploy its Objective Force Warrior system by 2010. This will be a radically expanded version of the current Land Warrior system for individual soldiers. It will be lighter, wireless, speech commanded and will be an integral part of the soldier's uniform. The current drop-down screen will be replaced by a visor, the computer integrated into ceramic body armour, the rifle replaced by a multi-function weapon and it will include 'intelligent' clothing capable of monitoring biorhythms and performing preliminary diagnoses in case of injury.[72]

This digitalisation of US armed forces is creating its own problems in terms of the size of bandwidth required by major force deployments. In the 1991 Gulf War, networked military computers transmitted information at the equivalent of 192,000 words per minute. As the new digital systems such as Land Warrior and Force XXI Battle Command become more generalised and the number of UAVs and UCAVs grows, US military computers will be transmitting 1.5 trillion words a minute – an almost eightfold increase of the data load on satellite systems.[73]

The Pentagon has decided that all this interconnected technology requires its own dedicated communications system. This US military version of a high-speed Internet has been baptised the Global Information Grid (GIG). A consortium including Boeing, Cisco Systems, General Dynamics, Hewlett-Packard, Honeywell, IBM, Lockheed, Microsoft, Northrop-Grumman, Oracle, Raytheon and Sun Microsystems was formed on 28 September 2004 to design and build this satellite-operated GIG at an estimated cost of $200 billion.[74]

Much of the above may sound like science fiction,

but it is science fact and will greatly enhance the striking power of US armed forces. The US Army will enter a level of technical ability unmatched, at least in the short term, by any other army on earth.[75]

A central element of the US philosophy is a faith in technology as a *Deus ex machina* that can solve all problems. Francis Fukuyama spells this out clearly in his introduction to *The End of History*:

> technology confers decisive military advantages on those countries that possess it, and given the continuing possibility of war in the international system of states, no state that values its independence can ignore the need for defensive modernization. Second, modern natural science establishes a uniform horizon of economic production possibilities. Technology makes possible the limitless accumulation of wealth, and thus the satisfaction of an ever-expanding set of human desires.[76]

Added to this faith is another ideologically driven one – privatisation.

The Privatisation of War

In 1995, Donald Rumsfeld wrote 'Thoughts from the Business World on Downsizing Government',[77] where he argued, 'Once one has determined the core functions to be performed by the federal government, all other activities should be scrutinized for...privatization.' As US Secretary of Defense, Rumsfeld has pursued this objective, trying to slim down the army by having private contractors take over as many functions as possible.

In the 1991 Gulf War, one in 100 US personnel was employed by a private contractor, whereas by the 2003 Iraq War that ratio had moved closer to one in 10. *The Washington Post* has estimated that as much as a third of the cost of the war is going into private US bank accounts. The US Army estimates that $30 billion of the $87 billion the US Congress voted for Afghanistan and Iraq in 2004 will be spent on contracts with private companies.[78]

The use of civilian personnel for non-combatant, or non-vital, services is common across many peacetime armies, particularly in their domestic garrison settings. Today's Pentagon is engaged in something quite different. Private contractors are being used to both service and operate weapon systems in combat zones. Technicians aboard US Navy vessels operated Predator and Global Hawks UAVs and some of the systems on the B-2 stealth bombers.

The 10,000 private employees deployed in Iraq make them the second largest contingent in the US-led Coalition. Private companies such as Military Professional Resources Inc. and Dyncorp are training the new Iraqi army and police forces, providing armed security guards for the Coalition Provisional Authority in Baghdad and bodyguards for the Afghan President Hamid Karzai and US diplomats in Israel.[79] Similar training and security operations are to be found in the Balkans.

The US Army is using a Halliburton subsidiary to purchase and transport fuel from Kuwait to its forces in Iraq, but according to Department of Defense officials, the army was paying $2.64 a gallon, or twice the market rate for its fuel.[80] There have been persistent reports of US troops lacking showers and being forced to live on combat rations because private contractors have failed to carry out tasks or deliver goods in combat zones.

The use of such contractors raises practical, legal and ethical issues. Practically speaking, private employees lack both the training and the *esprit de corps* of their military counterparts. Where an army driver may make heroic efforts to get fuel through to a unit, a civilian contractor can simply refuse. The worst sanction facing the civilian driver is that he can be fired. The Geneva Conventions prohibit the use of mercenaries, and although US contractors are not mercenaries, the line between being a civilian technician and a combatant gets blurred when the technician can push the 'fire' button. Who is liable for damage caused by a weapon discharged by a private employee?

The ethical issue is more complex, and more worrying. If a nation-state decides to declare war, then its responsibility is engaged. Its armed forces can be expected to discharge that responsibility. If a nation-state engages its sovereign responsibility which is then discharged by a private employee, we are getting ever closer to the medieval function of mercenaries. Peter Synger of the Brookings Institution in Washington has commented, 'This is a sea change in the way we prosecute warfare. There are historical parallels but we haven't seen them for 250 years.'[81]

The sea change has created the possibility of a use of force that is essentially disengaged from the normal life of American society. A small but highly trained elite will be able to conduct foreign wars almost by remote control, with limited American casualties and indeed limited direct involvement by ordinary Americans. The kind of social forces that became involved in the Vietnam War – a mass conscript army drawn from most American communities, a highly engaged media and consequently a profound national debate about national purposes and morality – can be kept at arm's length as war is waged by unmanned vehicles supported by private mercenaries. And the capacity of the American political system to control such forces is not at all clear.

Military Might and Political Weakness

The US went from being a small country to being one of several regional powers in the first 125 years of its existence. It then grew to become one of a handful of powerful nations in the half-century up to the end of World War Two. From 1945, until the collapse of the USSR, the US was one of two superpowers, and since the collapse of the Soviet Union, it has become the world's only hyperpower.

Its military power is planned, managed and operated by a political structure which was designed to govern a country of less than 2 million people over 200 years ago. Although the US sought to develop its power, its global predominance owes at least as much to accident as it does to design.

In the absence of broad political debate on foreign and security policy within the US, and indeed in the absence of any framework for such a debate, military power has come to be seen in Washington as almost an end in itself rather than as a political tool – Von Clausewitz's pursuit of political ends with the admixture of other means.

The political structures which operate this military power are essentially eighteenth-century ones, elitist and vulnerable to being controlled by a relatively small group of overwhelmingly unelected officials. In essence it is a twenty-first-century military hyperpower run by unanswerable eighteenth-century courtiers who owe their offices to the decisions of an elected monarch – the President of the United States.

Presidential Monarchy, Praetorian Weakness: Some Conclusions

A small group of appointed courtiers forms the Praetorian Guard of the US presidency when it comes to foreign and security policy. These presidential appointees direct the services, and thus control the information, on which the Congress bases its expenditure and political decisions. Much of the reasoning behind the praetorians' recommendations remains secret, as does the information on which they base that reasoning.

The US presidency exercises a degree of domestic and international power which those who drafted the US Constitution could never have imagined. This federal power has poured billions of taxpayers' dollars into creating the most technically capable armed forces in the world.

This amazing technical development has not, unfortunately, been matched by similar political developments. If anything, the US presidency has become more monarchical in recent decades. The US does not have a collegiate system of government along European lines. While there is a Cabinet of Secretaries appointed by the president, it meets infrequently, and rarely as a full body. The first US Cabinet meeting after the beginning of the Iraq War in March 2003 took place on 9 June 2003.[82] The president meets with specific members on specific issues, as with Truman making the decision on the use of atomic weapons in 1945.

There is no US equivalent to the UK's Prime Minister's Questions, where any member of the legislature may question the executive on any issue. Even in France's presidential system, the prime minister and other ministers must regularly face questions and challenges in the National Assembly or Senate. The French Cabinet meets weekly, chaired by the president.

Little executive power is shared with the Congress, and still less with other nations, even within particular bodies where the US has legal obligations to share decision making, such as the UN or NATO.

This war-fighting capability has a tendency to preclude political debate about war-fighting reasons. If, as Von Clausewitz suggests, the use of armed force is a political tool of government, then there must be a political mechanism for determining both the political reasons for using force in a particular situation and the political objectives such a use of force should achieve.

Weaknesses and Challenges

US military power increasingly drives US foreign, and indeed domestic, policies. Rather than being the scalpel, it has become the surgeon. This military power has two strengths which no other force on earth can match. Firstly, it has an ability to project its power almost anywhere in the world. Secondly, through investment in high-tech weaponry and systems, US forces are uniquely capable of locating, identifying and destroying 'hard' targets such as enemy aircraft or armoured vehicles. This second strength is also one of the US military's two major weaknesses.

As US armed forces come to depend more and more

on high-tech systems, they will inevitably become less able to cope should those systems ever fail – and all systems are vulnerable. A US artillery officer deprived of his or her computer system would be at a major disadvantage facing an enemy who had never had such systems to begin with.

High-tech systems demand highly competent engineers and technicians to maintain and repair them, yet the US educational system is less and less capable of producing such middle- and low-end engineers and technicians. The US will have to significantly invest in education and training, either in its general public systems or in providing graduate-level training for large numbers of its service personnel. Personnel with that training would of course attract higher salaries outside the services, thus US military and educational policies are in direct contradiction with each other.

At the moment, only British Forces can (just) manage to integrate with their high-tech US equivalents. Most of the world's armies cannot, and few countries are likely to make the necessary investments. As US armed forces become more high tech, they will be less and less able to operate with forces from other countries. Yet the US is chronically short of troops.

The US invasion and subsequent occupation of Iraq in 2003 illustrates this dichotomy. US forces quickly destroyed and defeated Iraq's regular army, but found themselves ill equipped and woefully under-strength when it came to governing an occupied Iraq.

Washington could reintroduce military service to provide the US with enough 'boots on the ground', but this would be both highly controversial in domestic political terms and highly expensive. As an alternative, Washington could expand its armed forces, creating two or three new army divisions of professional soldiers. While this would be less controversial, it would remain highly expensive.

We are now confronted with several new realities. The US government depends on the rest of the world for a significant, and growing, part of its income. This borrowed money is then directed to private defence corporations which are either completely or largely dependent on these dollars for their survival. The resultant armed forces are then directed by a significantly uncontrollable and unaccountable government system of eighteenth-century courtiers who depend on these same defence corporations for political contributions. When these courtiers decide on war, many of the functions of that war are then contracted out to another group of private corporations.

The use of force for no good reason has always been pointless and reprehensible. Given the levels of force available to the US in 2005, it is also extremely dangerous, for the US itself and for the rest of the world.

6

Whizzards and Wide Open Spaces: US Agribusiness

'Well, it turned my farm into a pile of sand,
Yes, it turned my farm into a pile of sand,
I had to hit that road with a bottle in my hand.'
— Woody Guthrie, 'Dust Bowl Blues'

In many ways, US agriculture is a microcosm of the US today. The US is still the world's greatest food exporter, but this status largely depends on public subsidies. Both the US and the European Union subsidise the export of surplus agricultural produce. The EU and the US, under considerable pressure from a global coalition led by Brazil, agreed at the World Trade Organization talks at Geneva in July 2004 to make deep cuts in these trade and development-distorting subsidies.[1]

Economically and ethically unjustifiable, these subsidies are on the way out. In the case of the US, the likelihood of their extinction is enhanced by the simple fact that Washington simply cannot afford to keep shelling out. In 2002, the US federal government paid $13 billion dollars to 700,000 farms.[2]

The US approach to agriculture is also a microcosm of US approaches to many other sectors. An extremist view of private property rights has been used to undermine individual farmers. Political cronyism has kept a river of federal dollars flowing to an ever smaller number of farming corporations. Food processing has been deskilled. The whole food industry is now so concentrated and so driven by high-volume, low-cost (and low-standard) production that it poses a real threat both to the survival of US agriculture and to the health of US consumers.

Stereophonic – or Schizophrenic – News

On 21 January 2004, the US Center for Disease Control (CDC) and RTI International, a leading American research organisation, issued a press release revealing that US states spend as much as $75 billion a year in medical expenditures related to obesity.[3] Much of the money comes from the US taxpayer through the Medicare and Medicaid systems. In 2003, obesity-attributable Medicaid expenditures ranged from $23 million (Wyoming) to $3.5 billion (New York), and Medicare expenditures ranged from $15 million (Wyoming) to $1.7 billion (California). The percentage of total annual Medicaid spending attributable to obesity ranged from 7.7 per cent (Rhode Island) to 15.7 per cent (Indiana). Obesity increases the risk of many chronic diseases, including type 2 diabetes, cardiovascular disease, several types of cancer, musculoskeletal disorders, sleep apnoea and gall bladder disease. According to CDC's 1999–2000 National Health and Nutrition Examination Survey, an estimated 64 per cent of US adults are either overweight (33 per cent) or obese (31 per cent). When the medical effects of obesity and being overweight are added together, the annual cost to the US public purse was estimated at $93 billion for 2002.

The price in both human and economic terms is clearly high and is obvious to at least one part of the US administration. Reacting to the RTI study, Department of Health and Human Services Secretary Tommy G. Thompson said, 'This report further drives home the point that we must stem the tide of the obesity epidemic in this country. These findings are a dramatic illustration of the devastating economic impact obesity has on health care delivery systems across the nation.' 'Epidemic', 'devastating', 'dramatic' – this is the language of urgency. Clearly, something was going to be done.

Scroll back five days, however, to a report that made a brief splash in the world's newspapers on 16 January:

> The Bush administration is challenging a World Health Organization report that outlines steps for nations to take to reduce obesity. In a letter to the United Nations agency that is meeting next week, Health and Human Services official William Steiger questioned the organization's findings, said they were based on faulty science, and called for changes to the report. The WHO report recommends eating more fruits and vegetables and limiting fats and salt. It also suggests governments limit food advertising aimed at children and encourage their citizens to eat healthier foods. Taxes and subsidies could be used to reduce the price of healthy food and make them more attractive to consumers, the report said...Steiger said in his letter that the WHO report did not adequately address an individual's responsibility to balance one's diet with one's physical activities, and objected to singling out specific types of foods, such as those high in fat and sugar.[4]

The contradiction is a good example of a serious structural weakness in the US. Power is about the ability to identify one's own interests and attain one's own ends. In this case, US interests are crystal clear – obesity hurts Americans and America, limiting the capacity of individuals and wasting vast amounts of public money. In Thompson's terms, it is a devastating epidemic. So what stops America from pursuing its interests? A mixture of ideological rigidity (fat is 'an individual's responsibility') and corporate interests. One of the most basic functions of a state – ensuring that its people are well fed – is being held hostage to the interests of an unsustainable industry.

The US Sugar Association says it will 'exercise every avenue available to expose the dubious nature' of the WHO's report on diet and nutrition, including challenging the WHO's $406 million in funding from the US. The industry is furious at the WHO report, which argues that sugar should account for no more than 10 per cent of a healthy diet. It claims that the review by international experts which decided on the 10 per cent limit is scientifically flawed, insisting that other evidence indicates that a quarter of our food and drink intake can safely consist of sugar.[5] The effectiveness of its lobbying was obvious in the Bush administration's wholesale adoption of its arguments, resulting in the letter of January 2004.

Fields of Dreams

We are our only link between our images of where we've come from, how we live and our desires for a better future. Reality is where we live. Images often focus on the past. Ideologies are about change, the future. Images, ideologies and reality are rarely in harmony. How we remember things as they were, how we know them to be and what we want them to become, often clash.

One of the most striking examples of this cacophony is food, and food industries, in the US. We have images of waving fields of grain stretching to the horizon and beyond, cattle roaming wide-open prairies, chickens and pigs rooting around farmhouses where families live and work. The houses may need a lick of paint, the vehicle parked out front may be a little dusty and perhaps not the latest model and a dirt track stretches to the nearest road. That traffic-free road will take you to a small town where most services are available, where people know each other and have both the time and inclination to stop and chat. Schools are simple but good, life perhaps a little rude, but healthy and free. Most city-dwellers are only a few generations removed from the land, and many quietly envy the freedom of rural life.

We know that this image is a little romanticised, that the rural US has its problems just like everywhere else. What few of us realise is just how far removed from reality our mental image has become.

Rural communities in the US are now the locus of the greatest social problems, the highest murder and crime rates, serious poverty and drug problems. Many US farmers have become modern-day equivalents of medieval serfs, working on contract for giant agri-businesses rather than farming their own land. Local communities are dying – their commercial tax bases destroyed, their employment opportunities restricted, the surviving jobs deskilled and their schools and public services crumbling.

Almost every aspect of US agriculture today – grain, soya beans, potatoes, beef, sheep, pigs and poultry – is dominated by a handful of giant, and often discreet, corporations. They focus on high-volume, low-margin, frequently subsidised production of the most standard-ised food possible. They form a circle – virtuous or vicious, depending on your outlook – with the fast and convenience food industries which have transformed diet and eating habits in under 50 years. These industries have helped turn obesity into an official US national epidemic. This concentration of production has increased both the scale of food-related illness outbreaks and the probability of such outbreaks occurring in the first place.

Family farms and family lives are menaced by corporate oligopolies. The scale of their production threatens the rural environment and, in some cases, the very ability of the land to continue producing food. These industrial oligopolies carry enormous political clout in Washington and beyond and form an important element of the US neoconservative deregulation crusade. They seek to overturn or weaken every aspect of federal or state law or regulation which imposes standards, duties or any form of restriction on them while fiercely defending those laws which suit them. Through the US government, they challenge global regulatory efforts like those proposed by the WHO.

Using federal and state dollars, they maximise their subsidies and export low-cost food worldwide, often undercutting local producers in Third World countries. Third World agriculture is forced to choose between permanent subsistence and producing cash crops for export, further reinforcing economic dependency.

This mass production of at best bland and at worst dangerous cheap food has transformed the face of US agriculture to such a point that the whizzard, a power-driven circular-bladed cutting knife used in industrial slaughterhouses, has become a more appropriate symbol of the US countryside than wide-open spaces once worked by independent-minded no-nonsense farmers.

If we are what we eat, we may not like the image of what we risk becoming.[6]

Family Farms Meet Fordism: Technical Limitations to Agriculture

By the middle of the nineteenth century, farming was running up against two technological barriers – power and fertilizer. The only mobile source of power apart from humans was animals, primarily horses. Animals were also the primary source of fertilizer (manure). Intensive crop production was impossible. There was only enough power to plough, sow and harvest a limited number of fields, and there was hardly enough manure to enrich those fields. Fordist production of artificial fertilizers and of farm machinery was to change all that.

Food was produced in the countryside and shipped to urban consumers. The development of railways facilitated the process, creating industrial-style power-houses such as the Chicago stockyards, from where cattle and pigs were shipped across the US. Almost 40,000 people worked in Packingtown, Chicago at the beginning of the twentieth century, slaughtering and packing beef for refrigerated shipment across the US and to Europe. The Chicago stockyards were then described as 'the greatest aggregation of labour and capital ever gathered in one place'.[7]

In the first half of the twentieth century there seemed to be no limit to the growth of output in US agriculture. While over-use of chemicals and land gave rise to many problems (like 1930s Dust Bowl erosion, whose cost in human misery was expressed in Woody Guthrie's ballads), family farming developed rapidly. Fordism transformed agriculture and rural life every bit as thoroughly as it had revolutionised industry and urban society.

World War Two was to deprive the US of certain traditional food imports and boost agricultural production. The 20 years from 1940 to 1960 were perhaps the golden age of US family farms, but two changes in the nature of agriculture at the beginning of that period were to herald major, perhaps terminal, challenges to what we might call 'modern, traditional farming' – feedlots and broilers. They would begin a process of transformation, of deskilling and industrial concentration, which would overwhelm traditional farming in the US and threaten it throughout the world.

Feedlots

During the 1930s Depression, Warren Monfort, a teacher from Greeley, Colorado, bought cheap grain from local farmers to feed his cattle. Up until then cattle had eaten hay in winter and outdoor grasses in the warmer months of the year. By feeding his cattle grain all year round, Mr Monfort was able to ship his cattle to Chicago when beef prices were at their highest.

There was another significant advantage to grain-fed beef. The meat was fatty and tender and unlike grass-fed beef did not need to be hung for weeks before being eaten. Slaughterhouses, meatpackers and butchers could lower their costs. Warren Monfort started feeding his 18 cattle cheap surplus grain, sugar beets and maize in the 1930s. By the end of the 1950s he was feeding 20,000 cattle in feedlots on crops grown specifically for that purpose. Feedlots were spreading across the US by the end of World War Two[8] and Warren Monfort had set up his own slaughterhouse in Greeley.

If you could feed cattle sugar beets, what else might they eat that would be even cheaper? Crowding that many cattle into restricted spaces makes them more prone to illnesses and infections while making it more difficult to treat individual animals. It became easier to add preventive medications, including antibiotics, to their feed.

Grass-fed cattle beef has lower saturated fat levels than their grain-fed counterparts, offers 400 per cent more vitamins A and E, is much richer in cancer-inhibiting beta-carotene and linoleic acids and has much higher levels of Omega-3 fatty acids, which inhibit cardiovascular diseases.[9] As grain-fed beef became the norm, human intake of saturated fats (and cholesterol) rose, just as work and lifestyle changes meant that humans exercised less.

Brazil overtook the US in 2003 to become the world's largest exporter of beef, and the Brazilian government predicted $2.5 billion in beef export earnings for 2004. Brazil's cattle herd, at 175 million head, is the world's largest – and Brazilian cattle are all grass fed.[10]

Finally, if you can feed cattle pretty well anything in a fixed location, you only need beef and dairy farmers to supply calves, at prices you can influence, if not control. Warren Monfort's pragmatic 1930s solution was to lead to the confined animal feeding operations (CAFOs) of the 1990s.

Broilers

The broiler industry is the US term for intensive indoor chicken farming. Raising chickens and collecting their eggs was traditionally an activity and source of cash income for farmers' wives. Chickens were fed close to the farmhouse, but left free to roam in search of seeds and grubs during the day before being collected into chicken houses to protect them from predators during the night, hence the term 'free range'.

During World War Two, pork and beef products were rationed in the US, but not chicken. The US government provided subsidies through Land-grant Agricultural Experiment Stations for developments in confinement housing, health, feeding and breeding to boost chicken production. The Farmers Home Administration subsequently provided low-interest loans for the construction of broiler houses and other buildings.

Broiler houses were initially operated as part of family farms. These independent farmers had supply contracts with the US government. Reduced costs, better reproduction rates and lower risks attracted new investors to the industry during and particularly after World War Two.

These new investors grew out of farm supply companies, particularly those dealing in animal feed. They sought to vertically integrate their industry by expanding into chicken production. This expansion involved reversing the farming order. No longer would farmers have contracts with their purchasers (the US government). Now corporations would supply the day-old chicks, the feed and medicines and buy the adult chickens from the farmer at a fixed contract price. Under this arrangement, authority and decision-making passed from the farmer to the corporate management. The original broiler farmers in Delaware, Maryland and Virginia refused to become employees, but without employees' security or rights.

The contracting firms moved south to where cotton had been devastated by the boll weevil and were welcomed by desperate farmers and county and state authorities. By 1960, more than 93 per cent of chickens sold in the US were being produced under contract.[11]

These two World War Two developments – feedlots and broilers – both helped by wartime food demand and guaranteed government prices, with the federal government investing directly in increased chicken production, opened the way for what was to become a total transformation of US agriculture into agribusiness.

Industrial Concentration and Deskilling

Working in an animal slaughterhouse is not one of the more attractive jobs available. Killing animals, cutting them open, removing skins and intestines and then cutting the carcasses up in a permanent atmosphere of blood, stomach contents, urine and faeces has to be one of the more unpleasant of human activities. Working with cutting tools is dangerous. Not surprisingly, workers in the meat industry were among the first to organise themselves into unions. By the end of World War Two, the US meatpacking industry was one of the most unionised in the country. Wages and benefits were high and workers could hope to train for more and more skilled jobs within the industry, work regular hours and attend night school.[12]

Swift and Company were one of the largest meat-packing companies in the US until the late 1960s. They were also the last family firm in the business. In 1961 two former Swift directors, Currier J. Holman and A.D. Anderson, opened the first Iowa Beef Processors (IBP) plant near Denison, Iowa with a $300,000 loan from the US Small Business Administration.[13] IBP was to revolutionise the beef business. IBP plants are located in rural areas, are non-union and pay around 50 per cent of the Chicago stockyard rate.[14] The whole organisation of the slaughterhouse was set up along McDonald's lines. Instead of having skilled workers, each operation was broken down to a series of single repetitive acts – a disassembly line. Each worker stood in one place, performing the same task over and over again. IBP co-founder A. D. Anderson was to later boast that IBP 'had taken the skill out of every step'.[15]

IBP integrated and expanded the feedlot approach. IBP did not content itself with producing carcasses, but went further, cutting the carcasses up into prime and sub-prime joints, vacuum-packing and boxing the cuts ready for sale to butchers. The IBP approach was to wipe out whole swathes of the meat industry. IBP installed 'grinders' to produce minced beef for hamburgers and transformed the scraps of meat, bone and offal it could not sell into pet food. Meat from different animals was mixed to produce a standard fat content in minced beef, making it impossible to trace food back from the final consumer to the farmer. IBP was to meatpacking what McDonald's was to restaurants. A pattern was set.[16]

This pattern has been duplicated across almost the entire range of US agricultural products in the last 40 years. Concentration has taken three main forms. Firstly, more and more produce is processed through fewer and fewer large installations. Secondly, an ever growing share of produce is handled by the three or four leading companies in each sector. Thirdly, mergers and takeovers have resulted in a few large companies that are active across several food sectors at a time. The figures below give a flavour of the degree of concentration which has taken place.

Table 6.1: Percentage of Animals Slaughtered in Large Slaughterhouses[17](Slaughterhouses Handling Up to 500,000 Animals per Annum)

Year	Bullocks and Heifers	Pigs	Sheep and Lambs
1977	16%	38%	42%
1997	80%	88%	71%

Table 6.2: Percentage of Slaughtering Handled by the Four Biggest Companies[18]

Year	Cattle	Pigs	Chickens	Turkeys
1963	26%	33%	14%	23%
1992	71%	43%	41%	45%

In 1960, 66 per cent of turkeys in the US were produced by independent farmers, but by 1980 that had fallen to 10 per cent, with the other 90 per cent being produced by contract labour or on corporate farms. The comparable 1980 figure for chickens was 99 per cent corporate and contract production.[19]

Three North American firms control 80 per cent of the US market for frozen french fries: Lamb Weston (owned by ConAgra, Nebraska), McCain (Canada) and the privately owned J.R. Simplot Company of Idaho.[20] One potato variety, the Russet Burbank, predominates.

Four US firms, ConAgra, IBP, Tyson and Excel, controlled 80 per cent of beef slaughtering in the US in 1995.[21] By 1999, three corporations controlled over 80 per cent of the market (Tyson bought IBP that year).

ConAgra of Nebraska is the largest turkey processor, sheep slaughterer, flour miller and seafood processor in the US.[22] In 2002, *Fortune* magazine ranked ConAgra number 61 in its Fortune 500 listing, with annual revenues of $27.1 billion.

This concentration is driven by desires for ever lower margins on ever higher volumes. The individual amounts are tiny. The US Department of Agriculture estimates that the largest meatpacking plants have margins of only 3 to 5 per cent lower than the smallest installations.[23]

In 1917, President Woodrow Wilson ordered the Federal Trade Commission to investigate the Beef Trust, a dominant cartel. The FTC investigation revealed that the five largest meatpacking companies of the day controlled 55 per cent of the market – as compared to the 80 per cent controlled by three companies today. The Trust negotiated an agreement to avoid a court case and sold off their stockyards, railway interests and other parts of their empires so that they no longer dominated the industry. The US Congress established the Packers and Stockyards Administration (later to become the Grain Inspection, Packers and Stockyards Administration – GIPSA) in 1920 to prevent price fixing and the emergence of monopolies in the beef industry. Under the Reagan administration, the GIPSA was to stand back as the meatpacking companies merged and grew to achieve the highest level of market concentration in US history.[24]

This corporate oligopoly can influence beef prices to the point of domination. Up to 80 per cent of the cattle being traded on any given day in the US are traded between these feedlots, and as they are private sales, the prices paid are not disclosed. As there is effectively no free market, independent farmers have to accept the prices offered by the oligopoly. Should prices start to rise in the 20 per cent independent sector, cattle are released from the corporate stocks.[25] One hundred and fifty-two beef sellers, or less than 1 per cent, account for over 40 per cent of all traded cattle.[26]

These corporations maintain several lobby operations in Washington and are major contributors to the US Republican Party. One Washington presence is the Farm Foundation. The Farm Foundation's Operating Vision talks of 'our mission to improve the economic and social well-being of U.S. Agriculture and rural people.' The chairman of the Foundation, William F. Kirk, was senior vice-president of DuPont Agricultural Products, and the 29-member Board included representatives from Gold Kist Inc. (Broilers), John Deere, Dow AgroSciences, Union Pacific Railroad, ConAgra and Novartis.[27]

Senator Phil Gramm (Republican, Texas), a member of the Senate Agriculture Committee, received more money from the meatpacking industry than any other US senator in the period 1987 to 1996. Former House Speaker Newt Gingrich (Republican) received more money from the restaurant industry than any other member of the House of Representatives.[28] Senator Gramm's wife, Wendy Lee, was a member of the IBP board.

The Fast Food Industry

Richard and Maurice McDonald reopened their McDonald Brothers Burger Bar Drive-In restaurant in

San Bernadino, California in 1948. It operated the Speedee Service System: no waiters, no cutlery, no crockery. There were no trained cooks. Every operation in the preparation of food had been broken down to a single task requiring little skill and less training. In 1956 the US Congress passed the Interstate Highway Act, investing $130 billion to construct over 74,000 kilometres of highway. The automobile had arrived, and with it came a lifestyle, suburbs and access to fast-food restaurants for working-class families.

McDonald's has grown to become, in its own words, 'the world's leading and best-known food service retailer with about 30,000 restaurants serving 46 million customers each day.'[29] It is estimated that one in eight workers in the US has worked for McDonald's at some point in their life. The three main fast-food corporations, Burger King, McDonald's and Triton Global Restaurants (which owns Taco Bell, Pizza Hut and Kentucky Fried Chicken), estimated that in 1999 they employed 3.7 million people worldwide in around 60,000 restaurants.[30]

The US restaurant industry (predominantly fast-food) is now the US's largest private employer, with about 3.5 million minimum wage employees. In 2000, the US federal minimum wage was $5.15 an hour, but for restaurants where the staff receive tips, employers are allowed to pay as little as $2.13 an hour, with the balance being made up from tips. If the tips do not lift wages, employers are expected to make up the difference.[31] Many workers on such wages cannot afford to rent, much less purchase, reasonable housing. They are therefore obliged to live in accommodation with minimum cooking facilities, meaning they have to eat as well as work in fast-food restaurants.[32]

McDonald's is the US's largest purchaser of beef, pork and potatoes and its second largest purchaser of chicken.[33] In 1968, McDonald's bought minced beef from almost 200 local suppliers across the US, but by the mid-1970s the number had fallen to 15.[34] In 1965, McDonald's in the US was buying potatoes for its french fries from about 175 local suppliers, whereas now it buys most of them from a single supplier, frozen, and they are all made from one potato species – the Russet Burbank.[35]

The fast-food industry has fuelled the concentration process in US agribusiness. Fewer and fewer producers and purchasers deal with each other, and in the process shape US agriculture. Although many of them grew from publicly funded changes in society, they have become fierce advocates of deregulation in ownership, health and safety and labour laws.

You Are What You Eat

The huge corporate concentration of the food industry into less than a dozen companies raises serious questions about competition and the very existence of a free market. This corporate concentration also gives rise to the production of standardised food. The role of the traditional butcher, selecting an animal for slaughter and processing the meat for his customers, has all but vanished in the US. It does not require any great degree of mathematical genius to work out that mass production does not allow for high-quality varied produce. Beef from animals that have grazed on one type of grass in Texas are bound to have a different flavour from cattle raised in Iowa. If the butcher, the restaurant chef or the final consumer has no way of knowing where their beef comes from, how can they exercise choice? As minced beef and minced beef products are made up with meat from different animals, the origins are even more obscure – and the fat content usually higher. Small-scale butchers and those selling organic meat can still discharge this traditional customer service and honour the guarantee that goes with it, but such suppliers are a tiny minority serving high-price niche markets in today's US.

Almost 65 per cent of adults in the US were reported to be either overweight or obese in 2002.[36] In 1991, just 12 per cent of the US population was obese, and even by

1998 this had only risen to 18 per cent. The US Center for Disease Control (CDC) cited 'a greater variety of foods, some with higher caloric content, the growth in the fast-food industry, the increased number and marketing of snack foods' as contributory factors.[37] In the period from 1973 to 2003, the proportion of obese children in the US increased from 5 per cent to 15 per cent.[38]

Jeffrey P. Koplan, director of the CDC, described the problem in the following terms:

> Overweight and physical inactivity account for more than 300,000 premature deaths each year in the United States, second only to tobacco-related deaths. Obesity is an epidemic and should be taken as seriously as any infectious disease epidemic. Obesity and overweight are linked to the nation's number one killer – heart disease – as well as diabetes and other chronic conditions.[39]

In 1984, US residents spent around 8 per cent of their disposable income on health care and 15 per cent on food. Those figures have been effectively inversed in the last 20 years.[40] The concentration of the food industry is a significant factor in this epidemic.

The concentration of food production in a small number of large production units poses other risks. Murphy's Law tells us that if anything can go wrong, it will, and the codicil adds that it will usually go wrong in the worst possible way at the worst possible time. Simple logic suggests that if food is processed at hundreds of different sites and contamination occurs at one site, the potential damage to human health is limited. The reverse is equally true. If food is processed at a few gigantic sites and contamination occurs at one site, the potential damage may well be nationwide.

As the main meat corporations seek to increase margins by 3 to 5 per cent through operating larger and larger plants and meatpacking remains labour intensive, reducing labour costs are of vital importance to the industry. If you can move carcasses through the plants faster, you may save an additional 1 per cent, or 1 cent on the dollar.

The Chicago stockyard plants slaughtered about 50 cattle an hour in 1900, whereas today's largest plants slaughter 400 an hour.[41] In order to achieve this, an average slaughterhouse worker may repeat up to 10,000 identical knife cuts in one eight-hour shift.

Stomachs and intestines are removed from carcasses by hand. If this is not done carefully, some of the contents can spill, contaminating meat with undigested food, faeces and urine. A single worker gutting cattle may handle up to 60 an hour. Experienced 'gutters' say that with six months' experience they have a spillage rate of around 0.5 per cent, while inexperienced workers have rates as high as 20 per cent.[42] The intestinal contents of one in five animals are spilled on a production line that does not stop. The USDA estimates that 1 per cent of cattle carry the food-poisoning pathogen *E. Coli* 0157:H7 in their gut during winter, but that figure can rise to 50 per cent in summer.[43]

Remember Warren Monfort, the inventor of feedlots? ConAgra bought his company in 1987. In July 2002, ConAgra had to recall more than 8 million kilos of minced beef because of *E. coli* contamination. The tainted meat was produced at the old Monfort plant in Greeley, Colorado. However, according to US Department of Agriculture regulations, this meat can still be used for people if it is cooked at a high temperature – and that's just what ConAgra did. A shipment of the recalled meat was sold to a Colorado prison, where it was cooked and fed to the prison inmates.[44]

In 1997 and 1998 alone, two companies, Hudson Foods of Nebraska (Tyson) and the Bauer Meat Company of Florida, recalled almost 19 million kilos of *E. coli*-contaminated meat. At the time, USDA inspectors did not have the power to order recalls. They had to negotiate the arrangements with the company concerned. The USDA's most potent weapon was to withdraw its health inspectors from a plant, which they did in the Bauer case, thus forcing the plant to close. A company can contest such a withdrawal in court, and many have.[45] In 1978, the

USDA employed approximately 12,000 meat inspectors, but by 1999 that number had fallen to 7,500.[46] The US Food and Drug Administration (FDA) inspected 21,000 food processing plants in 1981, yet by 1997 that number was down to 5,000.[47]

The USDA buys minced beef (assembled from different animals) for the US National School Lunch Program, serving around 27 million children. In 2002, the Department bought 62 million kilos of such beef. On 29 May 2003, the USDA decided to accept irradiated beef for its programme. The FDA approved food irradiation in 1997, but several consumer groups remain hostile. Critics of sanitary conditions in the US meat-packing industry have also expressed concern that the use of radiation to sterilise beef will allow the industry to further relax the already low level of attention it devotes to hygiene in its plants.[48]

US Secretary of Agriculture Dan Glickman complained in January 1998, 'We can fine circuses for mistreating elephants, but we cannot fine companies that violate food-safety standards.'[49] Cattle in feedlots are obliged to stand in their own faeces and urine, which contain several pathogens, including *E. coli*. In these confined conditions, illnesses can multiply rather as they did in unsanitary, overcrowded European cities of the Middle Ages. Pathogens live for several days in faeces. The beef industry deals with this problem by adding medications to the animal feed, including antibiotics. Scientific studies have shown that this contributes to the growing problem of antibiotic-resistant human infections and that the transfer of bacteria from food animals to humans is common. The use of manure from feedlots can release drug-resistant pollutants into the ground and into watercourses, and some drug-resistant human infections have been traced to specific meat and poultry operations.[50]

Feedlot operators are constantly seeking cheaper animal feeds than grains, maize and root vegetables. Before 1997, up to 75 per cent of cattle in US feedlots were fed with food that included rendered sheep and cow carcasses, and sometimes rendered cat and dog remains. The USDA banned such feeds following the BSE (mad cow disease) outbreak in the UK. However, pig, horse and chicken carcasses can still be rendered and fed to cattle, as can feed containing cattle blood and chicken manure.[51]

The highly concentrated US food industry favours those animal and plant species that produce the highest yields. There is far less genetic diversity in US agriculture than there was even 20 years ago. A *New York Times* 2002 editorial commented, 'The poultry and pork industries depend on just a handful of different types of turkeys, chickens and pigs. The beef industry is headed in that direction too. There has been a precarious narrowing of the genetic resources that supply most of America's meat.'[52] Different breeds have different levels of natural resistance to diseases. Having thousands of animals, all from the same breed, confined in a relatively small space where they cannot eat or move naturally is a recipe for a potential disaster.

Completely genetically engineered foods still belong in science fiction, but the food industry is already striding in that direction. Tyson Foods developed a new breed of chicken, the 'Mr. McDonald', with unusually large breasts to provide the meat for McDonald's Chicken McNuggets. The Harvard Medical School found that McNuggets hold twice as much fat per gram as a hamburger.[53]

A 1999 study, sponsored by the US Department of Agriculture, found that free-range chickens have 21 per cent less fat, 30 per cent less saturated fat, 34 per cent less cholesterol, 50 per cent more vitamin A and 400 per cent more Omega-3 fatty acids than battery-raised birds.[54] US Judge Robert W. Sweet, of the Manhattan Federal District Court, was to describe Chicken McNuggets as 'a McFrankenstein creation of various elements not utilized by the home cook.'[55]

Large meatpacking plants, open animal feedlots or

the huge buildings where animals are held in pens and fed by computer-controlled automated systems (confined animal feeding operations – CAFOs) are of such a scale that they have a direct environmental impact on those who work in them and those who live nearby. Transport of arriving animals, animal feed and outbound carcasses significantly increases traffic on local roads and railways, but some of the other environmental impacts are more directly noxious. Such plants are significant water consumers. For example, the IBP plant at Lexington, Nebraska uses more than 6 million litres of water a day from the Ogallala aquifer.[56]

One cow produces about 17 times the amount of faeces and urine as a human.[57] Using that ratio, a feedlot, or CAFO, holding 200,000 cattle produces the same amount of sewage as a city of 3.5 million inhabitants, or something approaching three times the population of Dublin. Since the feedlots or CAFOs are treated as farms, they are subject to far less regulation than sewage authorities in comparable towns or cities.

The Sierra Club (the oldest and possibly most prestigious environmental awareness organisation in the US) published a report in 2002 entitled 'The Rapsheet on Animal Factories'. The Sierra Club's attention was drawn to the issue as a result of a pattern of violations, many of which involved spills from waste-holding tanks, and resulted in criminal proceedings.

According to Iowa's Soil and Water Conservation Service, in 2001 half of the state's lake beaches were closed because of industrial agricultural pollution. From 1995 to 2001, the Service recorded 152 fish kills in Iowa, totalling almost 6 million fish. The United States Geological Survey reported in March 2002 that water downstream from industrial livestock facilities contained hormones and antibiotics administered to livestock – even after the water had been processed through treatment plants.

Farmers have traditionally spread animal manure on their land. Factory farms initially did likewise, and there were no regulations governing the practice. The volume of manure from factory farms (quite apart from the chemical composition of that manure) was such that the land could not absorb it. Spills from holding tanks and run-off from the land following rain have polluted watercourses across the rural US – and triggered the Sierra Club's interest.

One solution adopted in particular by the pig industry has been to store manure in open-air cesspits, each about the size of a football field. The industry calls such installations 'lagoons'. The contents of these lagoons are sprayed into the air, falling back into the lagoon. This assists in drying the sludge, which can then be disposed of as solid waste. The problem with this approach is the toxic air pollution it causes.

Iowa and North Carolina are the two biggest pork-producing states in the US. Iowa state officials monitored air quality around six lagoon locations in April 2003 and found that on 22 occasions the state's standards for hydrogen sulphide and ammonia were breached. Hydrogen sulphide and ammonia are poisonous. The highest level recorded for hydrogen sulphide was 70 parts per billion in an hour – Iowa's recommended standard is 15 parts per billion.[58]

Hydrogen sulphide can cause neurological disorders, vomiting and motor and co-ordination loss. According to Dr Kaye H. Hilburn of the University of Southern California, 'The coincidence of people showing a pattern of impairment and being exposed to hydrogen sulfide arising from lagoons where hog manure is stored and then sprayed on fields or sprayed in the air [makes a connection] practically undeniable.'[59] In May 2002, the Michigan State Medical Society called for an immediate phase-out of all open-air manure lagoons for CAFOs in Michigan.

Professor Viney Aneja, Professor of Marine, Earth and Atmospheric Sciences at the North Carolina State University, called for CAFOs to be treated as factories: 'It is no longer the mom-and-pop operation it used to be. This is a factory. Treat it as one. It should be under the same regulations as a chemical operation.' *The New York Times* reported in May 2003 that Bush administration officials were negotiating with lobbyists for industrial farming corporations to establish voluntary monitoring of air pollution at their sites.[60]

While much of what we have described above has global repercussions, the impact is most severely felt in small rural communities in the US itself.

Rural Life in Today's US

The general concentration of business in the US in the last 20 years is visible in a number of service areas, such as banking. The number of banks in the US more or less halved between 1980 and 1990. In this rationalisation process, the number of small banks and bank branches in small-town USA has been shrinking even faster. The reductions are even more dramatic when it comes to bank credit executives. Local banks where the executives knew their town and its surrounding farmers are increasingly a thing of the past. Decisions are now made in regional centres or state capitals. Loans to farmers have in some cases become conditional on the farmer producing a contract to supply a major producer.[61]

A major source of business development capital has effectively abandoned small-town USA. This has also impacted on local authorities. County and town authorities have long relied on issuing bonds to fund significant local developments. Local banks were often among the major purchasers of these bonds. In New York City, the number of clearing banks fell from 11 in 1975 to two mega-banks by the end of 2002.[62] If there was an almost 80 per cent fall in the number of banks in New York City over 17 years, something similar was happening across small-town USA.

The meatpacking and other food corporations can exercise considerable pressure at state and local level for legislative and fiscal measures to attract their investment, or to encourage them to retain their plants in given localities. ConAgra's Mike Harper effectively drafted a Nebraska state law (LB 775, the Nebraska Development and Investment Growth Act), which the state's unicameral legislature passed in 1990. This provided extensive tax breaks for the company, lower taxes on high (executive) incomes and even tax breaks for ConAgra's corporate jets.[63]

IBP's Lexington, Nebraska plant (opened in 1990) obtained property tax exemptions of $47 million.[64] IBP had been based in Nebraska since 1967, and following the adoption of LB 775, IBP paid no corporate taxes for the following 10 years and its executives paid state income tax at the maximum 7 per cent rate. IBP moved its headquarters from Nebraska to South Dakota in 1997, where there are no corporate taxes and no personal income tax.[65] IBP's Lexington plant also attracted $2 million in federal Community Development Block Grants (CDBGs). Nebraska state figures suggest that each meatpacking job generated cost approximately $20,000 in public funds.[66]

The number of farmers has been in steady decline in the US. In 1940 there were 6.1 million farms in the country, but by 1978 that had fallen to 2.3 million, and by 1998 to 2 million. Over the same 1940 to 1998 period, average farm size grew from 55 hectares to 190 hectares.[67] Family farms provide a range of benefits to their local communities. Virginia Tech University research showed that family livestock farms make 70 per cent of their purchases within a 30-kilometre radius, whereas the comparable figure for corporate farms was 40 per cent. Local farmers and their families make their own purchasing decisions, while corporate decisions are made at corporate HQ.

University of California anthropologist Dean MacCannell summarised the impact of these changes on local communities in the following terms:

> As farm size and absentee ownership increase, social conditions in the local community deteriorate. We have

found depressed median family incomes, high levels of poverty, low education levels, social and economic inequality between ethnic groups, etc....associated with land and capital concentration in agriculture...Communities that are surrounded by farms that are larger than can be operated by a family unit have a bi-modal income distribution, with a few wealthy elites, a majority of poor laborers, and virtually no middle class. The absence of a middle class at the community level has a serious negative effect on both the quality and quantity of social and commercial service, public education, local governments, etc.[68]

The progressive move by the meatpacking industry from the big cities to the Great Plains has been accompanied by a concerted, and successful, corporate policy to operate non-union plants. According to the USDA's Economic Research Service, wage levels in the meatpacking industry fell by between 40 and 50 per cent in inflation-adjusted dollars in the period 1972 to 1992.[69] The health and safety impacts of this non-union policy are striking. The USDA states that 'meatpacking has the highest rate of occupational illnesses and injuries of all U.S. industries. During the 1980's...the rate was 45.5 per 100 workers.'[70]

The meatpacking industry has had to cast its net further and wider to find workers prepared to undertake such demanding, high-risk and low-paid jobs. The answer has come from migrant labour. The US General Accounting Office describes the phenomenon in the following terms: 'Immigrants, primarily from Southeast Asia, Mexico and Central America, make up large and growing shares of the workforces in both hog and cattle slaughter plants. This has led to striking transformations in the rural communities that must provide schooling and social services to the workers and their families.'[71]An undercover federal investigation of Tyson Foods resulted in charges against six Tyson executives under immigration and racketeering statutes for recruiting and smuggling illegal migrant workers from Mexico into the US.[72]

In Lexington, Nebraska in March 1991, 9.56 per cent

of students in local schools were from racial minorities, and less than 10 per cent of that figure was Hispanic. By the following year, 23 per cent of students were from minorities, and 21 per cent of the minorities were Hispanic. Because of the high turnover of workers at the IBP plant (turnover in large plants can reach 84 per cent per year), about 20 per cent of the student population changed in Lexington in 1991–1992, making school budgeting extremely difficult. Lexington had become Nebraska's fastest-growing school district. Local health facilities have also felt the strain. Births at the local hospital have increased, as have problems with paying for them. In the 1980s, 17 per cent of natal bills at the hospital were covered by Medicaid and unpaid bills were rare. By 1992, 51 per cent were either not paid or covered by Medicaid.[73]

Town and county authorities are seeing their tax base contract as they offer incentives to attract meat-packers. These packers pay minimum wages to young, poor and often migrant workers. These wages are at or below taxation thresholds and the communities they support have little disposable purchasing power. Local retail sales fall and businesses close while local outgoings on health, social services and policing rise. The concentration of unregulated agribusinesses is undermining local democracy in the rural US.

Loup County, in the heart of Nebraska, earned the distinction of being the poorest county in the US in 2001. The US Department of Commerce found that average annual per capita income in the county was $6,606, or 22 per cent of the national average. A four-bedroom house there costs $30,000. The percentage of people living below the poverty line is 30 per cent higher in rural areas than in cities. Of the 25 poorest counties in the US, Nebraska and Texas have five each and South Dakota has four. Workers in rural areas are 60 per cent more likely to earn the minimum wage than their urban counterparts.

Dalhart, Texas, a town of 7,000 inhabitants, clocked in with twice the national average murder rate in 2001.

The rate of serious crime in Nebraska, Kansas, Oklahoma and Utah is 50 per cent higher than in New York state, according to the FBI. Towns between 10,000 and 25,000 inhabitants are the most likely places to experience a bank robbery. Drug-related homicides fell by 50 per cent in urban areas, but tripled in rural ones during 1991 to 2001.

Methamphetamine (meth), a drug easily made from chemical fertilizer, is a synthetic form of speed described by the Bush White House as the fastest-growing drug threat in the US. Meth has given some rural counties a higher murder rate than New York City. Nationwide meth production tripled during 1994 to 2001 and 300 times more meth labs were seized in Iowa in 1999 than in New York and New Jersey combined, according to the Drug Enforcement Administration (DEA). In Wyoming, state officials estimate that one in 100 people need treatment for meth addiction.

Meth users tend to be poor and white, are erratic, violent and can be borderline psychotic. 'We have serious drug crime in places that never used to have it. Meth seems to be everywhere in Nebraska right now. It's mostly Beavis and Butthead labs, with poor white kids making meth out of their cars,' Allen Curtis, executive director of the Nebraska Crime Commission, told *The New York Times*.[74]

One writer has synthesised the phenomenon in the following terms:

> formerly healthy, mostly middle class communities throughout the Midwest, the small towns that have given the area its distinctive character since its settlement, are being transformed into rural ghettos – pockets of poverty, unemployment, violence and despair that are becoming more and more isolated from the rest of the country.[75]

Two uniquely US forms of law have helped the development and consolidation of this form of agricultural production and ownership – Right-to-Work and Right-to-Farm laws. Twenty-two of the 50 US states have Right-to-Work laws of one form or other. While some of these laws were drafted to prevent union 'closed shop' agreements, the majority of them make it extremely difficult for workers to join or organise trade unions at their workplace.

Right-to-Farm laws first appeared in the 1970s to protect farmers from lawsuits where housing developments were being constructed in traditional farming areas. The rationale behind the laws was to protect farmers from legal complaints related to the use of agricultural machinery such as noise, dust from ploughing, harrowing and harvesting and odours from animal rearing and dung. One of their main results, however, has been to make it almost impossible to sue 'farmers' even where the farmer in question is a massive animal feedlot or a CAFO. Oklahoma, Wyoming, Tennessee and Kansas offer specific protection under Right-to-Farm laws for feedlots. Most states offer some protection for existing land use, so it is difficult to ascertain how many states have specific Right-to-Farm laws as such, but the figure would seem to be about 12. Some of these laws have been contested in court and the Iowa Supreme Court ruled that aspects of the state's Right-to-Farm laws were unconstitutional.[76]

Field of Nightmares

US agriculture and US agribusiness are disasters, in some respects waiting to happen, in others in full flight. The impact of some of these calamities will be largely confined to the US, others will hit neighbouring countries and some have global potential.

Domestically, the US has created a bizarre and potentially lethal cocktail of free enterprise and private property protections, intermingled with state aids, both current and historic, to produce the worst of both worlds – giant agribusinesses that dominate agricultural production and markets while protected by laws and customs designed for family farms. Family farming normally operates in some degree of harmony with the land, local climate conditions and market demand. Many countries have introduced and operate support systems to protect individual farmers from climatic hazards and fluctuating produce prices. In today's US, such systems tend to provide greater support for big business and wealthy landowners than they do for farmers. In 2001–2002, 25,000 US rice farmers received over $3 billion in federal subsidies.[77] Cotton growers received almost $4 billion, with the top 10 per cent of growers accounting for 73 per cent of that figure. The top 10 cotton farms (company farms) received on average almost $1.7 million each. According to Daniel T. Griswold of the free market Cato Institute, US cotton subsidies 'hurt some of the poorest countries in the world and benefit some of the richest [US] farmers.'[78] Subsidies are used as a tool to undermine, if not destroy, the very farmers they were supposed to protect.

Industrial farming and the fast-food industry contribute to the US obesity epidemic. The concentration of production into ever larger units depending on ever fewer animal species and plant varieties places the whole US food chain at risk. An animal epidemic or potato disease resistant to current treatments could wipe out a majority of the US food industry within years.

Canada and the US have had one confirmed case of BSE each to date. The first confirmed US case on 9 December 2003 was a 'downer animal' (a cow that cannot walk into the slaughterhouse) in Washington state.[79] US authorities, and most notably US Department of Agriculture spokesperson, Ms Harrison, have sought to play down the significance of this case, stressing that US beef is safe. Before joining the USDA, Ms Harrison was director of public relations for the National Cattlemen's Beef Association, the beef industry's largest trade group.[80]

The USDA carries out relatively few BSE tests. In 2003 it tested 20,526 US cattle for BSE out of the roughly 35 million slaughtered.[81] Belgium, with a cattle herd only a small fraction of the US one, tested almost 400,000 animals.[82] Following the outbreak, the USDA announced a ban on slaughtering 'downer' cattle (around 190,000 in 2003). A similar measure had been defeated in the House of Representatives in July 2003 by 202 votes to 199. In 2000, the US livestock industry had contributed $4.7 million to political campaigns, 79 per cent of it going to Republicans.[83]

A form of BSE, Chronic Wasting Disease (CWD), has been spreading though deer herds in the US midwest and in Canada since 1960, and the rate has accelerated since 1990.[84] Given the conditions in which cattle are raised and killed in the US and the absence of traceability from the plate back to an individual animal, a serious BSE outbreak would decimate the US beef industry – quite apart from the eventual human health impact of a Creutzfeld-Jakob Disease epidemic.

The concentration of economic agricultural power has produced influential lobbies, both at state and federal level. Adam Smith, often cited as the great apostle of free enterprise, warned, 'People of the same trade seldom meet together even for merriment or diversion, but the conversation ends in a conspiracy against the public; or in some contrivance to raise prices.'[85] Naturally, the companies that dominate US agriculture have no wish to see the policies that give them such wealth and control reformed or dismantled. US resistance to reducing export subsidies for agricultural produce was a major element in the collapse of the 2003 World Trade Organization talks in Cancun.

US agricultural policy, much of which operates to protect the interests of a privileged minority, is also having an increasing impact on US foreign policy. There are real tensions between the US and the EU, Latin American, African, Asian and Pacific countries over US food exports and US protectionist practices when it comes to food imports. These tensions can hinder other areas of policy co-operation.

If the US government persists in paying the 25,000 US rice growers \$3.10 a bushel for their crop while the world market price stands at \$1.40,[86] then West and Central Africa's 10 million rice farmers will not be able to compete. If 10 million human beings are driven out of rice production into poverty and forced to purchase US rice with dollars they do not have in order to support the lifestyles of 25,000 US millionaire rice producers, the consequences could include an increase in the very problem that the US says is its top priority – terrorism.

US agriculture is dangerous to the US population, massively expensive in its direct and indirect costs to the state and unsustainable. Gradual reform depends on a recognition in Washington that reform is necessary. There is little sign of such an awareness emerging, and many vested interests are working hard to make sure it does not.

If reform is not undertaken, and soon, US agriculture will crash – and food remains the last great physical export of the US. In June 2004 the US became a net importer of food for the first time in its modern history.[87] An imperium that cannot feed itself is not a pillar on which a world order can be built. An imperium that threatens the stability of global food production can come to be seen as a factor of global insecurity.

Global food insecurity is far more threatening to far more people's lives than terrorism has ever been. Former US Secretary of State Colin Powell described Brazil as 'an agricultural superpower' in October 2003. By 2010 Brazil will have overtaken the US as the world's largest food exporter (it's already the biggest exporter of chickens, orange juice, sugar, coffee and tobacco). Will twenty-first-century food power lie in the Matto Grosso rather than Montana? In a global economy, what would such a power shift mean in political terms? What relevance would armed superiority have for a nation lacking the foreign reserves necessary to pay for its imported food?

7

Evildoers Suck!

'The Son of man will send his angels, and they will gather out of his kingdom all causes of sin and all evildoers.'

> – New Testament, Matthew 13:41

'Men never do evil so completely and cheerfully as when they do it from religious conviction.'

> – Blaise Pascal[1]

'The law is not about forgiveness. It is oftentimes about vengeance, oftentimes about revenge.'

> – Former US Attorney General John Ashcroft

'We've lit our town so there is no
Place for crime to hide
Our little church is painted white
And in the safety of the night
We all go quiet as a mouse
For the word is out
God is in the house.'

> – Nick Cave, 'God is in the House'

Moving On: Facing the Future or Fleeing to the Past?

The US faces serious challenges to its economic and social well-being and to its place in today's world. Yet you have to search hard to find any recognition of that reality, much less debate over possible solutions, in the mainstream of American politics and media. The refusal to recognise that there is a problem has become a problem in its own right. If you do not, or cannot, recognise that something is broken, then you cannot even begin to think about fixing it.

There are many explanations for this continental blindness. The language of US politics has to be one of optimism. Those who are pessimistic, critical or even seriously questioning find themselves quickly labelled as extremists and/or traitors, then dismissed. Since such a label is a political kiss of death, it's easy to understand why few candidates for political office are willing to venture into such dangerous territory.

We all prefer simplicity to complexity – straight questions with clear yes or no answers are infinitely preferable to complex analyses which almost by definition lack straightforward answers. But many democratic societies have learned from bitter experience that in much of human life, questions resolve themselves into many shades of grey, rather than simple, crisp blacks and whites.

Much of American political culture has yet to come to terms with this reality. It doggedly insists on reducing the world to black and white, to good versus evil, with the US always and unambiguously on the side of good. Since the US is good, those who would question or oppose it must be bad. They are, in one of George W. Bush's favourite phrases, evildoers.

Evildoers Suck!

There is a web-based company in the US that sells a small but very popular line of products. All of them feature a lurid red and yellow illustration of the devil with the bold slogan: Evil Doers Suck! 'Do you wear your feelings on your sleeve? Then our EDS Tee (Just $16.95) is perfect for you! ...' Badges ('It's a full 3" round and can be seen from across the room! Kids absolutely love them and parents are happy to let them wear it!') go for $1.99 and 4x4" stickers ('high quality vinyl with UV ink for long lasting bright colors') are just 99 cents each. The products are not an exercise in satire. They are explicitly inspired by George W. Bush and the War on Terrorism and are intended to make clear the real object of the fight – not just the subjugation of an enemy, but the conquest of evil itself.

The difficulty the US has had in dealing with the very real threat of terrorism, and other threats perceived or real, is partly a conceptual problem. There is a deep-seated tendency in American culture to see crime of all kinds as a religious failure, a product of godlessness, a commitment to the Dark Side. George W. Bush's language is, in this regard at least, eloquent. He some-times talks of terrorism, but more often he talks of 'evildoers'. The phrase is biblical: 'And then will I declare to them, I never knew you; depart from me, you evildoers' (Matthew 7:23); 'The Son of man will send his angels, and they will gather out of his kingdom all causes of sin and all evildoers' (Matthew 13:41); 'They answered him, "If this man were not an evildoer, we would not have handed him over"' (John 18:30); 'Let the evildoer still do evil, and the filthy still be filthy, and the righteous still do right, and the holy still be holy' (Revelations 22:11).

Bush began to use and repeat the term immediately after 11 September 2001. A few examples from dozens will suffice: 'Civilized people around the world denounce the evildoers who devised and executed these terrible attacks' (14 September); 'We're a nation that can't be cowed by evildoers' (16 September); 'We're going to find those evildoers, those barbaric people who attacked our country and we're going to hold them accountable' (17 September); 'We're too great a nation to allow the evildoers to affect our soul and our spirit' (18 September); 'This is good versus evil. These are evildoers' (25 September); 'The evildoers struck, but they may have hurt our buildings, and they are obviously affecting some family lives in such a profound and sad way. But they will not touch the soul of America' (4 October); and so on.

It is quite simply impossible to imagine any European political leader from a German Christian Democrat through to a Turkish Islamic Democrat passing by way of a Spanish Socialist, a British Liberal and a Lithuanian Conservative employing in such an unsubtle way this kind of language drawn so directly from sacred scripture, whatever their personal religious convictions might be. Since the Enlightenment, religion in Europe has steadily become more and more a question of private belief, and less and less part of our public domain.

The same cannot be said for the US. Max Hastings, the former editor of Britain's *Daily Telegraph*, summed it up: 'A week in the United States…is enough to make anybody feel a trifle fed up with god, or rather with the relentless invocation of the deity by American politicians…The appeal to the faith, seldom mere ritual, is usually founded upon conviction.'[2]

This is one of the major differences between the US and the rest of the developed world at the beginning of our third millennium. It begs the question, asked by Professor Garry Wills of the US's Northwestern University, 'Can a people that believes more fervently in the Virgin Birth than in evolution still be called an Enlightened nation?'[3]

Religion and Supremacy

Religion is by definition exclusive. You cannot be both a Baptist and a Presbyterian – you must choose to be one or the other, although those two Christian religions are relatively close. The exclusive nature of religions becomes even more stark as the differences between the religions grows. You cannot be a Jew and a Roman Catholic, or a Muslim and a Shintoist. At their core, all organised religions claim a unique insight into truth and divine revelation. Each religion claims that only through its doctrine and rites can the individual reach heaven, or god, or whatever the higher state to which one wishes to accede to is called.

The step from this supremacist exclusivity to a position where you seek to impose your beliefs on others whose beliefs by definition must be inferior is a small, if distinct, one. Once you see your beliefs as being exclusively correct, it then follows naturally that you have a duty to impose these correct beliefs on others. From the harsh lessons of history, most of the world's religions have come to understand that this small step from belief to fundamentalist imposition is one that it is better not to take.

Religion, and in particular fundamentalist evangelical Christianity, is a major force in today's US. Forty per cent of the US population describe themselves as regular churchgoers, as opposed to 2 per cent in Britain.[4] According to recent polls, 94 per cent of the US population believe in god, 89 per cent believe in heaven, 86 per cent believe in miracles, 73 per cent believe in the devil and hell and 48 per cent believe that the US has a special protection from god.[5] Fifty-three per cent say religion is very important in their lives, compared with 16 per cent in Britain, 14 per cent in France and 13 per cent in Germany.[6] Forty-six per cent of the US population describe themselves as evangelical, or born-again Christians, and 48 per cent believe in creationism as opposed to the 28 per cent who see evolution as scientific fact.[7] President Bush has said that 'the jury is still out' on evolution.[8]

The dominance of religious discourse in American life is such that awkward realities are brushed aside. One almost invisible reality is those US residents who describe themselves as having no religion. If you identify such people as a group in a religious profiling of society, then those of 'no religion' are largely under thirty. They make up the fastest-growing group and are the third largest cohort after Roman Catholics and Baptists. Why is this group never mentioned?[9] Because its presence complicates the self-image of America as an essentially religious society.

Of course, the role of religion is not straightforward. Some of the most progressive movements in US history – the campaign to abolish slavery, the attempts by Quakers to stand up for the rights of Native Americans, the black civil rights movement of the 1960s – drew strength and courage from religious belief and language. Many of the bravest objectors to the Vietnam War, to US support for the dictatorships of Central and South America and to subsequent military adventures have been inspired by religious faith. But the power of religious conviction has been harnessed to an increasing extent not just by old-style conservatives, but by an extreme, and explicitly political, fundamentalism.

A particular phenomenon has emerged within evangelical Christianity in the US – the Christian Zionists. Their belief is that god granted the Jewish people a nation, Israel, and made no mention of Palestine. Polls show that 48 per cent of people in the US believe that god gave the land that is now Israel to the Jewish people, and 36 per cent believe that 'the state of Israel is a fulfilment of the biblical prophecy about the second coming of Jesus.'[10] The Christian Coalition of America's church liaison officer, Michael Brown, quotes the Book of Genesis: 'I will make of thee a great nation and I will bless them that bless thee and curse them that curse thee.'[11]

Conservative Protestantism has always existed in the US, but used to be both anti-Catholic and anti-Semitic. Conservative Protestants found common ground with conservative Catholics on the abortion issue, and have now found common ground with conservative Jews on Israel. A potent new political force has been born.

This support for Israel is amplified by the 'dispensationalist' belief that divides world history into seven sections, or dispensations. It first emerged in US evangelical Christianity during the nineteenth century.

According to this belief, the world is now entering the seventh, and last, dispensation. Jesus will return to save the chosen and will return to a Jewish state. A Middle East settlement allowing for a Palestinian state is not mentioned in the Old Testament, therefore evangelical Christians must support the most hawkish Israeli positions, and so should the US. (The rather awkward fact that America is not mentioned in the Bible either is brushed aside by the true believers.)

This current is not some extreme splinter group on the lunatic fringe of mainstream politics. Its 2002 Washington conference was opened with a message from President Bush, and the Republican leader of the House of Representatives, Tom DeLay, addressed the meeting.

The Left Behind series of novels setting out the dispensationalist view, written by Rev. Tim LaHaye and Jerry Jenkins, has sold over 60 million copies. *Desecration: Antichrist Takes the Throne*, one book from the series, was the best-selling novel in the US in 2001, and the latest volume, *The Remnant*, went straight to the top of *The New York Times* best-seller list in 2002.[12] The latest instalment in the series, *The Rising: Evil Unveiled*, published in March 2005, is also a best-seller. The Left Behind franchise, meanwhile, has been extended into video games, graphic novels, children's fiction and political novels with thinly disguised messages for voters. Their essential message is that violence and havoc are to be welcomed with joy as signs that the Last Days are upon the earth. These hard times will be followed by the establishment of a utopian thousand-year Reich in which the world is ruled by a totalitarian, theocratic monarchy.

Karl Rove, Bush's political guru, believes that evangelical Christians make up 18 per cent of the US electorate, and this in a country where 40 per cent turnouts in elections are normal.[13] The mobilisation by the Republican Party of this constituency of believers was one key element in President Bush's 2004 election victory.

In September 2002, President Bush met a group of

five clergymen, three Christian, one Jewish and one Muslim, in the Oval Office. He was frank about his divine mission: 'You know I had a drinking problem. Right now I should be in a bar in Texas, not the Oval Office. There is only one reason that I am in the Oval Office and not at a bar. I found faith. I found god. I am here because of the power of prayer.'[14]

There is a messianic strain to Bush's religion – the belief that god chose him to lead the US, and by extension the world, in a time of particular crisis. A flavour of Bush's Christianity can be found in his hometown of Midland, Texas. The town boasts three main churches. The Pilgrim Rest Baptist Church on Dixie Boulevard is predominantly black. The El Divino Salvador Roman Catholic Church on Muskingum Street is predominantly Hispanic. Bush's church is the all-white Belle View Baptist Church on Big Spring Avenue. The Belle View Church is part of the Anglo-Ulster-Scottish militant Protestant tradition which supported the Confederacy and has now become the millenarian Christian Right in Texas, treating the Bible as the literal word of god.[15]

Conservative Christians now exercise either 'strong' or 'moderate' influence in 44 Republican state committees, compared with 31 in 1994, according to a study in Washington magazine *Campaigns and Elections*. The man who used to run the Christian Coalition, Ralph Reed, is now the head of the Georgia Republican Party.[16]

This marks US society apart from Europe, Canada and much of the developed world. It is only in predominantly Muslim states that one finds similar patterns of religious belief and practice. Martin Amis observed, 'Doesn't Texas sometimes seem to resemble a country like Saudi Arabia, with its great heat, its oil wealth, its brimming houses of worship, and its weekly executions?'[17]

Following the 2004 US elections, several commentators remarked on the fundamentalist similarities between some US Christian extremists and their Islamic counterparts. Simon Schama was to label the two USAs that emerged from those elections Worldly America and godly America.

In Schama's terms, godly America is

> solidly continental and landlocked...turns its back on that dangerous, promiscuous, impure world and proclaims to high heaven the indestructible endurance of the American Difference...godly America is, at its heart...a church, a farm, a barracks; places that are walled, fenced and consecrated...Worldly America is about finding civil ways to share crowded space...godly America is about making space over in its own image. One America makes room, the other America muscles in.[18]

Susan Sarandon has expressed her fears as to where this mindset is taking her country. 'The thing that frightens me about the state of our dear nation and our world is this pre-emptive strike philosophy, and of violence as a means of solving everything, whether it is directed against the individual or a country. It is the elimination of all moderation.'[19]

Jailhouse Rot

Bush's religious language is so pervasive and sprang to his lips so quickly after the horror of September 11th that it cannot be dismissed simply as a rhetorical trick or series of quacks. It seems to come from somewhere much deeper in the psyche of conservative America, from a Biblical view of good and evil that is implicit in the peculiar vindictiveness of the American attitude to crime and punishment. A simplistic, vengeful attitude to the War on Terrorism is rooted in a simplistic, vengeful attitude to the pervasive American reality of crime. In this world view, it makes no more sense to ask about the causes of terrorism than to ask about the causes of crime in general. The answer is obvious – evil. The best place to look for an explanation of the fatal limits of the American response to terrorism is not in the White House or the Washington think tanks. It is in the vast network of prisons that contain a population larger than that of Slovenia. In all, more than 13 million US residents have been convicted of felonies and have spent time in prison.[20]

Daryl Matthews, a forensic psychiatrist based in Hawaii who spent a week at the Guantánamo prison camp in May 2003, commented that Europeans should not be over-enraged at conditions there, since

> prisons are a big industry in the US, we imprison a lot of people. People don't understand the extent and the misery of prisons in the US. People who are considered the most dangerous people in the US are moved in shackles. I've been in prisons in the US much more secure than Guantánamo. I've interviewed people in masks and shackles on the mainland US.[21]

Prison populations often represent an image of what we would prefer not to see in our societies – greed, violence, desperation and addiction. In societies where there are significant racial or ethnic tensions, those are also quickly reflected in the imprisonment ratio across different groups. Those who defraud people of millions are often less likely to do 'hard' prison time than those who steal thousands in an armed robbery. In US terms, those who fail, fail because they are weak, almost inferior, and most of those who fail tend to be at the bottom of the social heap and make up the majority of the prison population.

Laws and legal practices vary from country to country. Crimes punishable with a custodial offence in one jurisdiction may only attract a fine in others. Prisoners are a very particular group in any society. They are a reflection of their society while being both excluded from and forgotten by it. The gulags of Stalin's Russia, the concentration camps invented by the British Empire in South Africa and the death camps of Hitler's Germany bore witness to the horrors of those regimes. On a more benign note, the routine imprisonment of drunk drivers in the Nordic countries makes a clear statement as to how that offence is viewed in those societies.

However, the US is radically different in the numbers of people it incarcerates and in the number of people it executes. Its criminal justice system reflects its society in the disproportionate numbers of African-Americans and Hispanic-Americans it imprisons, in denying many of its offenders their right to vote, often for life, and in its refusal to face realities even, or perhaps particularly, when those realities cost US taxpayers dearly.

Operating expenses for the prisons of the 50 US states (as distinct from federal and local jails) amount to approximately $30 billion a year.[22] Maryland's Department of Legislative Services has calculated that it costs three times more to take a death penalty case through the courts to final execution than it does to lock up a prisoner for 40 years.[23]

The US imprisons more of its people than any other nation on earth. One in every 140 US citizens is currently in jail. As of 31 December 2003, 2,212,475 people were incarcerated in federal, state and local jails in the US, an increase of 2 per cent over 2002, and an increase which took place against a background of falling violent crime rates. FBI statistics show a drop of 16 per cent in violent crime in the US from 1994 to 2003, including a 36 per cent drop in murder arrests and a 25 per cent drop in robbery arrests.[24] The US prison population had risen to 2,212,475 in January 2004 from 501,000 in 1983. The annual average growth in the US prison population from 1995 to 2001 was 3.8 per cent.[25] The US has 5 per cent of the world's population, but 25 per cent of its prison population.[26]

Prison statistics are normally expressed in terms of numbers of prisoners per 100,000 population. In 2000 the average figure across 25 developed nations was 152. In the European Union it was 80 per 100,000, Canada imprisoned 123 people per 100,000 while the US imprisoned 702.[27] Is there really nine times more serious crime in the US than in the EU, or six times more than in Canada?

When the figures are broken down by race, the make-up of this enormous prison population becomes startling. In mid-2002 there were 3,535 sentenced black male prisoners per 100,000 black men, 1,177 Hispanics per 100,000 Hispanics and 462 white males per 100,000 white men.[28] Do these figures tell us that black men in the US commit eight times more crimes than their white counterparts?

The disproportionate numbers of blacks and Hispanics in the US penal and criminal justice systems reflects what is still a racist society to a significant degree. Political correctness may alter the labels and remove some terms from popular speech, but it does not, and cannot, address the underlying structure of a society. A US study in 1998 showed that the average black income was 61 per cent less than the average white income, a ratio that had not changed since 1880.[29]At the end of 2003, 44 per cent of federal prisoners were black, although blacks only make up 12.5 per cent of the US population; 35 per cent were white and 19 per cent were Hispanic. Ten per cent of all black American men aged 25 to 29 are in prison.[30]

Beyond its scale and inequity, however, what marks the American criminal justice system is its sheer vengefulness. Thirty-seven of the 50 US states have the death penalty, as does the federal government. At the end of 2001 there were 3,581 prisoners under sentence of death in US prisons. The youngest inmate under sentence of death was 19, the oldest 86. Sixty-nine men and two women were executed in the US in 2002.[31]

The US Supreme Court ruled in 1986 that it was unconstitutional to execute prisoners who were insane. However, in 2003 the US Federal Appeals Court ruled that it was legal to force insane prisoners to take anti-psychotic medication. Once medicated, the prisoner was no longer judged to be insane, and could then be executed. The court ruled 6–5 that the medication would be beneficial to a prisoner. The court did not need to consider the ultimate result of medicating a prisoner.[32] In May 2003, Utah's Corrections Department was looking for volunteers for a firing squad to shoot a condemned prisoner.[33]

An individual's risk of being arrested and sentenced to death is something of a lottery. If you're able to pay for your own legal representation and you're white, you are much less likely to be sentenced to death. A spate of releases, overturned convictions and pardons for wrongfully imprisoned individuals has rocked the US criminal justice system in recent years.

Illinois reintroduced the death penalty in 1977. By October 2002 it had executed 12 prisoners, but 13 condemned prisoners had been exonerated, one just 48 hours before his execution. These exonerations began when journalism students in Chicago reviewed cases for a project. Realising that the majority of convictions were unsafe, Illinois suspended executions in 2000 and undertook a full-scale review. Governor George Ryan described the state's capital punishment system as being 'putrid with racism, incompetent lawyers, overzealous prosecutors, bad judges and over-eager police.'[34] In his last days in office, Governor Ryan commuted the death sentences of 163 men and four women in the state's prisons to life imprisonment or less, saying, 'Our capital [punishment] system is haunted by the demon of error: error in determining guilt and error in determining who among the guilty deserves to die.'[35]

The US approach is in stark contrast to the European one. Forty-five countries have signed Protocol 6 (Abolition of the Death Penalty) to the European Convention for the Protection of Human Rights and Fundamental Freedoms. Article 1 of the Protocol states, 'The death penalty shall be abolished. No-one shall be condemned to such penalty or executed.' By June 2003, 41 countries had ratified the protocol (Armenia, Russia, Serbia, Montenegro and Turkey had yet to do so).[36] Article 2 of the protocol allows member states of the Council of Europe to retain the death penalty for use in time of war. However, some states have also abolished the death penalty for use in time of war. The Republic of Ireland did so by national referendum in 2002.

There is a biblical 'eye for an eye' element in US arguments for the death penalty, and this puritanical approach is reflected in the policies which have led to the explosion of the US prison population over the last two decades. In a number of areas, such as drug-related crimes, mandatory sentencing has been introduced – if the defendant is found guilty, the judge has little or no discretion when it comes to sentencing; the sentence is laid down by law. Several states have also introduced 'three strikes and you're out' laws, where a person convicted of a third offence is automatically sentenced to prison for terms ranging from 25 years to life. The best-known of these laws is the 1994 California statute. Governor Pete Wilson set out its purpose: 'It sends a clear message to repeat criminals. Find a new line of work because we're going to start turning career criminals into career inmates.'[37]

There is clear and growing evidence that harsh sentences or expanded use of custodial sentencing has, at best, a marginal impact on crime rates. Criminologists have long argued that the major deterrent for would-be criminals is their evaluation of how likely they are to be caught. If they believe they have a good chance of not being apprehended, then they clearly do not fear the sentencing which might follow. Statistics from California and Texas would seem to support this argument.

California led the way with 'three strikes' legislation and is the state which has made the most use of it, with over 40,000 inmates convicted under this law. The next state was Georgia, which had under 1,000.[38]

The approach is not working. Worse, it is compounding injustice in the system. 'Three strikes' has no discernible impact on the crime rate. Studies have shown that while crime rates fell by 36 per cent in California during the 1990s, they fell by 41 per cent in

New York, 33 per cent in Massachusetts and 32 per cent in Washington, DC, these latter three not having 'three strikes' legislation. The *Stanford Law and Policy Review* could find no independent effect of 'three strikes' legislation on crime rates.[39]

'Three strikes' tends to incarcerate prisoners who pose a declining threat. Not surprisingly, criminals are at their most active in their late teens and twenties. As people grow older, they tend to commit less crime. In California, only 22 per cent of felony arrests are for people over 39, and only 5 per cent for those over 50.[40] It obviously takes time to accumulate a criminal record involving prior convictions and prison sentences. Accordingly, the average age of a Californian criminal receiving a 'third strike' sentence is 36.[41] In other words, the state is locking away ageing criminals who are less and less likely to commit crimes.

'Three strikes' violates a basic principle of justice that there should be some correlation between the crime and the punishment. The 'third strike' does not have to be for a major or even violent crime – any conviction will do. The original California law was passed following the brutal murder of two young girls. The father of one of the victims, Mark Klass, has been highly critical of the use the law has been put to: 'In the depth of despair which all Californians shared with my family immediately following Polly's murder, we blindly supported the initiative in the mistaken belief that it dealt only with violent crimes. Instead three out of four crimes it addresses are not violent.'[42]

Scott Benscoter, who had two prior convictions for residential burglary, was sentenced to 25 years to life for the theft of a pair of sneakers in 2000. Arthur Gibson got a similar sentence the same year for crack possession, although his prior convictions for violent crimes dated from the 1960s.[43] Two California prisoners, Gary Ewing and Leandro Andrade, appealed their third strike sentences to the US Supreme Court. Ewing had been sentenced to 25 years without parole for stealing three golf clubs. Andrade got 50 years for shoplifting a few children's videocassettes from a K-Mart. The US Supreme Court rejected their appeal on a 5–4 decision, which *The New York Times* termed 'a clear miscarriage of justice.'[44]

'Three strikes' is extremely expensive for the prison system. Older prisoners are more expensive to incarcerate than their younger counterparts due to higher health and other costs. In 2001 California estimated that it cost the state $25,607 a year to imprison somebody. One study estimates that the annual cost of a prisoner sentenced at the average 'three strike' age of 36 could reach $60,000 a year in direct and indirect costs to the state.[45]

Texas enjoys being out ahead of other states, and has certainly achieved that distinction in terms of its prisons. Texas has 163,190 more people in prison than California, yet the population of California is 13 million more than that of Texas. At the end of 1999, 5 per cent of all adult Texans (706,000) were in prison, jail or on parole or probation. Throughout the 1990s, Texas added five times as many prisoners as New York, yet New York's crime rate dropped twice as much as it did in Texas. Texas also executed 227 prisoners between 1982 and 2002. Despite all that, the Texan crime rate had a lower percentage decline than the US national average – and Texas was seeking to build more prisons.[46]

This puritanical fixation with punishment, locking more people away for longer periods than other comparable societies, does not end with the prison sentence. As the numbers of inmates grow, so naturally do the numbers of former prisoners completing their sentences and re-entering society.

In 2003, around 650,000 former prisoners were released in the US. The comparable figure for 1994 was 272,000. According to US Department of Justice figures, over 60 per cent of released prisoners reoffend within three years. Others become crime victims. Forty-three per cent of Washington, DC's homicide victims had been released from prison within the last two years.

The 1998 US Higher Education Act bars those convicted of drug-related offences from ever receiving student loans. A 1996 federal law imposes a lifetime ban on those convicted of drug-related offences receiving family welfare benefits or food stamps. Paying your debt to society in the US can be a lifetime sentence. Charles H. Ramsey, Washington, DC police chief, argues that given a chance many convicts could make new lives: 'I think many of them, if given an opportunity and given a job, would not fall prey to this.'

A study of women convicted of drug-related offences in Philadelphia found that 80 per cent received their only drug addiction treatment in prison. Amy Hirsch, an attorney with Philadelphia's Community Legal Services, described the catch-22 situation these women faced upon leaving prison: 'They come out of jail hopeful, clean and sober, and then come out and run into this brick wall. All the things they need to get their life started back is off limits...They wind up homeless, back on the street.'[47]

The US has created a correctional monster that flies in the face of many of the norms of justice, incarcerates nine times as many people as EU countries, fails miserably in rehabilitation and has at best a marginal impact on serious or violent crimes. While this may make some puritanical points, it makes very little practical sense. The average cost of imprisoning a person in the US in 2002 was $21,000. The average cost of a year's drug treatment programme was $2,500. The US is now spending well over $30 billion a year it cannot afford on prisons.[48]

The punitive and discriminatory aspects of the US penal system do not end with the prison sentence, nor indeed with the denial of assistance for ex-convicts. It extends right to the heart of any democracy – denying the right to vote to convicted prisoners. Many countries have similar provisions, although they are usually restricted to offences connected with electoral fraud, and then require a specific sentence before they can be applied. Several countries, such as Germany, actively encourage prisoners to vote and participate in the democratic process as part of their rehabilitation.[49]

In 1998, 46 of the 50 US states and the District of Columbia removed the right to vote from convicted prisoners as part of their punishment. Massachusetts and Utah were considering such measures. Thirty-two states do not allow prisoners on parole to vote, and 29 states deny the right to vote to those on probation. Ten states – Alabama, Delaware, Florida, Iowa, Kentucky, Mississippi, Nevada, New Mexico, Virginia and Wyoming – disenfranchise ex-felons for life. Arizona and Maryland permanently disenfranchise those convicted of a second felony. Those convicted before 1986 in Tennessee and before 1984 in Washington state are disenfranchised for life. In Texas, a former prisoner remains disenfranchised for two years following the completion of their prison sentence, parole or probation.[50]

Almost 4 million electors in the US are thus permanently or temporarily disenfranchised, stripped of their right to vote. Around 73 per cent of these are not in prison. They have completed their sentences, have been released on parole or given probation by the courts. Given the disproportionate number of blacks affected by the US penal system, the impact of this denial of the right to vote is most acutely felt in that community. In Alabama and Florida, 31 per cent of black men are disenfranchised. In six other states – Iowa, Mississippi, New Mexico, Virginia, Washington and Wyoming – the figure is 25 per cent, falling to 20 per cent in Delaware and Texas.[51] Blacks are generally considered to vote Democrat in US elections.

The system was partly designed in the states of the old Confederacy to circumvent the Fifteenth Amendment to the US Constitution, which extended voting rights to blacks. It was this system which Florida abused to exclude upwards of 90,000 electors who were entitled to vote from the electoral rolls of the 2000 US presidential election. Many would consider that to constitute electoral fraud.[52]

The use of these laws to elect George W. Bush as president carried with it a particularly grotesque irony. In his thirties, Bush himself was a serious substance-abuser. He has acknowledged, with commendable honesty, that he had a serious alcohol problem until he was 40, when he found Jesus and went on the wagon. He was much more evasive, though, about his past use of cocaine and other illegal drugs. In the early stages of the 2000 presidential election campaign, Bush's 'youthful indiscretions' became a public issue when the Democratic Party's leader in the Senate, Tom Daschle, complained that the then Republican front runner was being given an easy ride by the press over the 'legitimate question' of his alleged use of cocaine in the past.

The *New York Daily News* then asked all the presidential candidates (back then, there were still 11 of them) whether they had ever used cocaine. All except Bush replied that they had not. Bush did not reply at all. The Associated Press then asked all 11 whether they had ever used any illegal drugs. Two acknowledged using marijuana, eight said they'd never used any drugs and, again, George W. Bush refused to answer.

Shortly afterwards, the *Dallas Morning News* asked a subtle and clever question of Bush. Would he, as president, insist on his appointees (judges, cabinet members, ambassadors and so on) passing the standard FBI background checks? Implied in the question was a query about whether Bush himself would pass these tests, one of which asked whether the subject had used an illegal drug in the past seven years. Bush, and his advisers, got the point and decided to take the opportunity for a carefully ambiguous denial. 'As I understand it,' Bush told a press conference, 'the current [FBI] form asks the question, "Did somebody use drugs in the last seven years?" and I will be glad to answer that question and the answer is No.' Taking him at his word, this meant that Bush had not used drugs since 1992. The following day, Bush shifted the boundary back farther, stating that at the time his father was inaugurated as president in 1989, he would have passed the background check that was then in force, which required a statement that the subject of the check had not used drugs in the previous 15 years. In other words, he was saying that he had not used drugs since 1974. And this, essentially, is his final word on the matter.

Again, since no one suggests that Bush now uses illegal drugs, he deserves credit for his ability to kick whatever kind of habit he once had. The problem is that instead of holding himself up as an object lesson in the ability of addicts to rehabilitate themselves, he has done the opposite. Towards those whose problems he once shared, he has been utterly merciless. Texas, of which Bush was governor, has the largest single prison system in the world. Counting those on parole, it contains well over half a million people. Texas is astonishingly punitive, with 700 adults out of every 100,000 currently incarcerated; 21 per cent of these prisoners are behind bars for drug-related offences. At the time of Bush's election as president in 2000, there were 8,800 people in Texas jails merely for possession of marijuana and 8,300 for cocaine possession alone. One woman was serving a 99-year sentence for the possession of one-tenth of a gram of cocaine. As the Texas journalists Molly Ivins and Lou Dubose put it, 'Because he was a rich white kid with an important daddy, Bush's chances of going to prison for drug use were nil. Yet there is no recognition anywhere in his record of "There but for the grace of god go I".'[53]

As governor, Bush upheld this system and if anything sought to make it even harsher. He personally insisted on a law debarring anyone convicted of a drug felony from ever again claiming welfare payments. That would mean, for example, that a woman caught in a car with a man who has a gram of cocaine in his pocket would be permanently debarred from the welfare rolls.

But even this hypocrisy was put in the shade by the spectacular hypocrisy of a president being elected with the help of laws that, but for his own good fortune, might have prevented him from even voting.

Vengeance and Terrorism

All of this may seem to fall outside the scope of any consideration of the War on Terrorism. Ordinary crimes, after all, are usually distinguished in most countries from terror-related offences, with the safeguards that apply in the first area softened or abolished in the second. In the US case, however, the official response to the atrocity of September 11th was determined above all by a biblical lumping-together of 'all causes of sin and all evildoers', in which Al-Quaida was seen as merely an exaggerated version of the badness that attacks American innocence simply because the evil hate the good. It followed that it should be dealt with in the same vengeful, simplistic and merely punitive spirit that brings the wrath of god onto the heads of domestic criminals.

Bruce Bartlett, a life-long Republican who served in the Reagan and Bush, Sr. administrations, described this phenomenon in 2004: 'This is why George W. Bush is so clear-eyed about Al Quaeda and the Islamic fundamentalist enemy. He believes you have to kill them all. They cannot be persuaded, that they're extremists, driven by a dark vision. He understands them, because he's just like them.'[54]

As it happened, these notions came together in the person of the Attorney General in Bush's first term, John Ashcroft. Ashcroft himself is a spectacular example of the power of unelected courtiers, for he was actually voted out of the Senate just before he was appointed Attorney General. Moreover, he lost the race in Missouri to a dead man, the Democratic challenger Mel Carnaghan having been killed in a plane crash late in the campaign. The Missouri electorate, given a choice between a corpse and

Ashcroft, chose the corpse. Never before in US history had a dead man been elected to the Senate. In a normal democracy, such a humiliation would have been the end of a political career. Instead, rejection by the voters in these mortifying circumstances was actually a huge boost to Ashcroft's career. He got a job much more powerful than that of a senator, taking charge of the entire justice system.

Even before September 11th, Ashcroft was big on evildoers. He is a devout member of the Assemblies of god, a fundamentalist Pentecostal sect that regards, for example, line-dancing as the work of Satan. He never went to the movies as a child because, as he recalled, his parents told him, 'If you pay 15 cents to get into a movie, 7 cents of that will go to support a Hollywood lifestyle we disagree with.' When he became senator for Missouri in 1995, he was anointed by friends with Crisco oil from the kitchen (like 'the ancient kings of Israel', he noted).[55] He instructed employees of the Justice Department not to use the phrase 'We are proud of the Justice Department' because pride is one of the seven deadly sins. He instituted regular prayer meetings for Justice staff in his office, with the implication that non-attendance was unwelcome.

More importantly for the War on Terrorism, Ashcroft holds to the fundamentalist view that misery is a punishment for bad behaviour and success a reward for righteousness. As governor of Missouri in the late 1980s, he twice vetoed a state grant for a Kansas City home for AIDS patients. When the state senator who proposed the grant asked him why, he replied, 'They're there because of their own misconduct, and it wasn't very reputable misconduct either.'[56] On the other hand, he saw the workings of god in all aspects of the life of the faithful, telling the Justice Department prayer group on one occasion that his wife had been bumped off a flight but given extra frequent-flyer miles and a free ticket because 'god is working for her.'

This fundamentalist view of the world, in which god

gives the righteous frequent-flyer air miles and Satan sends his minions to crash planes into buildings, shaped Ashcroft's, and the administration's, response to September 11th. On any rational level, it should be obvious that a crude world view in which everything is either good or evil does not accord with the need to understand your enemies which is so central to effective counterterrorist action. The conservative religious mindset embodied by Ashcroft was also directly damaging to the American capacity to respond to the threat of fundamentalist Islamic terrorism. The fatal lack of Arabic speakers in the armed forces, for example, was seriously exacerbated by the fact that 20 Arab experts were thrown out of the US military since 1998 merely because they were found to be gay.[57]

Such considerations did nothing to limit the crudity of the official response to September 11th. Ashcroft's department drafted the Uniting and Strengthening America by Providing Appropriate Tools to Intercept Terrorism Act (colloquially known, perhaps because no one can remember its official title, as the Patriot Act). It permitted the government to listen in on attorney–client conversations, to conduct secret searches, to demand of libraries and bookshops information on the reading matter of clients, to compel those who have been searched not to tell anyone else about it, to jail Americans indefinitely without access to lawyers and to detain immigrants on secret charges while keeping their identities and even the number so detained secret. The Patriot Act was rushed through Congress with very little dissent. Who, after all, wants to vote against patriotism? Especially when, as Ashcroft warned critics, 'your tactics aid terrorists'.

In this view of the world, defending the US Constitution and its guarantees of civil liberty and protections against an oppressive state is itself a form of terrorism. Since only evildoers have anything to fear, objecting to measures designed to root them out is itself prima facie evidence of evil intent. Arguably, however, more harm is done by these revocations of long-cherished liberties to America itself, its distinctive political and civil traditions, than to terrorists. Even basic principles of justice systems in all democratic countries, like the idea that justice should be seen to be done, have been set aside. In late 2003, for example, it became evident that at least one court district, Southern Florida, had two court lists – one for public trials and one for secret cases. Mohamed Kamel Bellahouel, an Algerian-born waiter living in Florida, was arrested for violating his student visa a month after the September 11th attacks. Although he sought his release in the District Court and appealed to the 11th Circuit, no public record of his case existed until his appeal to the US Supreme Court.[58]

Aside from all questions of principle, however, the construction of a huge, secretive and virtually omni-potent apparatus of state security is in fact extremely ineffective and inefficient in combating terrorism. By early 2004, over 18,000 anti-terrorism subpoenas and search warrants had been issued. Vast amounts of data and documentation have been seized and intercepted, though since gagging orders are issued to many people who are searched, preventing them from informing even a lawyer or a member of Congress, the precise numbers are a secret. Some thousands of detainees have been rounded up and placed in preventive detention. Again, even Congress does not know how many. But by early 2004, all of this activity had resulted in very few prosecutions and just two guilty verdicts.

The huge amount of information being processed seems to have achieved very little other than to clog up the investigative system and distract federal agencies from the real job of protecting Americans. A report by the Inspector General of the US Department of Justice released in September 2004 showed that the FBI had a backlog of over 123,000 hours of untranslated, un-reviewed recordings in Arabic, Farsi and other lang-uages associated with known terrorists – about 20 per cent of its total intercept 'take'.

Since terrorists might use other languages, the FBI

holds nearly 500,000 hours of recordings in languages that have yet to be reviewed or translated. Worse still, as the FBI's computer systems have relatively limited storage capacity, older recordings are regularly dumped *before* they are reviewed to make room for newer material, this three years after the September 11th attacks.[59]

Meanwhile, other vital lessons of September 11th have not been learned. The simple, unglamorous but obviously crucial step of putting effective security into US airports, with well-paid, well-motivated and well-trained staff, has not been taken. Coming up to the second anniversary of the attacks, a time when heightened security might be expected, the *New York Daily News* sent its reporters to board 14 domestic flights. Each carried contraband items in hand luggage, including box cutters, razor knives and pepper sprays. Not a single airport security checkpoint spotted or confiscated any of the dangerous items. The security systems at the four airports where the September 11th terrorists boarded planes – Newark International, Boston's Logan Airport, Washington's Dulles International and Portland International Jetport in Maine – were all breached:

> A security agent at Newark insisted on passing our bag through an X-ray machine twice after spotting a tape recorder, cell phone, two-way pager and radio inside. She remarked: "You're pretty loaded up." It was 5 a.m. Few others were on line. But she never opened our bag – and had no idea she missed a rubber-handled razor knife and box cutter. At Portland, two guards painstakingly picked through a reporter's laptop computer case and purse as other passengers filed onto a jet scheduled to depart for Boston at 1:50 p.m.
>
> When one of the guards came across a matchbook in one of the bags, he said we had to carry it in a jacket pocket.
>
> Neither of them found our rubber-handled razor knife.
>
> At Santa Barbara, a ticketing agent escorted us to a security checkpoint around 4:40 a.m. We had been randomly selected to have our check-in and carry-on

luggage searched. On the way, the agent joked: "You haven't taken any flying lessons recently, have you?"

The utility knife in our carry-on would not be discovered – despite X-ray and hand searches.[60]

Before boarding, however, guards at several airports chose to search at least one passenger who appeared to be of Middle Eastern or South Asian descent. The reporters, on the other hand, did not look like they might be Muslims.

With such glaring failures, it is hardly surprising that the very people who have demanded more and more powers to stop terrorism also predict on a regular basis that more attacks are inevitable.

In three days in May 2003, for example, three senior officials warned the American public that a repeat of September 11th on some scale was inevitable. Vice-President Dick Cheney said on 19 May, 'The prospects of a future attack on the United States are almost certain…not a matter of if but when.' The next day, FBI director Robert Mueller stated, 'There will be another terrorist attack. We will not be able to stop it.' The day after, Secretary of Defense Donald Rumsfeld acknowledged that another attack was 'only a matter of time.'[61]

Admissions of failure do not come much more stark. If this really is a war, those who are running it seem pretty sure that they're losing, yet no debate on the nature or the objectives of the US Global War on Terrorism takes place in the US; it was at most a minor part of the 2004 presidential campaign. More strikingly, many key US voters saw the terrorist threat as a reason for supporting President Bush in the 2004 presidential election.

Ohio should have been a natural state for the Democrats, with its ageing industries, semi-crumbling cities, high unemployment and growing poverty. 5.6 million Ohio voters turned out and George W. Bush won that key state by around 130,000 votes.

The pro-Kerry America Coming Together organisation did a post-election poll in Ohio to determine the reasons behind voters' choices. Fifty-four per cent thought the US was safer in 2004 than it had been in 2001, 55 per cent saw the war in Iraq as part of the War on Terrorism and 58 per cent thought George W. Bush could be trusted to lead the War on Terrorism, against 40 per cent who expressed similar confidence in Kerry.

Why?

The fact that evildoers suck is one part of the answer. It provides the intellectual framework for the easy answer, the good guys versus the bad guys. But it does not completely answer the question.

The nature, possibilities and forums for political debate in today's US are strikingly limited. That limitation helps turn the easy answer into the correct one – and into the only correct one.

8

See No Evil, Hear No Evil,
Speak No Evil: US Elections,
Media and Think Tanks

*'George Bush is the president…Wherever he wants me to line up,
just tell me where and he'll make the call.'*
– CBS news anchor Dan Rather, 17 September 2001

The Guardian's G2 section marked the election of George
W. Bush as the 44th President of the US in November
2004 with a black front page carrying the headline 'Oh
god'. Many shared that sentiment, including over 55
million US voters.

The 2004 elections had been one of the hardest
fought in US history, with a controversial president
seeking a second term and a clear contender emerging
well before the summer. It was probably one of the most
closely followed elections in the world, with media
from all continents deploying special teams and
presenting background reports from communities
across the US.

Yet it was largely a campaign without content. In a
presidential contest, the primary focus is on the
candidates, but in theory at least, candidates' records
and proposals should also feature. If there were serious
policy confrontations about the future of the US or any

attempt to critically analyse the role of the US in the world, they certainly were not to the forefront of either campaign, or of the media coverage.

The language of optimism precluded consideration of potential US failure in any domain. Once the idea that the US faced serious challenges, other than those of crazed Islamic fundamentalist terrorists, was excluded, the campaign was doomed to become a political beauty contest.

US voters are neither less intelligent nor less literate than their counterparts elsewhere. They are, however, less informed, and alarmingly, more misinformed, than comparable electorates. Misinformed or ill informed, they stay with the comforting myths of American exceptionalism, then select the president they identify as being the best equipped to give life to those myths.

If the only real problems flow from evildoers, the best president thus becomes the one most likely to zap those evildoers, whoever or wherever they are to be found. Voters trusted Bush to do just that, and so he was elected as the 44th President of the United States of America in November 2004.

Polls, Participation and Pennies

The 2004 US elections provided a stark picture of a society deeply divided in political terms – red and blue America, or Simon Schama's Worldly and godly Americas. This is not an altogether new phenomenon, but it is one that is becoming starker. The 2000 US presidential election divided the country – 48.4 per cent for the Democrats and 47.9 per cent for the Republicans (Gore vs. Bush). In November 2004, almost 59 million voted for Bush (51 per cent), while over 55 million (48 per cent) chose Kerry.[1] It was a mandate, a clear popular mandate, but hardly a landslide.

US voter registration systems often seem designed to dissuade rather than encourage potential voters. The US Census Bureau produces a 'voting age population'

(VAP) figure as distinct from registered voters. For the 2000 presidential elections, the Census Bureau estimated the US VAP at 205,815,000, as opposed to the 156,421,311 registered voters. This figure would suggest that there are over 49 million US voters who are not registered. Four million of these are disenfranchised prisoners or former prisoners. North Dakota does not have voter registration, so that accounts for 500,000, and in Wisconsin voters register on polling day, accounting for another 4 million. There are therefore over 40 million people of voting age in the US who are not registered to vote – or almost 20 per cent of the voting population.[2]

Even allowing for a slight over-estimation by the US Census, this is a frightening figure. When coupled with the adverse effects of negative television advertising, this gives rise to a further weakness in the US democratic system. Fewer and fewer US voters are going to the polls. In the 1992 US presidential election, 76 per cent of registered voters turned out. By 2000 that had fallen to 67.5 per cent,[3] and only 17 per cent of 18- to 29-year-olds turned out.[4] In the 1994 midterm legislative elections, 68.5 per cent of registered voters turned out, whereas in the 1998 midterms that was down to 51.6 per cent.[5]

In the 2002 midterm legislative elections, with Democrats smarting over the allegations of electoral fraud in Florida which had cost them the 2000 presidential elections and with the country poised to invade Iraq, it would not have been surprising to witness an increase in voter turnout. The parties spent an estimated $1 billion on their campaigns, achieving a turnout of just under 40 per cent.[6] The hotly contested 2004 elections reached a turnout figure of almost 60 per cent, still down on the 65 per cent turnouts of the 1960s and towards the lower end of the average European turnout.[7]

Under George W. Bush and his neoconservative allies, the Republican Party has moved to the right, but not to such a degree that it has alienated Republican support. In January 2004, 91 per cent of Republican supporters approved of the job the President was doing, 85 per cent of Republicans supported the war in Iraq, 83 per cent believed pre-emptive war was justified and 81 per cent agreed that terror suspects should be held without trial.[8]

The very system of presidential elections mitigates against real campaigning. The electorate votes by state, and each state has a given number of electoral college votes in proportion to its population. The winning candidate collects all the electoral votes from that state. Campaigns therefore focus on 'swing states', more or less abandoning those states where their candidate stands little chance. The University of Wisconsin's Advertising Project monitored campaign television advertising and found that almost 60 per cent of voters (the more than 80 million residents of states such as California, New York or Texas where the result was taken to be a foregone conclusion) had not seen a single campaign ad.[9]

US elections cost a lot of money. The election campaigns to become governor of New York state cost over $120 million in 2002.[10] The Senate race to defeat outgoing Senate Democratic Leader Tom Daschle in South Dakota (pop. 700,000) was the most expensive of 2004, clocking in at $31.5 million, or almost $45 per vote. The total campaign costs for the November 2004 elections, as calculated by the Federal Election Commission, amounted to over $2 billion.[11]

Large chunks of this money come from corporations, wealthy individuals and interest groups. Naturally, those who pay for the winning campaign come looking for something in return afterwards. There are relatively strict laws about campaign finance and limits on the amount individuals, corporations and others can contribute to candidates. These direct contributions are known as 'hard' money in US political campaigning, but they only represent a fraction of the total outlay.

'Soft' money does not go directly to candidates, and thus escapes many of the funding rules. The standard vehicle for 'soft' money is a Political Action Committee

(PAC). After Watergate, the rules on direct contributions were further tightened and the PAC boom started. Their number quadrupled by the 1980 presidential election, with 88 per cent of the funds going to Republican candidates.[12]

A corporation (such as Enron) seeking deregulation of the energy and utility market will naturally fund candidates who have declared themselves favourable to such deregulation. The corporation must abide by strict rules on direct donations to candidates. But Enron, or Enron executives, can form a PAC. This PAC can create and air television advertising promoting an issue their candidate favours, or attacking the opposing candidate. In recent campaigns this negative advertising has grown exponentially.

Enron's Kenneth Lay was one of George W. Bush's 'Pioneers', the wealthy individuals who contributed $100,000 each to kick-start Governor Bush's 2000 presidential campaign. Enron donated over $1 million to the Republican Party and made its corporate jets available to the Bush campaign. Enron and its executives kicked in another $300,000 to help fund the Bush inaugural festivities in Washington.[13]

The Texas Wyly family are oil and energy traders, Republicans and supporters of George W. Bush. The US Federal Elections Commission records them as the eleventh largest donors to his 2000 presidential campaign, with donations totalling $250,000. The Wyly family felt their interests would be best served by having George W. in the White House, and became anxious when Republican Senator John McCain started to draw ahead of their preferred candidate in the Republican primaries. They then spent $2.5 million on negative advertising against Senator McCain in March 2000.[14] George W. won the nomination.

Individuals may be encouraged to consider making a donation. In early June 2003, E. Stanley O'Neal, the chief executive of Merill Lynch, wrote to his company's senior management suggesting they might like to donate to the Bush campaign. O'Neal is one of nine

'Bush Rangers' on Wall Street, each of whom raised a minimum of $200,000 to qualify for the title. Between 12–30 June 2003, the Bush–Cheney campaign was to receive 157 cheques from Merill Lynch executives and at least 20 from their spouses. One hundred and forty of them were for the maximum amount allowed by law, $2,000. In three weeks Merill Lynch personnel donated $279,750, part of almost $500,000 in private donations flowing from this one company. The finance and insurance companies were reported to have donated over $12 million to Bush. The same sectors raised just under $3 million for Kerry.[15]

A new feature of the 2004 elections was the scale of contributions from wealthy individuals to organisations assisting the Kerry campaign. A section of the US tax code, section 527, imposes no limits on donations to campaigning organisations. Such organisations, called 527s, must not be an integral part of a candidate's campaign, but may work freely on related topics or activities.

Financier George Soros was one of the individuals who collectively donated over $70 million to bodies such as America Coming Together (ACT) and The Media Fund, an activity criticised by some Republicans. It would seem that it is politically acceptable to fund Republican-related activities, but not Democratic ones. In one sense these 527s can be said to simply be a method of addressing funding legalities. In the 2004 elections, in addition to traditional areas like television advertising, these bodies undertook activities such as canvassing and voter registration, which in the past were largely carried out by local party organisations.

Initially, most of the 527 money went to pro-Kerry groups, but Bush supporters were quick to react. The most famous of the pro-Bush 527s was the Swift Veterans for Truth, which ran the ads challenging Senator Kerry's Vietnam War record. In the third quarter of 2004, $62.8 million was donated to pro-Bush 527s, with $36.5 million going to pro-Kerry ones.[16]

US television has been axing current affairs coverage, particularly at local and state level, as it is expensive to produce and, with a few exceptions, does not attract large audiences. University of Wisconsin students monitored the campaign TV coverage, tracking 325 hours of TV news daily. They also had access to material from the Nielsen Monitor-Plus professional television figures. They found that only 44 per cent of 122 TV stations in the top 50 US TV markets offered any campaign coverage at all. Most of the coverage offered was about races between candidates in the closing days of campaigns. On the rare occasion a candidate got to speak on air, they averaged 12 seconds – a sound bite.[17]

The primary campaigning medium thus becomes television advertising, much of which is used to attack opponents. Up to the end of May 2004, *The Washington Post* calculated that in the top 100 TV markets, 75 per cent of Bush's 2004 advertising, or 49,050 ads, had been attacks on Kerry. The equivalent figure for the Kerry campaign was 27 per cent, or 13,336 negative ads.[18]

Politicians and parties have to buy this air time, and they have to find the money to do so. Here we encounter a primary difference between European and US political campaigns. Political advertising is illegal on European stations, either public or commercial. During election campaigns, equal air time is made available for party political broadcasts by all the contenders. These broadcasts air on both commercial and public channels. Candidates and parties do not raise large amounts of money to buy air time because it's not for sale.

The continuous nature of US elections – with some seats coming up for re-election every two years and with local and state elections and the four-yearly presidential elections – has turned many US politicians into permanent campaigners. In national terms, the only real battles left are the presidential and senatorial ones. As the House is responsible for drawing up the constitutional (district) boundaries for the election of its members, both parties have become extraordinarily gifted at designing constituencies which lock in a majority for the incumbent. In 2002, only 22 to 25 of the 435 House seats were genuinely contested, or less than 5 per cent.[19]

Their primary sources for ideas are professional think tanks or the professional lobbyists in Washington, DC and many state capitals. Political parties, in the European sense of organisations of ordinary members providing the backbone of a policy development and political campaigning machine, are less and less important in the US.

The media, and in particular television, is candidates' main avenue of access to the electorate, and the US media, primarily for commercial reasons, have become rather particular animals.

The US Media

The media is the prism through which we view our society. In democratic countries the polling booth is where we select our leaders and policies. There is a symbiotic relationship between media and politics – to flourish each needs the other, yet each distrusts the other. It is a dynamic relationship, constantly changing, inherently conflicting and democratically essential.

The very scale of the US makes this role even more vital. Dubliners used to joke that had Watergate happened in Ireland, everybody would know who Deep Throat was and Nixon would still be in power. In a continental polity, only the media can relay and interpret political messages between the electorate and its representatives.

NEWSPAPERS

In the young US strong local papers quickly emerged as watchdogs of democracy, to scrutinise and challenge the actions of the elected leadership. The First Amendment to the US Constitution (freedom of speech) was to provide US newspapers with legal rights long before their European counterparts. Titles such as *The New York Times, The Washington Post, The Los Angeles Times, The Philadelphia Enquirer, The Boston Globe, The Miami Herald* and many others are recognised around the world. Modern print and communications technology has made possible the closest thing the US has to a national newspaper, *USA Today*, but it remains a newcomer to the field.

If the myth of eagle-eyed independent newspapers coupled with a nation of newspaper readers has survived, today's reality is somewhat different. Only 34 cities in the US still have two or more competing newspapers.[20] In 1998, 1,054 daily newspapers were published in the US. Of these only 300 were independently owned, and only 15 of them, or just over 1.5 per cent, had circulations of more than 100,000.[21] In 1998, 57 per cent of *The New York Times* and 52 per cent of *The Washington Post* was owned by institutional investors.[22] Only 11 per cent of the US public reads a daily newspaper beyond the cartoons and advertisements.[23]

TELEVISION

Television is the primary forum for US political debate. As Frank Rich, a senior US media commentator, wrote, 'news doesn't register in our culture unless it happens on television.'[24]

The approach to broadcast media naturally grew from the experience with print media. Broadcasting was a private enterprise occupation in the US, although a Public Broadcasting Service (PBS) did also emerge. While National Public Radio (NPR) receives public funding, the PBS television service receives only 12 per cent of its funding from the federal government. The different states provide differing amounts of support, but at least 50 per cent of PBS television is financed by private donations.

Television is the dominant mass medium in the US today. On average, most US homes receive 45 channels and the average US viewer 'watches' four hours of television per day. Half the population watches television during dinner and a third over breakfast. Just over 2 per cent watch public television. The remainder watch commercial channels which screen 1,500 advertisements a day.[25] The average US adult devotes 99 hours a year to reading books compared to 1,460 hours watching television.[26] For most people in the US, television is the primary news source. A *Los Angeles Times* poll in March 2003 asked people what their three main news sources were: 69 per cent selected cable TV news, 23 per cent local broadcast TV news and 18 per cent national network news.[27]

US television is dominated by five media corporations: CBS (owned by Westinghouse-Viacom), ABC (owned by Disney), NBC (owned by GE), the AOL-Time-Warner conglomerate (including CNN and HBO) and Fox (owned by Rupert Murdoch's News Corporation, which is in the process of taking over DirecTV, the biggest US satellite delivery system).[28] Viewers in the US get over 80 per cent of their news information from television stations owned by five media corporations. These media giants, effective oligopolies, own the broadcast networks, the local stations and the cable companies that pipe in their own, and their competitors', signals. They also increasingly own the studios which produce their programmes. In 1990, ABC, CBS, NBC and Fox owned 12.5 per cent of the new series they aired. By 2002 that figure had surged to 77.5 per cent. Ninety per cent of the top 50 cable companies are owned by the same groups which own the broadcast networks. These same media conglomerates also own the top 20 US Internet news sites.[29]

RADIO

Since the Federal Communications Commission's rules on radio ownership were relaxed in 1996, the two biggest radio groups went from owning 130 stations to owning more than 1,400.[30] Two-thirds of radio news listeners are tuned into stations owned by just four companies. The largest, Clear Channel Communications, based in Texas, is co-chaired by Tom Hicks, who bought the Texas Rangers sports franchise from George W. Bush in 1998, making the future president a multimillionaire. Clear advised their stations not to play 'deviant' records such as John Lennon's *Imagine* after September 11th.[31] They sponsored pro-war Rallies for America around the country. Roxanne Cordonier, co-host of the morning talk show on Clear Channel's station WMYI-FM in South Carolina, was fired in April 2003 after publicly opposing the invasion of Iraq.[32] Another of the dominant conglomerates, Cumulus Media, banned the Dixie Chicks from its 42 country music stations after the group's lead singer, Natalie Maines, criticised President Bush for the war in Iraq.[33]

Some observers argue that the 'sameness' of radio broadcasts accounts for the fact that radio audiences have fallen to a 27-year low.[34] A study by the FCC noted that the inflation-adjusted price of radio advertising rose by 68 per cent in the five years following the 1996 deregulation, following a steady decline in advertising prices over the three previous decades.[35] Concentration of ownership and competition are not natural bedfellows.

As radio stations are taken over, costs are trimmed and editorial functions are often outsourced. McVay Media of Cleveland, Ohio describes itself as the largest radio consulting firm in the world. A McVay 'War Manual' advised radio stations how to handle the 2003 Iraq War: 'Get the following production pieces into the studio NOW...patriotic music that makes you cry, salute, get cold chills! Go for the emotion...Air the National Anthem at a specified time each day as long as the U.S.A. is at war.'[36]

NEWS AND ENTERTAINMENT

Television is entertainment, and TV news is part of that entertainment provision. Disturbing and difficult stories, or ones that clash with the official mantra of the day, are shunned, avoided or eviscerated until they become bland, upbeat and entertaining.

News must be entertaining to maximise audience figures and thus drive up advertising rates. Veteran US broadcaster Bob Edwards describes the approach:

> But remember what the news looked like in the days and weeks before the [Iraq] war began? Television news was consumed with the fate of Elizabeth Smart and other kidnapped girls. There was a lot about that woman who accidentally ran over her husband three or four times with the family car until his cheating butt was good and dead. And then there were all those interviews with the yutzes who are on those so-called 'reality' TV shows. In other words, what passed for news was a lot of stuff that had no bearing on your life whatsoever. But it was titillating, and it might have kept you from reaching for the zapper and tuning in the ballgame — which is the whole point of doing tabloid stories and celebrity gossip and calling it news.[37]

Attracting and holding audiences is the name of the game. US television does not sell programming to audiences - its commercial *raison d'être* is to sell audiences to advertisers. The advertising rates a station charges vary in function of the size of its audience. Losing audience by programming too much news costs the station money. Reuven Frank, the former NBC News president, summed up this reality: 'The product of commercial television is not programs. If one thinks of making goods to sell, the viewers are not the customers, those who buy the product, pay money for it. Programs are not what they buy. What they buy, what they pay for, is audience.'[38]

A six-year study of TV programme content (Project for Excellence in Journalism) found that 35 minutes out of every broadcast hour was devoted to direct advertising or direct selling. As four of the five channels are part of larger conglomerates, they promote their conglomerate's products and services. In only around 10 per cent of cases was this corporate relationship disclosed.[39]

US television companies use consultants to advise them on editorial approaches to find out what their viewers want to see in terms of news coverage. This approach means that news ceases to be driven by facts and instead becomes driven by consumer interest. 'The influential television news consulting firm Frank N. Magid Associates recently put it in even starker terms: covering war protests may be harmful to a station's bottom line...Magid says only 14 percent of respondents said TV news was not paying enough attention to anti-war demonstrations and peace activities; just 13 percent thought that in the event of war, the news should pay more attention to dissent.'[40] Frank Rich commented that TV news anchormen were now 'eager to hunt down an audience, not a story.'[41]

When Oprah Winfrey, the hugely popular talk-show host, was granted unprecedented access to National Security Adviser Condoleezza Rice in October 2003, the show did not explore US foreign and security policy, nor venture down any dangerous, controversial roads. Ms Rice's most stunning revelation was that President Bush was a fast eater – 'If you're not careful, he'll be on dessert and you're still eating the salad.'[42]

Media Ownership

The US Federal Communications Commission (FCC) was partly inspired by US anti-trust legislation of the early twentieth century. In the 1940s, shocked by the totalitarian misuse of broadcasting in Europe, the FCC set strict rules as to how many radio and television stations could be owned by the same corporation in the same cities. There were also strict rules governing cross-media ownership. Powerful newspapers could not own, and thus dominate, broadcasting in their own cities. These rules have been progressively relaxed, with the Commission voting 3–2 along party lines to further deregulate ownership conditions in June 2003. Companies are now allowed to own sufficient television stations to reach 45 per cent of the national audience, to both own several stations and to own newspapers, radio and television stations in the same catchment area.

These media groups have been assembled through mergers, takeovers and buy-outs, frequently leaving the new owners heavily indebted. The natural result of this is a management drive to cut operating costs and boost profits.

News Coverage is Expensive

News coverage involving journalists and crews is expensive. Ted Turner, the founder of Turner Broadcasting and CNN, warned of 'more consolidation and more news sharing. That means laying off reporters or, in other words, downsizing the workforce that helps us see our problems and makes us think about solutions.'[43]

The television groups have severely cut back on foreign correspondents. Tom Fenton of CBS said that in 1970 he had been 'one of three correspondents in the Rome bureau. We had bureaus in Paris, Bonn, Warsaw, Cairo, and Nairobi. Now you can count the number of foreign correspondents on two hands and have three fingers left over. Before, we had stringers all over the world. Now no one can afford that.'[44] Commenting on the CBS coverage of the sixtieth anniversary of the Normandy D-Day landing, the Irish columnist Kevin Myers, who describes himself as 'an ardent friend and admirer of the US', was forced to observe that 'if that bulletin was your only source of information about the landings – and for millions of Americans it probably would have been – Operation Overlord consisted entirely of American soldiers.' He added that this poor coverage made a 'massively important cultural statement about the US; that Americans genuinely don't see other people if they share the picture with Americans.'[45]

Investigative journalism is perhaps the most expensive news-gathering activity of all. Teams can work for months on a story, getting information, checking sources, researching, travelling. Perhaps the most famous investigative story is that of the Watergate scandal that eventually forced President Nixon to resign. *The Washington Post* supported its Woodward and Bernstein team for months as they built the story.

The Project for Excellence in Journalism found that investigative reporting in US local television had declined by 60 per cent and the percentage of stories with a correspondent at the scene had fallen by 30 per cent. Material supplied by other stations within the same group, but not necessarily flagged as such, had doubled, and this over the five-year period from 1997 to 2002.

The Watergate story compares poorly with the story of the 2000 US presidential election in Florida. London-based US journalist Greg Palast broke the story that the Florida state government, headed by Governor Jeb Bush, had worked to eliminate 90,000 electors who were entitled to vote from Florida's electoral register. Fifty-four per cent of those were black or Hispanic, and Palast's team reckoned that the electors denied their vote were overwhelmingly Democrat supporters. Florida Secretary of State Katherine Harris (who had co-ordinated much of the electoral register clean-up) declared the Republican candidate, and brother of the Florida governor, George W. Bush the winner of the Florida election, and thus President of the US, by a margin of 537 votes.

This was a major news story and it made front-page news and featured on national television – in the United Kingdom (*The Guardian, The Observer, BBC Newsnight*). CBS television was naturally interested, but they informed Greg Palast that they had checked out his story and it did not hold up. The CBS investigation? They called Governor Jeb Bush's office, and the governor's office denied it. The story finally ran in the US on the front page of *The Washington Post* in June 2001 after the US Civil Rights Commission had conducted an official in-vestigation which confirmed the BBC story. Greg Palast commented, 'Three elements of investigative reporting: risk, time, money. Our BBC/Guardian stories required all of those, in short supply in U.S. news operations.'[46]

In October 2003 the small, independent, family-owned Toledo, Ohio newspaper, the *Toledo Blade*, broke the story of the US Tiger Force's massacres in Vietnam following months of investigative journalism across the US and in Vietnam. The *Toledo Blade*'s executive editor, Ron Royhab, explained, 'We have the resources to do this. There are no shareholders to worry about.'[47]

Dissent is Dangerous

The role of the media in the US has changed from being one of critically challenging official policies to one of transmitting those policies to the population. Av Westin was a producer at CBS for 20 years, then a producer at ABC for 21 years. Mr Westin's comment on current US news coverage is:

> Since 9/11, the press has been watching the opinion polls almost as much as the administration, which explains why it has taken quite a while to assume the kind of normal adversarial relationship, much less the kind that was rampant during the Clinton years and the Nixon years. There is a considerable amount of self-censorship going on in terms of pushing government officials on certain topics. But I've always believed our job was to ask questions that need to be asked, regardless of official reaction or public opinion.[48]

It is clear that even some of the most distinguished organs of the American media abrogated this responsibility in the run-up to the invasion of Iraq. *The New York Times* in particular put its hard-won authority behind stories about Iraq's weapons of mass destruction which, as it turned out, were simply government propaganda dressed up as investigative reporting. In September 2002, immediately after Bush and Tony Blair held a joint press conference to warn of Iraq's supposed nuclear weapons programme, the *Times* reported as fact the apocalyptic prediction that 'the first sign of a smoking gun...may be a mushroom cloud.' It also quoted a pseudonymous Iraqi scientist to the effect that 'all of Iraq is one large storage facility' for chemical weapons. Over the succeeding months, the *Times* ran exclusive stories, most of them by Judith Miller, claiming that 'Iraq obtained a particularly virulent strain of smallpox from a Russian scientist'; that Iraq had hidden its WMD weapons in Syria; that Saddam Hussein was working closely with Al Quaida; and that American forces in Iraq had captured a scientist who had given them definite proof of the existence of WMDs.[49]

Such uncritical stories in such a respected newspaper indicated the oppressive atmosphere for the reporting of unwelcome facts. CNN executives faced a real quandary as the 2003 Iraq War approached. They understood that the White House, and many US viewers, would be less than understanding – or for-giving – if they departed from the official US line. They also understood that the war was viewed with deep suspicion right across the world outside the US. They solved the problem by not only editing two completely different newscasts on CNN and CNN International, but also by deploying two different teams of journalists.

The CNN International edition, the one broadcast to the world at large, has been described as 'far more serious and informed than the American version.' *The New York Times* faced a similar challenge on a smaller scale. Its *International Herald Tribune* comes with the locally produced *Daily Star* insert in Qatar. On 7 April 2003 the *IHT* headline was 'For US Soldiers, Therapy Helps Ease Battle Stress', while the *Daily Star* ran 'Iraqi Hospitals Offer Snapshot of Horror'. Michael Massing summed up his observations: 'US News organizations gave Americans the war they thought Americans wanted to see.'[50]

There is a curious gap between US public opinion as revealed in polls and the often self-imposed 'patriotic' straightjackets applied by editorialists. A national poll just six weeks before the US invasion of Iraq showed US public opinion far from convinced of the need for imminent war: 59 per cent believed the President should give the United Nations more time, 63 per cent said Washington should not act without the support of its allies and 56 per cent said President Bush should wait for United Nations approval.[51]

Peter Beinart, editor of the liberal magazine *New Republic*, cautioned contributors, 'This nation is now at war, and in such an environment, domestic political dissent is immoral without a prior statement of national solidarity, a choosing of sides.'[52] During the first three weeks of the war, the major evening news shows on US television drew overwhelmingly on pro-war sources. Sixty-four per cent of those interviewed were for war, with just 10 per cent against. Forty-seven per cent were from the military and 63 per cent were former or current government employees.[53] The US public, however, demonstrated with its zappers that it wants more objective coverage. BBC World television attracted more viewers than CNN during the 2003 Iraq War.[54]

The distinction between news and entertainment is increasingly blurred. The coverage of national and global politics is less and less critical, but more and more disparaging. Political reporting is reduced to sound bites and sarcasm. This media approach becomes self-perpetuating – if serious political debate is to go unreported, then why engage in such debate in the first place? When serious debate is engaged, as in the case of Senator Byrd's critical speech on war in Iraq, it goes virtually unreported. When the actor Sean Penn challenged the White House line on Iraq, it went unreported. Had he been getting married or divorced or arrested, coverage would have been coast to coast. Mr Penn finally paid $125,000 to have his essay published as a full-page advertisement in *The New York Times* in May 2003.[55]

The nature of the US media influences, even determines, US politics. Since US media is driven by shareholder profit requirements, maximising audience ratings has triumphed over content quality. For a TV station or newspaper to challenge a general consensus is to risk accusations of being unpatriotic, and more seriously, is a threat to its share price. Viacom chairman, self-styled liberal Democrat Sumner Redstone, announced his support for George W. Bush's re-election on the basis that he 'votes for what's good for Viacom.'[56]

US Justice Hugo Black wrote in a 1945 judgement that 'The First Amendment rests on the assumption that the widest possible dissemination from diverse and antagonistic sources is essential for the welfare of the public.'[57] Almost 60 years later that antagonistic diversity seems sadly absent from mainstream US media.

Lens and Mirror

If our media is a lens through which we view our societies, it also acts as a mirror, reflecting those societies back to us. US television projects a distorted image of US society to the US and the world. The image is distorted because it is partisan. There is no US equivalent of the BBC's long-running soap *EastEnders*. As the name suggests, *EastEnders* is set in a (fictional) working-class district in the East End of London. Hopefully, for the sake of residents of London's East End, the level of drama and violence portrayed in the series does not accurately reflect everyday life. The series does, however, project a national (and even international) image of ordinary people struggling to make ends meet.

US equivalents either show wealthy families, as in *Dallas*, or skip over the details of everyday life. *Friends* shows a struggling actor living in a Manhattan apartment which must cost at least $5,000 a month in rent. Mary Maher, describing her experience on returning to canvass in the US 2004 elections, wrote, 'To court the alienated Democratic voter, you have to slog through some stretches of urban USA never featured in *Sex and the City* or *Friends*.'[58] Subscriber television in the US is slightly freer, so in the HBO series *The Sopranos* we hear people swear and glimpse partial (female) nudity. Yet the New Jersey gangsters who rob, murder and blackmail in urban streets all leave after work for their suburban homes. The title sequence of the series depicts the transition from city to smart suburb perfectly.

Barbara Ehrenreich describes this clash of reality and

189

image as she and a colleague catch snippets of TV soaps while cleaning hotel rooms.

> It is the TV that keeps us going...In Room 503, Marcia confronts Jeff about Lauren. In 505, Lauren taunts poor cheated-on Marcia. In 511, Helen offers Amanda $10,000 to stop seeing Eric...The tourists' rooms that we clean and, beyond them, the far more expensively appointed interiors in the soaps begin after a while to merge. We have entered a better world – a world of comfort where every day is a day off, waiting to be filled with sexual intrigue. We are only gate-crashers in this fantasy, however, forced to pay our presence with backaches and perpetual thirst.[59]

Hyper Impotence

BBC World Affairs editor John Simpson was to write of the 15 February 2003 peace demonstrations: 'The actions of 10 million people worldwide received relatively little attention on American television news. The networks tended to ignore them as weirdos and malcontents. The American media were getting ready for war, not for a discussion about the merits of peace.'[60]

Following the fiasco of the invasion of Iraq and the embarrassingly absent weapons of mass destruction, some of the US media faced up to their editorial shortcomings. *The Washington Post* admitted in August 2004 that 'the voices of doubt were effectively drowned by the din created by the beating of war drums.' *The New York Times* acknowledged that it too had failed to properly handle views and reports which challenged the assertions of the US administration.[61] Others adopted a different approach. The Murdoch-owned *New York Post* covered the important report by the CIA's chief weapons inspector, Charles Duelfer, that Iraq had not had any WMD before the US invasion, but the story appeared on page 8. Even then, the phrase 'while no stockpiles of W.M.D. were found in Iraq' did not appear until the sixteenth paragraph of the page 8 story.[62]

US media, and its broadcast media in particular, has

become all but structurally incapable of considering the weaknesses which threaten the US. In the run-up to the 2003 invasion of Iraq, only a small minority of the US media seriously reported the growing level of dissent and criticism within the intelligence, military and civil service over the White House's shrill assertions of the real threat posed by Saddam Hussein's regime.[63]

The reality that private enterprise exists within a social setting is one which many on the US political right seek to deny. This reality is particularly evident when it comes to broadcasting. Broadcasters are regulated in terms of content and in terms of licences and frequencies. US broadcasters thus operate with one eye on audience figures and another on federal regulators and their political bosses.

The huge dominance of privately owned broadcast media in the US now actively works against the very freedom of expression this private ownership was supposed to guarantee. To the extent that the corporations that own these networks actually compete with each other, they compete for audience. Quality current affairs coverage is expensive to produce and only rarely attracts significant audiences, therefore commercial stations offer very little. When a major and complex issue arises, there is simply no show for people to watch. British viewers may not watch *Newsnight* every evening, but they know it will be there when they wish to inform themselves. The commercial network that has axed its foreign correspondents and its in-house editorial team has to reach for outside experts to offer any background at all, an approach that carries its own risks, as we demonstrate below.

The US Conservative Agenda: Tools and Think Tanks

The 1960s was a time of significant social change around the world. The baby boomers, those born immediately after World War Two into a period of unprecedented prosperity and growth, were coming of age. Laws, social conventions and personal and political approaches were challenged and changed. As always in times of change and questioning, there are those who disapprove, who long for a return to an often mythical period of calm *avant la déluge.*

The US was no exception, but at least three exceptional factors came into play there. One was the significant presence of conservative religions. Another was the fact that many of those who followed such religions and largely disapproved of the 'Swinging Sixties' had great personal wealth, if less political influence. The third exceptional factor, and the one that acted as a catalyst for turning the other two into an active force, was the US war in Vietnam. For many on the US right, the defeat of their country in South-East Asia was due less to the implacable resistance of Vietnamese nationalism, or even the support it received from Moscow and Beijing, but more to domestic left-liberal opposition to the war which had grown right across the US political spectrum.

Since the US could not by definition be on the side of the bad guys, the US should have prevailed in Vietnam, Cambodia and Laos. The US had been betrayed by many of its own citizens, and this betrayal had suborned whole swathes of US society – the media, academia, the Democrats and to a large extent the Republicans, the civil service (partially including the armed forces) and a whole misled element of the US population.

According to this view, when Richard Nixon won the White House for the Republicans in 1968, he took command of a country so much in the thrall of this left-liberal decadence that he had no option but to negotiate US withdrawal from South-East Asia as skilfully as possible. His re-election in 1972 should have allowed for the balance to be redressed. Nixon was forced to resign in 1973 to avoid being impeached for illegal use of executive power (burglary of the Democrats' offices in the Watergate Building, illegal wire taps, etc.). The

Watergate scandal was broken and pursued by *The Washington Post* and followed up on by a largely Democratic House and Senate.

Those on the US right felt cheated, victimised and outmanoeuvred. Their candidate had won the election only to be forced from office by the left-liberal media and their allies in the Democratic Party. This was a call to arms for those on the right, or far right, of the US political spectrum, a spectrum already considerably to the right of any European norm.

The vehemence of their feelings was summed up by one of their newspaper columnists, Frank Pastore, a Christian broadcaster in California whose material is often offered by the *Los Angeles Times/Washington Post* service. Writing after George W. Bush's November 2004 victory, Mr Pastore warned this was no time for compromise:

Christians...are against false ideas that hold good people captive. Last Tuesday, this nation (the US) rejected liberalism, primarily because liberalism has been taken captive by the left. Since 1968, the left has taken millions captive and we must help those Democrats who truly want to be free to actually break free of this evil ideology...Conservatives must not compromise with the left. Good people holding false ideas are won over only if we defeat what is false with the truth...The left hates the ballot box and loves its courtrooms...The left bewitches with its potions and elixirs, served daily in the strongholds of academe, Hollywood and the old media. It vomits upon the morals, values and traditions we hold sacred: god, family and country...Americans have rejected John Kerry and John Edwards and the left because they are wrong...We are one nation under a god they reject. We remain indivisible despite their attempts to divide Americans through their relentless warfare against class, ethnic and religious unity...We are unique and we are the greatest force for good in the world, despite what the left, the terrorists or the United Nations may claim.[64]

Frank Pastore is a writer's dream – from the extreme end of the US Christian Right mainstream, he states in clear terms what others only suggest. His thesis that misguided Democrats, the courts, academia and the old media pose a threat to American values is more than borne out by the millions of dollars his fellow believers have donated to combating that threat.

Twelve of the most conservative private US foundations, collectively holding more than $1 billion in assets, set out to change the terms of political and social debate in the US. They, and others, provided over $80 million for conservative policy institutions dedicated to promoting anti-government deregulation policies. $89 million went to support conservative scholars and academic programmes, $27 million to support conservative lawyers (and thus future judges) and nearly $50 million went to support publications and websites.[65]

Material developed by four of these private institutions – the National Bureau of Economic Research, the Hoover Institution on War, Revolution and Peace, the American Enterprise Institute and the Center for Study of American Business – were the champions of Ronald Reagan's supply-side trickle-down economics, in particular his Economic Recovery Tax Act of 1981. The Manhattan Institute was to lead the charge on the US's 1996 welfare reform.

Since the established media, academia and public research bodies are not to be trusted, these institutes specialise in neutral or official-sounding titles, provide article kits or pre-written articles to magazines and local, national and international papers. A study of media citations of private research and campaigning institutes in 2003 showed that 86 per cent of such citations came from centre, centre-right and conservative bodies, whereas only 13 per cent came from progressive or centre-left ones.[66]

Funds also flow towards publications such as *The New Criterion* and through the American Studies Center, producing conservative radio programmes for 2,000 US radio stations. Money was also made available to assist with the creation of conservative TV programmes such as *Firing Line* (William F. Buckley). Bodies such as the Center for the Study of Popular Culture (CSPC), Accuracy in Media, the Center for Media and Public Affairs, the Media Research Center and the Media Institute all received funding with the particular aim of challenging 'the left-wing bias' of the US Public Broadcasting Service.

The impact of this carefully constructed and self-reinforcing media web is clear to all who follow US media coverage. A 2004 survey by the Program on International Policy Attitudes at the University of Maryland found that almost 70 per cent of President Bush's supporters believe that the US has demonstrated 'clear evidence' of active co-operation between Saddam Hussein's Iraq and Al Quaida. One-third believe that WMD have been found in Iraq and over a third believe that a substantial majority of world opinion supported the 2003 US invasion of Iraq.[67]

The Institute on Religion and Democracy (IRD) argues that 'the National and World Council of Churches are theologically and politically flawed.' The American Legislative Exchange Council and the State Policy Network have developed more than 150 pieces of model legislation which they distributed for free to over 26,000 state legislators across the US. The Institute for Justice (IJ), the Centre for Individual Rights and the Washington Legal Foundation are funded to challenge government programmes and to attract the brightest conservative law students.

In terms of their ability to influence policy, think tanks have several advantages over universities. They can hire staff without committee procedures, which allows them to build up teams of researchers that share a similar political orientation. They can also publish books themselves without going through the academic refereeing processes required by university publishers. As academic careers are partly built on publication of books and journal articles, mainstream academic publishers insist on works being reviewed by the author's peers. In this way blatantly one-sided arguments are either avoided or clearly presented for what they are.

The whole purpose of the centres, think tanks and foundations is to provide the veneer of academic achievement while avoiding any presentation, much less consideration, of opposing arguments. The majority of these bodies usually site themselves in Washington, close to government and the media.

The American Enterprise Institute (AEI) had assets of $35.8 million and an income of $24.5 million in 2000. It received seven donations of $1 million or above in cash or shares, the highest being $3.35 million.[68] The Senior Fellow of the AEI is Lynne Cheney, wife of Vice-President Dick Cheney. Twenty of the AEI's fellows hold posts in the George W. Bush administration, and many of its long-argued goals have become official US policy.[69]

The impact of the AEI's 'professional' image was to be seen in *The New York Times*'s coverage of the build-up to the invasion of Iraq. Judith Miller was one of the senior correspondents whose work was later criticised for being uncritical of US government positions. Miller had earlier co-authored the book *Saddam Hussein and the Crisis in the Gulf* with Laurie Myrolie, one of the AEI's Middle East Scholars. Judith Miller had met Ahmad Chalabi through AEI contacts, and some of the weaknesses in her reporting could have flowed from her having her facts confirmed by three 'different' sources – the US government, the AEI and the Iraqi exiles. The problem was, as it frequently is with this web, that apparently different sources were all singing from the same centrally scripted hymn sheet.[70]

The Washington Institute, which deals only with Middle East policy, had assets of $11.2 million and an income of $4.1 million in 2000. The institute says its donors are identifiable because they are also its trustees, but the list of trustees contains 239 names, which makes it impossible to distinguish large benefactors from small ones. The smaller Middle East Forum had an income of less than $1.5 million in 2000, with the largest single donation amounting to $355,000.[71] The most famous, and certainly the most influential, think tank operation is the one launched by the out-of-power Republican neoconservatives themselves, the Project for a New American Century (PNAC).

One illustration of this interlocking web of research, policy formation, advocacy and media influence is the range of positions held by one of Washington's best-known hawks, Richard Perle. Perle is a board member of the AEI, a consultant to the US Secretary of Defense, former chairman and member of the Pentagon's Defense Policy Board, a board member of the Hudson Institute and a Resident Fellow at AEI. He is also co-chairman of Hollinger Digital, Inc. and a board member of Hollinger International, Inc. (publishers of *The Daily Telegraph*) and a director of *The Jerusalem Post*.[72]

The impact of these apparently neutral/scientific bodies has been described as follows:

> [a] cosy and cleverly-constructed network of...'experts' who pop up as talking heads on US television, in newspapers, books, testimonies to congressional committees, and at lunchtime gatherings in Washington. The network centres on research institutes – think-tanks that attempt to influence government policy and are funded by tax-deductible gifts from unidentified donors.[73]

In 1984, the moderate Republican senator John Saloma warned of the effect of this approach, saying it constituted 'a major new presence in American politics', a presence he described as being a 'new conservative labyrinth' that would pull the centre of gravity of US politics far to the right.[74] Twenty years later, his prediction echoes eerily around the US Senate, where the newly elected Republican senator from Oklahoma has warned of the 'gay agenda' that threatens the US and has publicly called for the death penalty for doctors who perform abortions.[75]

A weakened political debate, often misleading or

misled media and an aggressive, well-funded network of private institutions were to provide the incubator and life support for a particular group of individuals eager to exercise power through unelected offices in the executive branch of the US government – the neo-conservatives. Their primary focus of interest was less on the US itself than on the role of the US in changing the world. They are Washington's revolutionaries.

9

The Neoconservatives and US Power: Washington's Revolutionaries and Their Hyperpower Village

'Boom goes London and boom Paree
More room for you and more room for me
And every city the whole world round
Will just be another American town
Oh, how peaceful it will be
We'll set everybody free
You'll wear a Japanese kimono
And there'll be Italian shoes for me.'
— Randy Newman, 'Political Science'

Perceptions, Power and Threats

The neoconservatives were politically conceived in the humiliation that was Vietnam and born into what was, for them, the treachery of Nixon's disgrace and resignation during the early 1970s. The United States of America they believed in was under attack, from within and without. While some saw the omnipotent hand of Moscow, all agreed that the US had lost its way and that the path back to righteousness involved the reassertion of Washington's dominance.

In the temporary interregnum of the Ford presidency (1974–1976), with George H. Bush as the director of the CIA, they found their first organisational niche. They saw the process of détente, the thawing of the Cold War, as betrayal, playing into the hands of the Kremlin. CIA Director Bush dealt with their challenge by forming what came to be known as 'Team B'. Team B's task was to challenge the accepted intelligence and foreign policy view, to look for evidence to counter the status quo. They argued that armed force was the only answer. Donald Rumsfeld, as Ford's Secretary of Defense, was one member of Team B. So were his now Deputy, Paul Wolfowitz, Vice-President Cheney's now Chief of Staff, Lewis ('Scooter') Libby, and the ubiquitous Richard Perle.[1]

When Jimmy Carter won the 1976 presidential election they found themselves briefly removed from access to power, but the Reagan victories in 1980 and 1984 and the George H. Bush victory in 1988 restored their right of entry, their shadowy glory. Throughout most of this time, their essential prerequisite, an existential enemy, existed in the form of the rival superpower, the Soviet Union. This was a given, something which needed to be neither explained nor defended within the US or its Republican Party.

At what should have been the zenith of their power, what they portrayed as US victory in the Cold War, the very democracy they claimed to champion dealt them a body blow. Bill Clinton not only won the 1992 election, but went on to win the 1996 one as well.

Much of the Republican Party never forgave him. If there was Republican anger at Clinton's electoral victories, for the neoconservatives there was absolute fury. Clinton was robbing them of a once-in-a-lifetime opportunity to shape not just the US, but the entire world. The Cold War was over, leaving the US as the world's only hyperpower with a crushing advantage over other states in terms of its military supremacy. For the neoconservatives this advantage had to be maintained, then expanded and used to create a global order tailored to their perception of US interests. The neoconservatives used these wilderness years to develop on the ideas they had begun to formulate when in power. They needed to define a project, political power to implement that project and a new existential threat to validate it.

They refined their project through a web of right-wing think tanks and publicised their message through a related network of right-wing journals, radio and television shows and websites. They would use their network to achieve significant political power without ever having to face the ballot box – they formed the backbone of the George W. Bush-appointed US foreign and security policy government team of 2000.

The existential threat eluded them. Rather like the thriller writers whose Cold War-based works had become international best-sellers, they floundered in the post-Cold War era. Post-Soviet Russia was in chaos, the EU hardly marketable as a threat, China a hard-sell future possible, India unconvincing, other potential candidates too small. During the 2000 election campaign, George W. Bush was to remark, 'When I was coming up, with what was a dangerous world, we knew exactly who the they were. It was us versus them, and it was clear who the them were. Today we're not so sure who the they are, but we know they're there.' Vice-President Dick Cheney echoed this in his address to the Council on Foreign Relations in February 2002: 'When America's great enemy suddenly disappeared, many wondered what new direction our foreign policy would take.'[2]

This sentiment, that the primary role of foreign policy is to confront an enemy, speaks volumes for their thought processes. Theirs is a Hobbesian view of the world, with them cast in a double Nietzschean supremacist role. The role of the US is to lead the world, since it encapsulates all that is best on our planet. The role of the neoconservatives is to lead the US, since they epitomise all that is best in the US. Many of them claim inspiration from the teachings of Leo Strauss (1899–1973) at the University of Chicago, and those of his acolyte Albert Wohlsetter – although Strauss scholars dispute this.[3] Former Cold War hard-liner Senator Henry ('Scoop') Jackson was one pivot in the interwoven network of personal relationships, mutual hirings and promotions which have propelled the group onwards and upwards since their early days in the Nixon White House.

Understanding something of their motivation, their methods and their understanding of our world at the beginning of our third millennium is vital to an understanding of US foreign and security policy today and why it is failing.

The Neoconservatives

There is an interlocking web of personal networks. Donald Rumsfeld and Dick Cheney have been friends for more than 30 years. Rumsfeld recruited Cheney to the Nixon White House staff in 1969.[4] Secretary of Defense Rumsfeld appointed Paul Wolfowitz as his deputy. Wolfowitz had served as Cheney's Undersecretary of Defense for Policy during the Bush, Sr. administration.[5]

There is a clear career pattern amongst many of those who make up the current foreign and security policy community: start out as a Congressional staffer, move to very junior appointments in one Republican administration, then more senior appointments in the next (Nixon, Ford, Reagan or Bush, Sr., depending on the age of the individual). Pass through industry, law firms, academia or a think tank and then back into senior positions in the current Bush administration. Only two of them have held elective office, Dick Cheney and Donald Rumsfeld as Congressmen.

Their wilderness years of the Clinton 90s were spent working in and around the right-wing think tanks, in particular the Project for a New American Century

(PNAC). PNAC's policies were disseminated directly through conservative circles and via sympathetic journals such as the Murdoch-owned *Weekly Standard* edited by Bill Kristol.[6]

Rumsfeld and Wolfowitz appointed Douglas Feith as Under Secretary of Defense for Policy. Under Reagan, Feith had been Deputy Assistant Secretary of Defense for Negotiations Policy. Before becoming Deputy Assistant Secretary, he was Special Counsel to the then Assistant Secretary of Defense, Richard Perle.[7]

Rumsfeld appointed J.D. Crouch to Perle's old job as Assistant Secretary of Defense for International Security. Crouch was Associate Professor of Defense and Strategic Studies at Southwest Missouri State University. He had also been Principal Deputy Assistant Secretary of Defense for International Security Policy under Bush, Sr.[8]

Apparently at Cheney's insistence, John R. Bolton, a protégée of Senator Jesse Helms and senior vice-president of the American Enterprise Institute (AEI), was appointed as Under Secretary for Arms Control and International Affairs, the number three post at the State Department.

Out of the 34 individuals who signed either or both the Project for a New American Century 1997 Statement of Principles and its 1998 Letter on Iraq, 10 served in the first Bush administration, but only one can be described as having been elected– Vice-President Dick Cheney.

The other nine were appointees or staffers – Donald Rumsfeld, Secretary of Defense; Paul Wolfowitz, Deputy Secretary of Defense; Paula Dobriansky, Under Secretary of State for Global Affairs; Peter Rodman, Assistant Secretary of Defense for International Security Affairs; John R. Bolton, Under Secretary of State for Arms Control and International Security; Robert B. Zoelick, the US trade representative; Zalmay Khalilzad as Special Presidential Envoy for Afghanistan and to the Iraqi Opposition; Elliott Abrams, senior director for Near East and North African Affairs at the National

Security Council; and I. Lewis 'Scooter' Libby, Vice-President Cheney's Chief of Staff.

A further three hold advisory or related posts – Richard Perle, formerly chairman and then member of the Defense Advisory Board; R. James Woolsey, former director of the CIA and now a member of the US Interim Authority in Iraq; and William Schneider, chairman of the Defense Science Board in the US Department of Defense.

President Bush's brother, Jeb, governor of Florida, and former US Vice-President, Dan Quayle, were also signatories, as was multi-millionaire and one-time Republican presidential contender Steve Forbes. A further six of the signatories had served in the Reagan and/or Bush, Sr. administrations.

The remaining 12 signatories include a cross-section of neoconservative academics and senior members of right-wing think tanks, such as neoconservative guru Francis Fukuyama, author of *The End of History*, who argues that free enterprise democracies represent the nadir of human political development, and Robert Kagan, author of *Paradise and Power: America and Europe in the New World Order*. Former US President Jimmy Carter has warned of 'a core group of conservatives who are trying to realize long-pent-up ambitions under the cover of the proclaimed war against terrorism.'[9]

These unelected courtiers and think tank gurus effectively control the formulation and the implementation of much of the US's security and foreign policies. Their stated goals are abundantly clear, and their actions have all been about achieving them.

The Project

They based themselves on the 1992 Defense Policy Guidance drafted by the then Under Secretary of Defense for Policy, Paul Wolfowitz, for the then Defense Secretary Dick Cheney.[10] That document argued that the US had to 'discourage the advanced industrial nations from challenging our leadership or even aspiring to a larger regional or global role.'[11]

The PNAC published its two-page Statement of Principles on 3 June 1997. The following quote conveys the essence of the PNAC statement:

> conservatives have not confidently advanced a strategic vision of America's role in the world...they have not fought for a defense budget that would maintain American security and advance American interests in the new century...We aim to make the case and rally support for American global leadership...Having led the West to victory in the Cold War, America faces an opportunity and a challenge...We seem to have forgotten the essential elements of the Reagan Administration's success: a military that is strong and ready to meet both present and future challenges...we need to increase defense spending significantly...we need to accept responsibility for America's unique role in preserving and extending an international order friendly to our security, our prosperity, and our principles.[12]

In January 1998, the PNAC wrote to President Clinton, urging him to

> enunciate a new strategy that would secure the interests of the U.S. and our friends and allies around the world. That strategy should aim, above all, at the removal of Saddam Hussein's regime from power...removing Saddam Hussein and his regime from power...now needs to become the aim of American foreign policy...American policy cannot continue to be crippled by a misguided insistence on unanimity in the UN Security Council.[13]

In September 2000 the PNAC was to publish its *chef d'oeuvre*, *Rebuilding America's Defenses*.[14] The following are some key excerpts.

On the global role of the US:

> Today, the United States has an unprecedented strategic opportunity...to provide adequate resources for the full range of missions needed to exercise U.S. global leadership...The true cost of not meeting our global defense requirements will be a lessened capacity for American global leadership and, ultimately, the loss of a global

security order that is uniquely friendly to American principles and prosperity...After the victories of the past century – two world wars, the Cold War and most recently the Gulf War...there has been no shortage of powers around the world who have taken the collapse of the Soviet Empire as an opportunity to expand their own influence and challenge the American-led security order...deter the rise of a new great-power competitor; defend key regions of Europe, East Asia and the Middle East, and to preserve American preeminence through the coming transformation of war made possible by new technologies...security can only be acquired...by deterring or, when needed, by compelling regional foes to act in ways that protect American interests and principles...America's current geopolitical preeminence will be extended...If American peace is to be maintained, and expanded, it must have a secure foundation on unquestioned U.S. military pre-eminence (pp. iv, v, 1, 2, 3, 4).

On nuclear weapons:

...[the] Clinton Administration has put its faith in new arms control measures, most notably by signing the Comprehensive Test Ban Treaty (CTBT)...whose principal effect would be to constrain America's unique role in providing the global nuclear umbrella...if the United States is to have a nuclear deterrent that is both effective and safe, it will need to test...need to develop a new family of nuclear weapons designed to address new sets of military requirements...maintaining American strategic superiority – and, with that superiority, a capability to deter possible hostile coalitions of nuclear powers. U.S. nuclear superiority is nothing to be ashamed of; rather, it will be an essential element in preserving American leadership in a more complex and chaotic world (pp. 7–8).

On regional conflicts:

adversaries like Iran, Iraq and North Korea are rushing to develop ballistic missiles and nuclear weapons as a deterrent to American intervention in regions they seek to dominate (p. 4).

One of the architects of the PNAC, Robert Kagan, was to write *Paradise and Power*,[15] where he argues that the US and Europe no longer share the same view of the world. As a former diplomat, Kagan does not attack Europe's inferior military power as such, rather he notes it as a reality which prevents Europe, with the possible exception of the UK, from playing in the First Division. Europe can get on with the exciting task of building its island of Kant's 'perpetual peace' – the Paradise of the title – while the US faces the Hobbesian reality of the world – the Power.

Europe places its faith in negotiations and the rule of law, while the US places its faith in the strength of its armed forces and the political will to use those forces. Kagan argues that this is a reversal of their previous roles. When the young US was militarily weak, it placed more emphasis on the rule of law while the strong European empires relied more on force.

European powers grew militarily weaker after the two World Wars, Kagan argues, and 'their postwar inability to project sufficient force overseas to maintain their colonial empires in Asia, Africa, and the Middle East, forced them to retreat on a massive scale...perhaps the most significant retrenchment in history.'[16] The European Union, Kagan argues, became an economic giant while remaining a military pygmy in part because Europeans failed to 'shift significant resources from social to military programs.'[17]

These political arguments, developed outside government, have now come to represent official US policy. The National Security Strategy of the US states: 'Our [US] forces will be strong enough to dissuade potential adversaries from pursuing a military build-up in hopes of surpassing, or equaling, the power of the United States.'[18]

The Hyperpower Village: Power without Electoral Risk or Mandate

The US was never designed to be a world power. The role of the initial federal government was small. The

Supreme Court was a watchdog tasked with keeping it so. In 1894, in its Pollock judgement the US Supreme Court ruled that a federal income tax was unconstitutional. It took the Sixteenth Amendment to the US Constitution to introduce such a tax.[19] The US Constitution was drafted over two centuries ago for a country with a (white) population of around 1.8 million, and whose largest city, Philadelphia, had a population of 20,000. In 1784 the US Army numbered 80 officers and men.[20] By 1789 it had expanded to 700.[21]

In the words of France's former Foreign Minister, Hubert Védrine, today the US is 'our world's only Hyperpower',[22] but it is a hyperpower operated by political structures designed to govern a small country with a standing army of less than 1,000 troops.

The radical growth of US power since the late nineteenth century has not been matched by commensurate changes in the US system of government. In the original US, fiscal and military power was vested in the 13 states. The states decided upon and collected their various taxes and the young nation's military power was largely composed of its state militias. The power to sign international treaties was, and still is, vested in the US Senate, where the representatives of the states gather as senators. The presidency was designed by the country's founding fathers as a form of chairmanship, arbitrating between the states. The balance of power within the US government has completely changed; the structures have not.

Political control of the US's foreign and security policy is vested in the elected president. He (up until now it has always been a he) then selects his cabinet members and their deputies. While most senior positions are subject to confirmation by the Senate, few junior ones are. The appointees then have almost complete freedom to hire their staffs and to award contracts to outside bodies. The neoconservative control of the Bush White House since 2000 has thus provided government jobs for many neoconservatives: 'Two-thirds of those working for the US Federal Government today are not on the federal payroll...Private contractors write budgets, manage other contractors, implement policy – and sometimes essentially make it as well.'[23]

Once the appointee has been confirmed, they depend on the president for their authority, and he depends on them for policy suggestions. In his book *War in a Time of Peace – Bush, Clinton and the Generals*, David Halberstam describes the US recruitment process as presidential hopeful Bill Clinton began to assemble his foreign and security policy team in 1991.[24] George W. Bush's team came almost ready assembled from the neoconservative organisations, journals and think tanks of the greater Washington area. The structure of the US executive has handed them almost uncontested control of the machinery of government.

As big players in the relatively small community of US Republican foreign policy hawks, they have been able to support, defend and advance each other, rather like party managers in a town where a single party has been in power for generations. The difference is one of scale – their village hyperpower seeks to control our world. The following presents some of what they administer today.

Administering the Village Hyperpower

INTELLIGENCE

The US National Security Act of 1947 combined the former Departments of the Army and of the Navy into a single Department of Defense under a Secretary of Defense appointed by the president, subject to confirmation by the Senate. It also established the National Security Council (NSC) as an advisory body to the president, bringing together the intelligence, foreign policy and military communities. The president appoints the NSC, may add specialist advisers and is its chairman. The role of National Security Adviser grew out of the NSC and is also appointed by the president.

The Act also established the Central Intelligence

Agency (CIA) with a wide remit to conduct operations outside the US. The CIA is an agency of the executive branch of the US government, answerable to the president. The president appoints its director, subject to confirmation by the Senate. The Act specifically states that the CIA 'shall have no police, subpoena, law-enforcement powers, or internal security functions.' In 1949 the CIA had a staff of 302 and a budget of $4.7 million; by 1952 it had grown to over 6,000 personnel with a budget of $82 million.[25]

The Federal Bureau of Investigation (FBI) retained its domestic counterintelligence and security functions. The US Secret Service (part of the Department of the Treasury) retained its VIP protection functions. The idea of a single agency was to give way to that of an 'intelligence community'.

The National Security Agency (NSA) is the electronic and signals intelligence organisation, monitoring broadcasts, Internet and telecommunications. It is the equivalent of the UK's GCHQ and has a staff of around 20,000, a figure that does not include service personnel assigned to the NSA.

The Defense Intelligence Agency (DIA) was established in 1961 to centralise the strategic work of the different armed services' intelligence divisions. However, the Army, Navy and Air Force all retained their intelligence divisions, such as the Office of Naval Intelligence (ONI).

The National Reconnaissance Office (NRO) is a joint Air Force Intelligence–CIA operation and is responsible for operating spy satellites and aircraft. The National Geospatial-Intelligence Agency handles photographic interpretation.[26] A section of the US Department of Agriculture works closely with the NRO, estimating foreign harvests (it originally monitored Soviet agriculture).

The Department of State has its own Bureau of Intelligence and Research, relying mainly on input from US diplomats around the world. The Department of Energy has a foreign intelligence section focusing on energy questions, particularly on nuclear energy.[27] In 1998 it was estimated that over 100,000 people with a budget of over $27 billion worked in 13 agencies grouped within the National Foreign Intelligence Program and the Joint Military Intelligence Program.[28]

MILITARY

The US divides the globe into a series of military commands with geographical responsibility for planning and executing operations in most (if not all) of the world's nation-states:

- USJFCOM (United States Joint Forces Command) is the former Atlantic Command.
- USEUCOM (European Command) is responsible for Europe and Africa.
- USPACOM (Pacific Command).
- USCENTCOM (Central Command) is responsible for the Middle East, Horn of Africa and Central Asia.
- USSOUTHCOM (Southern Command) covers Latin America.

The four other commands are Space, Special Operations, Transport and Strategic.[29]

CENTCOM has its headquarters in Tampa, Florida. The 1991 Gulf War, the 2002 Afghanistan War and the 2003 Iraq War were organised under CENTCOM. In 1998 it had a staff of more than 1,000 and a special Commander's budget of more than $50 million a year.[30] Its staff are governed by military discipline and/or the National Security Act and is only answerable to the commander-in-chief, i.e. the president.

DOMESTIC SECURITY

When the National Security Act was debated in the US Congress in 1947 it came in for serious criticism on two main grounds. One was the warning of the US founding fathers that the maintenance of a large military in peacetime was a potential threat to democracy. The other was that this outgrowth of the executive branch, subject to only limited congressional supervision, might lead to abuses of government authority.

Criticism was more muted in 2002 when Congress created the Department of Homeland Security in response to the 11 September 2001 attacks. The Department's brief covers the FBI, 650,000 state and local law enforcement officials, federal agencies such as the Drug Enforcement Agency, the US Border Patrol, Bureau of Firearms, Tobacco and Alcohol, US Customs, US Immigration Service and elements of the National Guard (the volunteer reserve – the successors to the old state militia). The Department groups 22 agencies and nearly 170,000 government workers into a giant new bureaucracy, has a budget of $35.5 billion and its own intelligence service – the Information Analysis and Infrastructure Protection Division.[31]

The US armed forces, its enormous intelligence 'community' and now its newly created Homeland Security apparatus are all led by the president, the commander-in-chief. This executive branch of the US government was designed by the country's founding fathers to act as a form of moderator between the 13 component states, not to govern the globe. If the US armed forces numbered under 1,000 when the Constitution was adopted, today those forces, together with the intelligence and security communities, number over 1.6 million men and women with a collective budget of around $550 billion.

This enormous defence machine, funded in part by US taxpayers and in part by the rest of the world, has grown, topsy-like, under the executive branch of the US government – the president. It operates with little political oversight and almost no policy control.

The Boys and the Mistress: Weaknesses and Failings of Neoconservative Thought

The neoconservative policies contain two startling central assumptions, outrageous factual errors and omissions and the kernels of extremely radical and highly dangerous policy departures.

The first startling assumption is that at the beginning of the twenty-first century armed conflict between states is still seen as being at the core of our world order. Such an assertion might have been valid in Aristotle's Athens or Caesar's Rome, but coming from today's Washington it reads as though there has been no human progress. In Peter Shaffer's *The Gift of the Gorgon*, the heroine, Helen, points out that the ancient Greeks 'had the gods to take the big view for them. Athena could come down suddenly and stop the boys fighting, like a schoolmistress in a playground. We haven't got anyone to do that. We're the boys and the mistress, both.'[32]

Kagan shares with other US neoconservatives a fetishisation of military power in which the distinction between right and might disappears. Military power is the essential ingredient of global order, and since the US has more such power than any other state, the US should then lead the world, free of Lilliputian restraints.

The second startling assumption is that the US has both the right and the duty to order the rest of the world. For whatever reason, the US has the power, and therefore it must unilaterally lead the world.

The US most certainly did not win 'two world wars, the Cold War and most recently the Gulf War.' In World War One the US played a pivotal role in the last year of that conflict. In World War Two the US played a major role, but it was no less a Conservative icon than Winston Churchill who recognised that it was the USSR that 'tore the guts out of the Nazi war machine'.[33]

The argument that the US won the Cold War has more to do with neoconservative ideology than with reality. The Cold War was a stalemate in which the two superpowers avoided direct conflict and fought each other by proxy. Why is there no mention of the Korean War? Is it because it was fought under a UN mandate? Or because the stalemate ceasefire that ended that war is not seen as a victory in neoconservative terms? Did the US win in Vietnam, a war it fought explicitly as part of its broader crusade against communism? The US's craziest imperial venture to date is not mentioned at all. Because it was a defeat? Or because it shows that military power alone can never provide a comprehensive solution to conflicts?

Did the US win in South Africa, where for most of the Cold War period it supported the apartheid regime and the Soviet Union gave military and economic aid to the ANC? Did anyone at all win in the grisly conflicts in Latin America in which US-sponsored military juntas murdered, raped and tortured to their heart's content? One could argue the degrees forever. Did the US 'win' the Cold War by 51 points to the USSR's 'losing' it by 49? Or perhaps it was 60–40? Or 40–60? Claiming a US victory may sound good on an electoral campaign, but it is not a sustainable policy argument.

In the 1991 Gulf War the US played a determinant role, supplying over 500,000 of the 1.3 million troops committed under the UN Security Council resolution. Under President Bush, Sr. and his Secretary of State, James Baker, it played a crucial role in building, managing and leading that broad coalition of states which saw US, French, British and other NATO troops work with former Warsaw Pact units, plus 400,000 Egyptian and Syrian troops. It could be argued just as convincingly that the 1991 Gulf War was a victory for the UN system.

The most radical and dangerous policy departure is over nuclear weapons, both in the doctrine governing such weapons and in their testing. Supercomputers and lasers have replaced the need to test such weapons. The US neoconservatives apparently do not accept that such computer testing is valid, while at the same time being prepared to spend billions on a computer-dependent national missile defence system (which keeps failing its tests). If the US returns to nuclear testing, other states will almost certainly follow.

Nuclear weapons are of little military use and have

been relegated to the role of strategic deterrence – mutually assured destruction (MAD). State A has nuclear weapons and can thus threaten State B, which also has nuclear weapons, but State B equally threatens State A, and so a balance of terror is created, a balance which has contributed to maintaining a form of global peace since 1945.

The development of new 'usable' nuclear weapons could break that balance of terror, with untold risks for global security and possibly for global survival. Under a 2002 US Secret National Security Directive, President George W. Bush has made the use of US nuclear weapons more possible.[34] Only one country has ever used nuclear weapons – the US in 1945. Only one country has ever completely dismantled its nuclear arsenal – the Republic of South Africa under President Nelson Mandela.

Kagan ignores the primacy of political choice and thus Von Clausewitz's dictum of war being the pursuit of policies by other means. In the first 20 years of the Cold War, 1945–1965, Western European countries maintained large armed forces configured to resist a Warsaw Pact invasion. From the late 1960s onwards, through Brandt's *Ostpolitik*, the CSCE and the general détente process, Western Europe's political evaluation of the Warsaw Pact threat declined, and with it Europe's defence spending. It's true that this was comforted by the US strategic umbrella, but it was a political choice which naturally came to be reflected in defence posture.

Similarly, the European decolonisation process has its roots in political choices. Colonised peoples demanded their right to self-determination as guaranteed in the Universal Declaration of Human Rights. Most Europeans came to recognise that right and to believe that their countries had no business ruling over other peoples around the globe. General De Gaulle and Major Harold Macmillan discussed decolonisation in Algeria in 1943. De Gaulle went on to propose greater autonomy to French colonies in his Brazzaville speech in January 1944.[35] Macmillan, as UK Prime Minister, was to go further with his famous 'The wind of change is blowing through this continent, and, whether we like it or not, this growth of national consciousness is a political fact' Cape Town speech in 1960.[36]

Decolonisation came not from failure to project military force – the French contingent in Algeria reached almost 500,000 in 1958 – but from an evolving political choice. France hovered on the brink of civil war over Algeria until French public opinion no longer supported the retention of millions of Algerians within France against their will. Algeria voted by 5,975,581 votes in favour to 16,534 votes against for independence from France on 1 July 1962. Eight hundred thousand Europeans had fled Algeria by then, but even had they stayed their votes would not have changed the outcome.[37]

The Portuguese dictatorship was the last European government to fight colonial wars. It was swept away by a military coup in 1976 because Portuguese soldiers and Portuguese society no longer believed it had the right to try and retain Angola, Mozambique, Guinea-Bissau, the Cape Verde islands, Sao Tome, East Timor, etc. within a Portuguese empire by force of arms.

Military force is the expression of a political will, of political choices. The political choices come first and the military posture follows. Many US neoconservative hawks view Europe's concern with the rule of law, politics and diplomacy as the primary tools of conflict resolution as a form of weakness. Terrorists often fall into the same trap, mistaking restraint for weakness or even for decline. When our societies are threatened, they respond. That response may finally have to involve the use of force, but that remains a choice as to which instruments are best suited to achieve a desired goal. The selection of an instrument – negotiations or force – is a political one to be made by people. People should choose the instrument; the instrument should never impose itself.

The EU's de facto Foreign Minister, Javier Solana, notes:

> There is no inherent opposition between power, supposedly the 'US method', and law, the 'European method'. Law and power are two sides of the same coin. Power is needed to establish law, and law is the legitimate face of power. Sometimes European countries have tended to forget that law and international norms have to be backed by force. And occasionally I have heard American voices that seem to have forgotten that, if it is to have a lasting effect, force needs to be backed by legitimacy.[38]

Ideological Fervour

One definition of an ideology, belief or faith is that it seeks to provide both a comprehensive value system and to lay claim to perfection. It is not based on rational argument or scientific deduction, although these may play a role – its core energy comes from belief. Belief is not open to argument. Many people believe in a god or several gods while others believe in none. What all have in common is an inability to scientifically prove their respective cases.

When general beliefs metamorphose into their intense form of ideology or faith, their acolytes believe and argue that their ideology is perfect. If applied with sufficient rigour, the ideology will create a perfect society. Should the ideology fail, the failure must belong to those who applied it, since the ideology is by definition perfect.

In the final analysis, the clearest definition of a faith-driven perfect ideology comes from its interactions with reality. When a faith-driven ideology clashes with an obvious reality, the ideologues deny, airbrush out or change the reality, never the ideology. In the Ireland of the 1950s, 'good Catholic girls' did not have sex before marriage. In the workers' paradise of communist Poland there was no need for trade unions as workers were all blissfully happy. Yet babies were born to single mothers in the Ireland of the 1950s and Polish workers marched in their thousands to challenge the state in the Poland of the 1980s. In both cases, the challenged ideological authorities sought to alter reality rather than question their faith.

The George W. Bush administration is the most ideological government in the world today. Its ideology is biblical – biblical in its absolutism and partly biblical in its inspiration. The neoconservative label is as misleading as its 'conservative' element is vaguely reassuring. This is the most revolutionary government in the world today, more threatening than the Jacobins of the revolutionary Paris of 1787 or the Bolsheviks of Petrograd in 1917. A leading neoconservative, Kenneth Adelman, described this reality in April 2003: 'The starting point is that conservatives are now for radical change and the progressives – the establishment foreign policy makers – are for the status quo.'[39] Former Spanish Prime Minister Felipe Gonzalez has described their ideology as 'converted Trotskyism'.[40]

Given that its ideologues are predominantly white, male and wealthy, it comes as no surprise that the ideology is significantly macho, or at least hirsute. It is supremacist and partly puritanical. There is no hidden conspiracy, but the ideology is packaged very skilfully and sold very smoothly.

Free market enterprise is social perfection. Where market systems have shortcomings it is because of the moral failures of individuals (Enron, etc.) or because the state has intervened in the market process, thus corrupting it. For Bush extremists, such as the Federalist Society, taxation, any taxation, is a form of state interference in the market. In a perfect world where the state took no money from its citizens, those citizens would then be perfectly free to dispose of all their wealth in whatever way they saw fit. People would thus provide their own schools through paying fees and schools would become perfect since failing schools would not attract fees. Compassionate conservatives would allow the state to distribute vouchers so that parents who lacked the necessary money would be able to participate as 'customers' in this educational market. The examples continue through health care, transport, environmental issues, etc. The US model is the best – 'America is not just a stronger, but is a freer and more just society.'[41]

Underpinning much of this approach is the puritan concept that those who fail do so because of their own incompetence, weakness or sin. If your factory closes, get in your car and drive to wherever one is opening. Compassionate free marketeers allow for (tax-deductible) charity for those at the bottom of the social heap, but this charity should never allow anybody to become comfortable. That would rob them of their freedom, their incentive to participate in the employment market.

The ideology owes much to a vulgar version of Nietzsche, and by extension to Hobbes. Without any sense of the philosopher's use of irony, it takes Nietzsche's contention that man has allowed himself to become soft, his strength sapped by morality, concern for the weak and concepts of justice. For Nietzsche, leaders were a natural aristocracy who proved and forged themselves in asserting their leadership. This natural aristocracy 'accepts with good conscience the sacrifice of innumerable men who for its sake have to be suppressed and reduced to imperfect men, to slaves and instruments.'[42] Nietzsche argued that this natural aristocracy, the leaders, needed to prevail to preserve our species: 'Accordingly we must agree to the cruel sounding truth that slavery belongs to the essence of culture...the wretchedness of struggling men must grow still greater in order to make possible the production of a world of art for a small number of Olympian men.'[43]

War and the veneration of combat was a central element of Nietzsche's argument: 'That lambs dislike great birds of prey does not seem strange: only it gives no ground for reproaching those birds of prey for bearing off little lambs'[44] and 'You should love peace as a means to new wars. You say that it is the good cause that hallows even war? I tell you: it is the good war that hallows every cause.'[45]

If a deadpan version of Friedrich Nietzsche's nineteenth-century German philosophy without Nietzsche's countervailing opposition to all ideologies provides one element of the dominant ideology of today's Bush administration, seventeenth-century England provides another through Thomas Hobbes. Hobbes believed that war was the normal state of things, causing 'continualle feare, and danger of violent death; and the life of man, solitary, poore, nasty, brutish and short.'[46] For Hobbes the answer to this natural state was the creation of a dominant power which would impose its rule and order on the world – a benign absolute ruler, a Leviathan.

The US neoconservative ideology finds its roots in these two philosophies. There must be a natural group of leaders, wealthy, powerful and necessarily ruthless. These leaders need to impose order through a benign imperium on their own people and on the rest of the world. They are the ones who define the parameters of their own debate and of their own power. They pass seamlessly from private industry to government office, awarding contracts to sympathetic bodies to carry out policies which they have determined. The neo-conservatives have established a system where there can be no argument, no challenge, no conflict of interest, for as one Washington sympathiser expressed it, 'There is no conflict of interest, because they define the interest.'[47]

It is an interest they define narrowly, and frighteningly. The US author Ron Suskind found himself confronted with a senior George W. Bush adviser following a 2002 *Esquire* article on White House communication director Karen Hughes which had not pleased the inner circle. The adviser warned that critics of the Bush administration were wrong because they worked from 'what we call the reality-based community', people who

> believe that solutions emerge from...judicious study of discernible reality. That's not the way the world works anymore. We're an empire now, and when we act, we create our own reality. And while you're studying that reality – judiciously, as you will – we'll act again, creating new realities, which you can study too, and that's how things will sort out. We're history's actors...and you, all of you, will be left to just study what we do.[48]

The Threat

The first eight months of 2001 must have been progressively more frustrating for the neoconservatives. They were back in power, the Vice-President was clearly on their side, the President sympathetic. They had their project and they had their power – what they lacked was a credible and immediate threat.

For the neoconservatives, the 11 September 2001 attacks on New York and Washington were a moment of destiny, an opportunity to be seized, manipulated and exploited to implement their long-prepared agenda. The threat was obvious, real, frightening. The question was how frightening?

They needed it to be very frightening indeed. The threat from Islamic fundamentalist terrorism had to be sufficiently frightening to justify taking the US to war. Above all, it had to be sufficiently frightening to unify the US people behind the administration. In a curious reversal of scientific practice, the neoconservatives set to work with a will to establish first a result and then find the evidence to satisfy that result.

They created a reality which did not bear much studying because it was false. As ideologues, they have come, fatally, to believe their own declarations. The rest of the world has no choice but to live with reality; the neoconservatives have opted to create their own and sought to impose it on the rest of humanity.

Their desires, their prejudices, their ideological preferences and what the rest of us might recognise as truth have all become hopelessly blended to the point where reality no longer has any meaning for them. In a sense they are not telling lies, they're just no longer capable of distinguishing the truth.

10

Global War On Terrorism (GWOT):
Down Jungle Trails or
Up Garden Paths?

*'We are going to fight them…and we will capture or…kill them.
We dominate the scene and we will continue to impose our will on
this country.'*

– Paul Bremer[1]

*'The American psyche is an extreme expression of a condition
endemic in societies which need to believe themselves terminal
and invincible, and which are therefore prone to perpetual
anxiety.'*

– Eric Mottram[2]

*'Terrorism by definition strikes at the innocent in order to draw
attention to the sins of the invulnerable.'*

– Chalmers Johnson[3]

The Day We Were All Americans

Against the wall is a huge 20-ton double column of
steel, misshapen, mangled and shrivelled like a dry
stick thrown casually into a fire. It was part of the
perimeter wall of floors 71 to 74 of the north face of the
north tower of the World Trade Center. Beside it is a

damaged sign for a bicycle rack near the base of the towers, warning evildoers not to park their bikes elsewhere: 'Violation will result in removal of equipment and a $30 fee.' The sense of lost innocence is heartbreaking.

Opposite is what's left of a fire engine that was hooked to a hydrant under a footbridge when the north tower fell on the bridge. More moving still are the odds and ends of human detritus: the half-crushed remnant of a payphone, the twisted stub of a red umbrella carrying the logo of an investment company, the floor number signs from the elevators, the broken-off head of somebody's golf club. And, almost unbearable to contemplate, stray pieces of the fuselage and engine of a Boeing 767.

Looking at all of this you get a weird sense of archaeology as current affairs. These relics – and that is exactly the right word – of September 11th on display at the New York State Museum in Albany were excavated from the now gaping site of the atrocity and from the hauntingly named Freshkills dump on Staten Island to which the rubble was removed. In a country with a thin layer of historical memory, they are sacred objects, radiating the mystery and solemnity of the recovered remnants of a lost civilisation. Yet they are also today's news, exhibits in a sensational trial that is still in progress.

It is hard for anyone to look at an exhibition like that or visit the bleak, awful absence of Ground Zero without understanding how copiously the wounds of 11 September 2001 still bleed for Americans or to reflect in sadness on the simple act that those wounds once bled for humanity in general. On that day, Americans seemed to people everywhere to be living at the epicentre of a terrible experience that belonged to us all – quite literally in the sense that the victims came from every corner of the globe. Theirs was not an American tragedy but a human tragedy. The foolishness and the weakness of the Bush administration's response is that it made September 11th an exclusively American tragedy again. In less than two years, a world that had felt complete solidarity with the US now felt threatened by the US.

The four aircraft attacks of 11 September 2001 stunned the world because of the powerful imagery and the scale of the devastation they produced. Because of the fortuitous presence of a French cameraman with the New York Fire Department we were able to later witness that first airliner flying level and straight into the tower. By the time its lethal sister arrived, myriad television cameras were focused on the World Trade Center. The world was able to watch a disaster movie nightmare unfold in living, and dying, colour. The after-the-attack images of the Pentagon and tragic detritus of the heroic 'Let's Roll' passengers and crew in a Pennsylvania field seemed almost routine by comparison.

New York, that amazing, cosmopolitan city, has become the capital of our world, its skyline, with the Twin Towers, familiar to billions around the globe. This is a place where even first-time visitors from thousands of kilometres away have a sense of déja vu because the buildings and streets, the architecture and the attitudes are stored in the memory banks from repeated exposure to sitcoms and movies. The attack on New York was, and was intended to be, an attack on the entire Western world. *Le Monde* may have slightly exaggerated with its 'We Are All Americans' 12 September 2001 headline, but that florid linguistic gesture had a genuine resonance for hundreds of millions of non-Americans. As with the unexpected news of the death of a close relative or a good friend, all that had dominated our thoughts and senses in the minutes before, suddenly seemed trivial.

The scale of the carnage, with early reports talking of over 30,000 dead, was beyond anything we had ever witnessed, and scale is always a major element of our reactions. Three thousand people died in what are euphemistically referred to as the Northern Ireland

'Troubles', but they died over 30 years, one here, three there, never making triple figures in a single day, or even a single week. The *drip, drip* of horror became routine.

This was disaster, real, live disaster, not some Hollywood pastiche. There were no scenes of mass hysteria, no movie extras screaming in their seats and no superheroes. We were confronted with ordinary people, shocked, covered in ghostly grey dust, quietly walking home. New York City policemen and firemen calmly went about doing the jobs they were trained to do, trudging up the unending stairs of the towers, many of them to their deaths. The sangfroid of brokers, secretaries, janitors and executives calmly helping each other down those same stairs in an orderly evacuation played a central role in keeping the casualty figures as relatively low as they turned out to be. People around the world were touched by their courage and resilience. At that moment of supreme vulnerability, ordinary Americans were admired more than their nation tends to be in its moments of triumphant power.

The US government and its President understandably faltered on 11 September 2001. Had the attackers done their worst? Were there another 10 aircraft out there zeroing in on other targets? The system wobbled, recovered and went to work. Men and women took deep breaths, wiped tears from their eyes, pointlessly tried to swallow the lumps in their throats, made the phone calls, drove the ambulances, scrambled the F-16s and excavated the rubble of Ground Zero with their hands in a frantic search for survivors.

George W. Bush finally became the President of the United States of America in the afternoon of Friday, 14 September 2001 at Ground Zero. He climbed onto a charred truck beside New York fireman Bob Beckwith. Bush-the-Uncertain started to deliver the speech he had been giving over the previous three days. Someone in the crowd interrupted him, shouting, 'Can't hear you!' Bush-the-President shouted back, 'Well I can hear you!

The rest of the world hears you, and the people who knocked these buildings down will hear from all of us soon!' Karen Hughes, a senior Bush communications staffer, beamed in satisfaction.[4] Her President was no longer just in office, now he was in command.

Al Quaida at Its Ghastly Zenith

Al Quaida, as a handy label for a network of fundamentalist Islamic terrorists dedicated to the destruction of the last remaining superpower and the creation of a global caliphate, is ironically a child of the Cold War superpowers and their extremists. The Soviet 1981 invasion of Afghanistan was a product of Kremlin hard-liners. The Soviet adventure had more to do with intervening in an internecine struggle within Afghanistan's communist government than with any strategic Soviet interest.

The official US response to the Soviet move was a relatively low-level CIA programme to provide arms to those Afghan tribes which resisted both the Kabul government and its Soviet backers. An extraordinary coalition of conservative Texan interests, including a powerful east Texas Congressman, mavericks in the CIA, Pakistan's military junta plus its semi-autonomous secret service, the ISI, and Islamic conservatives (most notably in Saudi Arabia), was to convert this trickle of arms and assistance into a torrent. The Reagan administration, struggling to muster Congressional majorities to deal with a cascade of controversies surrounding its illegal supplies of arms to Iran (to generate illegal funds for Nicaragua's counter-revolutionaries) bought part of the support it needed by agreeing to several funding increases for the Afghan resistance.[5]

Disaffected young men streamed to Afghanistan for a jihad or holy war against the 'Little Satan', as Iran's Ayatollah Khomeini had baptised the USSR. Several Arab governments were happy to see their hotheads vanish into a grisly faraway war, while others actively encouraged them. The US provided money, weapons, training, medical assistance and even mules to keep the conflict going. Rich conservatives across the Arab world chipped in, and all this had to pass through Pakistan and its military rulers, who took a cut.

Following the Soviet withdrawal in 1991, the Kabul government staggered on, increasingly harassed by a range of Afghan movements, until the USSR imploded. Thereafter, Afghanistan descended into a bloody civil war until the Pakistani-sponsored Taliban took power in 1996. US interest and presence virtually ended with the Soviet withdrawal. The Islamic jihadists could claim to have destroyed one superpower; now their sights shifted to the second. Osama bin Laden declared in a 1977 CNN interview that 'the myth of the superpower was destroyed not only in my mind but also in the minds of all Muslims...Our battle with the United States is easy compared to the battles in which we engaged in Afghanistan.'[6]

Bin Laden and his close assistant, Khalid Sheik Mohammed, agreed to prepare an attack on the US using hijacked airliners in late 1998 or early 1999.[7] By this time, Al Quaida was safely ensconced in the Taliban's Afghanistan – which the USSR and the US had done so much to help create. The US National Security Council reported, 'Under the Taliban, Afghanistan is not so much a state sponsor of terrorism as it is a state sponsored by terrorists.'[8]

Al Quaida had a state sanctuary within which it could operate freely, run training camps and provide a beacon for jihadist volunteers. Elements within the Pakistani, and possibly the Iranian, authorities provided Al Quaida members with anonymous, unrecorded transit across their respective territories. Although it was attracting the interest of several intelligence and security services, Al Quaida was not seen as a priority threat. Its activities were only partially understood and even less monitored. Immigration authorities, including US ones, were not overly vigilant in scrutinising visa applications from young Arab men, although Al Quaida activists were already encountering problems with US visas by 1999.[9]

Yet given these almost idyllic operating conditions, it would take Al Quaida almost three years to plan and mount the September 11th attacks. Its greatest handicap was an absence of volunteers who could easily move across Western frontiers and integrate themselves into Western societies. Simply put, Al Quaida had to scale back its plans for aircraft attacks in the US from 12 to four aircraft because it could not find enough appropriate candidates who could train to become pilots without risking detection.

Three of the four September 11th pilots, Mohammed Atta, Marwan al Shehhi and Ziad Jarrah, were 'walk-ins' – volunteers who arrived in Kandahar to train for the Chechen War in late 1999. They had all lived and studied in Hamburg and had decided to become Islamic combatants themselves. Their first contact with Al Quaida took place in Afghanistan.[10] This was the best Al Quaida could manage under optimum conditions from a state sanctuary against an unprepared world.

The September 11th attacks grew from an observation of weaknesses in US domestic air security. Security for US domestic flights was somewhere between light and non-existent, enforced by badly paid, shifting members of the working poor, people who cannot afford to ride the planes they protect. Getting small craft knives or box-cutters on board was no problem at all. Airline crews had standing instructions to accede to hijackers' demands. The attackers were also probably aware of the delays before air traffic control would alert the Air Force, the delays involved in getting fighter aircraft airborne and the comforting delays which, at least pre-September 11th, meant that the order to shoot down a commercial airliner would normally be hours, rather than minutes, in coming.

Former CIA director R. James Woolsey described the September 11th team as 'very smart and very evil men'.[11]

229

The attack had been worked out in considerable detail. The Twin Towers collapsing was a bonus for the attackers, as Osama bin Laden was to later admit. Several experts have drawn attention to inadequate or worn fire-proofing on the lightweight steel floor trusses of the towers. These buckled in the intense aviation fuel fires, causing the floors to collapse in the house-of-cards images we have all become familiar with.[12]

The hijackers were certainly fanatics, but they were not psychopaths. Some, perhaps all, of them knew they were embarked on a suicide mission. They saw themselves as soldiers, desperate soldiers in a holy cause. To dismiss them as being crazy is to avoid the question of why a group of young men with promising lives before them would willingly sacrifice themselves to attack the US. It is vital to answer that question, to understand your enemy, before you can hope to counter, much less defeat, him.

Terrorism and Counter-terrorism

Writing in 1999, Professor Chalmers Johnson observed, 'Most Americans are probably unaware of how Washington exercises its global hegemony...Many find it hard to believe that our place in the world even adds up to an empire.'[13] Such ignorance provided no shield from the 'blowback' he wrote of, warning:

> The innocent of the twenty-first century are going to harvest unexpected blowback disasters from the imperialist escapades of recent decades. Although most Americans may be largely ignorant of what was, and still is, being done in their names, all are likely to pay a steep price – individually and collectively – for their nation's continued efforts to dominate the global scene.[14]

The majority of the attackers were citizens of Saudi Arabia, an ally of the US since 1944. Many of them came from well-to-do families and had studied in Western universities. The US was seen as being the prop that maintained the Saud family monarchy in control of

Saudi Arabia. Thomas L. Friedman expressed this thought: 'The Saudi rulers are insignificant. To destroy them you have to hit the hegemonic power that props them up – America.'[15]

The US was seen by the September 11th hijackers as being largely or partly responsible for the disturbing and depressing reality that is today's Arab world. Arab nationalistic socialism has been seen to fail in Egypt and Iraq and to a lesser extent in Syria. 'Moderate' Arab governments have largely proved incapable of satisfying the demands of their young populations. As David Hirst wrote, 'popular disgust with governments – failed, corrupt, tyrannical – runs incomparably deeper in this [Arab] region than almost anywhere else.'[16]

Avishai Margalit, the Schulman Professor of Philosophy at the Hebrew University in Jerusalem, commented:

> The Islamic world, which consists of a seventh of the world's population, is on the verge of what in the old-fashioned jargon was called a 'revolutionary situation.' Lenin characterized the revolutionary situation as one in which the masses can't stand the regime anymore, and the regime finds it very hard to control them. In almost all the Islamic countries, over 50 percent of the population is made up of young people under eighteen. Their prospects in life are very bleak, and yet they have a sense of a glittering life elsewhere...when secular ideologies fail, as they have so miserably in the Islamic countries, the attraction of the dreams encouraged by religious ideologies increases many times over.[17]

Global War on Terrorism or a US Worldwide War?

The initial response to the attacks was heartening, a global coalition against a global terrorist threat. For the first time in its 50-year history, NATO invoked Article 5 of its Treaty. The attack on the US was now considered as an attack on every NATO member. The democratic world, and most of the semi-democratic one, was united as it had not been since World War Two.

There was already a problem with the title – War on Terrorism. How do you wage war on an 'ism', particularly on a notoriously slippery concept that is usually employed as a subjective value judgement? One person's terrorist is another's freedom fighter, or as the BBC's World Affairs editor John Simpson put it, 'if it's done by our side it's not terrorism.'[18] During the 2003 US–UK invasion of Iraq, when BBC correspondent Paul Adams was asked if Iraqi fighters were using quasi-terrorist tactics, he replied that it would be more accurate to speak of 'asymmetrical warfare'.[19]

A war on terrorism is by definition never-ending. A war on terrorists is something quite different, more defined, more finite. A war on particular terrorists is even narrower in its definition. Tackling a terrorist threat requires a three-pronged approach: security, intelligence and political action. One of the best-known descriptions of this approach comes from Britain's Brigadier General Frank Kitson in his 1971 book *Low Intensity Operations*.[20]

SECURITY

Security is tightened across the targets the terrorists have chosen, making it progressively more difficult for them. There is, of necessity, a catch-up element to this approach in that as security at one type of target is tightened, the terrorists switch to others.

The state must proceed carefully, balancing security needs against over-response and curtailment of normal life and civil rights. The terrorist wants the state to over-respond, wants draconian searches and intrusions, wants to be able to demonstrate the validity of their basic argument – that their target state is an oppressor.

The Italian response to its Red Brigade terrorist campaign is a good example of this careful balance. Post-fascist Italy deliberately created different and competing police and security forces as a bulwark against future totalitarian excesses. Italy passed hardly any emergency legislation, but Italy's security forces defeated the Red Brigades with only minor interference in normal life.

INTELLIGENCE

By definition, terrorists have far fewer resources than the state they are attacking, otherwise they would not need to act as terrorists. Defeating terrorist cells means preventing them from implementing their plans. This requirement is reinforced in the case of terrorists undertaking suicide missions. Since the terrorists' scale is small, penetrating a handful of cells can prevent myriad attacks.

Outside penetration of terrorist groups is difficult and slow, particularly where the attacked state is from a different culture. Co-operation, however difficult, between different security services is essential. The input of the various Mukhabarat (security and intelligence) services of the Arab world is vital in tracking an Islamic group. Obtaining this co-operation requires some walking on diplomatic eggshells and a willingness to take on board some of the security concerns of these different Arab states.

Where intelligence allows for the capture of terrorist suspects, the capturing state must proceed carefully to avoid its captives being seen as martyrs. Martyrs only feed the terrorist cause – witness the political fall-out from the H Block 'dirty protests' and hunger strikes in Northern Ireland.

Terrorists operate in a legal twilight zone between criminality and war. Terrorist suspects are often difficult to bring to trial in ordinary courts. Again, the attacked state must tread a careful line between providing special court procedures and not leaving itself open to even semi-founded accusations of rough justice.

The state represents an ordered and legally regulated society. Terrorists are free of such restraints. The state must be careful not to descend to the level of the terrorist. If it does so, the terrorist has won a potent political victory.

Circumstances may arise where the state, being at war, determines that it must eliminate suspected or potential terrorists. The temptation always exists to 'fudge' this issue, operating nod-and-wink shoot-to-kill policies. History shows that such approaches usually rebound negatively on the initiating state. If the state, and in particular its leadership, is satisfied that such conditions apply, that its soldiers, security police and others are to be asked to kill suspects, then that policy must be formalised. The cases must be considered and a political decision taken for which those who take it are responsible. Otherwise, the state once again descends to the level of the terrorist and runs the risk of unleashing death squads, squads which in the nature of things tend to broaden their informal remit to eliminate an ever growing number of 'undesirables'.

POLITICAL ACTION

Effective terrorists exist at the apex of a pyramid, where they articulate generally held grievances. For every terrorist who goes into action, there are tens of volunteers who would willingly do likewise. The next layer of the pyramid is made up of hundreds who while not ready to act at the cutting edge are prepared to assist, to drive cars, scout locations, pass documents and store ammunition, weapons and explosives.

Below that layer are tens of thousands of passive supporters, ones who broadly share the terrorists' aims but have difficulty with their methods. They will warn of approaching patrols and look the other way if they happen to spot weapons being moved or people arriving at neighbours' houses in the dead of night. Most importantly of all, this layer will almost never voluntarily co-operate with the security forces and will not provide that vital flow of information on which most successful investigations depend. At the bottom of the terrorists' pyramid stands hundreds of thousands, perhaps millions, who understand where the terrorists are coming from, even if they publicly or privately condemn their actions, but because they like the terrorists' enemies no better than they like the terrorists themselves, they do not tell the authorities what they see and hear.

This process is well described by one of the most effective critics of the IRA's long terror campaign in Northern Ireland, the journalist Malachi O'Doherty, who grew up in the IRA's heartland of Catholic West Belfast. In his book, *The Trouble with Guns*, he wrote,

> By 1971 I could for instance have been well able to point the police towards men on the run and to the likely positions of stores of arms and explosives. I didn't do that because I didn't trust them to come in and deal fairly. I wasn't siding with the IRA but I wasn't siding with anybody.[21]

The borders between these layers of the pyramid are permeable, with people moving backwards and forwards in response to particular events. How the state handles its security and intelligence operations will have a significant impact on movement within this pyramid. If it is seen to be heavy handed and oppressive, more and more individuals will move upwards through the pyramid from political understanding to passive support, and from passive support to action.

Carefully balancing the security and political aspects of counter-terrorist actions is not about being 'hard' or 'soft', it is about being effective.

Terrorists need popular support to carry out their campaigns. Mao Zedong talked of fighters swimming in a sea of peasants. Stella Rimington, the former head of the British Security Service (often referred to as MI5), wrote that 'a war on terrorism cannot be won unless the causes of terrorism are eradicated.'[22] The most effective way of eliminating terrorist mosquitoes is to drain the swamp where they breed.

Islamic fundamentalist terrorism has shown itself to be a dedicated and effective enemy. If it did not reflect and exploit widely held grievances, it would not pose such a serious threat. Removing dangerous individual terrorists and terrorist leaders from circulation, even without the over-reaction of creating semi-police states, can only buy the world some time at best.

The war, or at least its major battles, can be won or lost in that time. That is the choice Washington and the rest of the democratic world faces. We must make every effort to bring about an equitable settlement to the Israeli–Palestinian conflict. We must engage with reformers in Islamic countries. The West has always opted for 'stability' in its relations with the Islamic seventh of our world's population. When it involves repressive or totalitarian Mukhabarat states, short-term stability has shown itself more than capable of producing long-term carnage. To quote former CIA director R. James Woolsey, we must 'stop treating the area [the Middle East] as a gasoline station.'[23]

The US War on Terrorism

The Al Quaida attacks on the US in 2001 were not so much concerned with domestic US security reactions as with provoking US actions in the Islamic world. However, there is room for genuine concern over some of the domestic actions of the Bush administration, such as holding US citizens incommunicado without trial or charge.

The non-person status of prisoners at the US Guantánamo naval base and elsewhere, together with the proposed military trials of such prisoners, raises real questions both as to the current US government's interpretation of human rights standards (including such central elements as the Geneva Conventions) and over the competence of US anti-terrorist tactics.

The whole web of non-prisons the US has created flies in the face of the very democratic values it claims to defend. This is no haphazard occurrence with some overzealous junior officers or exasperated troops getting out of control. This is official US government policy, the creation of an ultra-secret Special Access Program (SAP) within the US Department of Defense based on a presidential 'finding' signed in late 2001 or early 2002. When Donald Rumsfeld was questioned on criticisms of these policies in early 2002, he dismissed those criticisms as being 'isolated pockets of international hyperventilation'. Under this SAP the US has snatched prisoners around the world and is holding them in various facilities at Guantánamo and in Afghanistan, Egypt, Thailand, Singapore, Jordan, Pakistan and, of course, in Iraq.[24] One estimate places the number of people being held in the US's modern gulag at over 2,500.[25] It's not about bad apples, it's a whole rotten orchard.

In his previous role as a US government counsel, John Ashcroft's successor as US Attorney General, Alberto Gonzalez, determined that prisoners in Afghanistan should be denied the protection of the Geneva Conventions. He also urged US Justice Department lawyers to redefine torture as meaning only procedures which would produce pain 'of an intensity akin to that which accompanies serious physical injury such as death or organ failure.'[26] His definition allows myriad interrogation procedures which most people would regard as torture.

Long before the Abu Ghraib scandal blew up in Washington's face, a group of senior military legal officers from the Judge Advocate General's (JAG) Corps of the US Army were so worried about the programme and the conditions of detention within it that they took the, for them, extraordinary step of by-passing the military command system. In a desperate attempt to get something done they visited and briefed Scott Horton, the then chairman of the New York City Bar Association's Committee on International Human Rights. In May 2004, Mr Horton stated, 'They were urging us to get involved and speak in a very loud voice...the message was that conditions are ripe for abuse, and it's going to occur.'[27]

The US is well on the way to producing several

hundred Islamic martyrs from dozens of countries, martyrs who will either become terrorists should they be released or who will inspire further terrorists if they are not. A highly respected CIA analyst who reviewed conditions in Guantánamo 'came back convinced that we were committing war crimes.' He is reported to have commented that 'if we captured some people who weren't terrorists when we got them, they are now.'[28]

The International Committee of the Red Cross (ICRC), a body normally known and often criticised for its discretion, has been particularly blunt on conditions for detainees. In a 24-page report submitted to US and UK authorities in early 2004, the ICRC wrote of 'a variety of ill-treatments ranging from insults and humiliation to both physical and psychological coercion that in some cases might amount to torture…methods of physical and psychological coercion used by the interrogators appeared to be part of the standard operating procedures by military intelligence personnel to obtain confessions and extract information.'[29]

There is even greater room for concern over US actions in the Islamic world, notably its invasions of Afghanistan and Iraq. Has the US danced to an Al Quaida tune? Senior Middle East journalist and commentator Robert Fisk asks, 'Has anyone noticed that Mr bin Laden is writing the script? Al-Qa'ida attacks New York so we attack Afghanistan. Al-Qa'ida attacks in Bali and the Australian government re-pledges its support for America…How Mr bin Laden – hardly a man of humour, as I can personally attest – must be smiling.'[30]

The US pursuit of other geopolitical goals under the banner of a War on Terrorism has placed considerable strains on the vital co-operation between American, European and Arab security services. An outraged Iraqi may appear as an Al Quaida terrorist on the FBI's system, but to an Egyptian Mukhabarat officer at Cairo airport he may have more the allure of a resistance fighter, someone to be nodded through unless they work really hard at calling attention to themselves.

Al Quaida is No Islamic Pentagon

Paul Wolfowitz, seen by many as the intellectual force behind George W. Bush's foreign and security policy, built part of his reputation by attacking the tendency of foreign policy, intelligence and security services to undertake 'mirror reasoning'.[31] This describes the natural tendency to base projections about how an enemy may react on one's experience of how one's own country acts.

US National Security Adviser Condoleezza Rice told US television host Matt Lauer that since Saddam Hussein had refused to account for missing stockpiles of botulinum toxin and anthrax even though he knew he would face serious consequences, 'I don't know how you could have come to any other conclusion but that he had weapons of mass destruction.' *New York Times* columnist Maureen Dowd succinctly suggested that other conclusions were possible when she wrote, 'Condi Rice made a tyro error. She mirrored. A conservative, ice-skating Brahms aficionada from Birmingham had assumed that a homicidal, grenade-fishing Sinatra aficionado from Tikrit reasoned just like her.'[32]

In Vietnam the US came to believe that their enemy had a headquarters structure like the US Military Assistance Command Vietnam (MACV). This was dubbed the Central Office for South Vietnam (COSVN). US military units searched for this headquarters complex for years, and failing to find it argued that it had to be based across the border in the Parrot's Beak area of Cambodia. Destroying COSVN and shortening the war was one of the factors in the Nixon decision to invade Cambodia. This was pure 'mirror reasoning'. COSVN had never existed.

Much US comment on Al Quaida falls into the same trap of 'mirror reasoning'. Perhaps subconsciously, Al Quaida is seen as a monolithic organisation with a headquarters, committees and directorates, something between US Special Forces Command and CIA headquarters at Langley, Virginia. Most observers agree that the reality is quite different, a frequent English translation of Al Quaida being 'The Base'. Al Quaida is about networks, contacts and resources, particularly money. Before the 2001 invasion of Afghanistan, Al Quaida also benefited from an environment where it could openly run training camps and retreat to lick its wounds. Al Quaida is better understood if seen as a loose franchise rather than as a centralised corporation. In American terms, it is more McDonald's than Intel.

Jason Burke, a specialist in terrorist organisations and author of *Al-Qaeda: Casting a Shadow of Terror* (2003), spells this out:

> Al-Qaeda, conceived of as a tight-knit terrorist group with cadres and a capability everywhere, does not exist in that form. It barely existed before the war in Afghanistan in 2001 destroyed Osama bin Laden's carefully constructed infra-structure there. It certainly does not exist now. Instead, we are facing a different kind of threat. Al-Qaeda can only be understood as an ideology, an agenda and a way of seeing the world that is shared by an increasing number of predominantly young, predominantly male Muslims. Eliminating bin Laden and a few hundred senior activists will do nothing to counter this al-Qaeda…the President and the men who answer to him and his allies are not winning the war on terror, they are losing it…He [Bush] believes eliminating al-Qaeda will end the threat of Islamic militant terrorism. Though this is rubbish, as a close analysis of recent terrorist attacks shows, it is the conventional wisdom among most of those charged with ending the violence that we are now being subjected to.[33]

Many states around the world have had to respond to terrorist threats, both internal and external. Over the years significant experience has been accumulated, security forces trained and quite spectacular results achieved.

After September 11th the US needed the expertise and support of its allies, friends and others in London, Dublin, Paris, Berlin, Rome, Madrid, Amman, Cairo, Damascus, Jerusalem, Islamabad and a host of other cities. It needed the co-operation of their domestic security services, their foreign intelligence services, their anti-terrorist units and a dozen other agencies. All that help was more or less readily forthcoming.

Services co-operated as they had never before, and an awesome coalition was put in place, albeit an odd coalition where the US as the victim was at the centre, but where the US was in some operational senses a junior partner. It was a coalition where knowledge was more important than force. When it comes to dealing with a terrorist cell, an experienced team of specialists is more effective than a B-52. Perhaps it was this very notion of the US being a partner rather than the dominant leader which the neoconservatives found so abhorrent. The neoconservative agenda is about the US leading the world, not about it being part of an interdependent one.

Managing and leading such a coalition requires special talents, leadership, understanding, patience and the odd dose of humility. The US had demonstrated these skills in building and leading the 1991 Gulf War coalition. Would the George W. Bush administration be able to repeat the achievements of the George H. Bush one? 'To lead is to heed. This is not the counsel of wimpishness, but of wisdom,' Josef Joffe, editor of *Die Zeit*, remarked.[34] The George W. Bush White House was to clearly show it had no intention of heeding, and in that demonstration was to throw away the unique opportunity it was offered to lead.

Afghanistan

The US had been attacked by a terrorist group based in Afghanistan, and one that was an integral part of what passed for a government in that unfortunate country under the rule of the Taliban. Kabul refused to either arrest or extradite the Al Quaida leadership based in Afghanistan or to close Al Quaida camps. Faced with these refusals, Washington was left with the military option. The decision to intervene militarily in Afghanistan fell rather clearly into one of the two cases foreseen in the UN Charter when a state may employ armed force – self-defence. The US had been attacked and the attackers had been identified and were promising further attacks. The US had the right to respond, and many countries around the world were willing, even eager, to assist in that response.

The central objective of the US in this invasion was the elimination of the Al Quaida infrastructure in Afghanistan, including the capture or death of the main Al Quaida leaders. Achieving this objective involved defeating and toppling the Taliban regime, but that was a secondary goal, a necessary and desirable by-product, but nonetheless a by-product of its primary goal.

A third and longer-term objective should have been assuring the emergence of a relatively stable post-Taliban country capable of satisfying the US's three main interests. Firstly, ensuring that neither the Taliban nor the warlord anarchy which had helped bring them to power in the first place would have a chance to re-emerge. Secondly, continuing the Taliban success in prohibiting cultivation of the opium poppy, thus helping reduce the international flow of heroin. The third US interest was the potential use of Afghanistan as a route for gas and possibly oil pipelines from neighbouring countries.

Washington chose to pursue only its secondary goal, toppling the Taliban, and it pursued even that rather half-heartedly. Apart from one brief raid by US Rangers (which lasted a few hours), no US troops were inserted into Afghanistan until 25 November 2001, seven weeks after the offensive began. These were US Marines inserted near Kandahar, a city they did not invest until 7 December when they found, not surprisingly, that the Taliban and Al Quaida leaderships had vanished.[35]

Most of the ground fighting was carried out by the Afghan Northern Alliance, aided by regional warlord units which the US had spent $70 million 'encouraging' and supported by US air power. Northern Alliance forces around Kunduz watched helplessly as aircraft evacuated Al Quaida personnel. Other Taliban and Al Quaida leadership elements retreated into the Tora Bora mountains near the Pakistani frontier, where US Special Forces and Afghan fighters made a desperate attempt to surround them in mid-December 2001. It was not until March 2002 that the US had deployed enough of its own troops to conduct another sweep through Tora Bora.[36] Although it met with heavy resistance, it also failed to capture any Al Quaida or Taliban leaders. In all the US was to send fewer troops to Afghanistan than the New York Police Department normally deploys in Manhattan.[37]

The US was not short of troops nor of offers of assistance from its allies. Britain's Royal Navy fired its stock of non-nuclear Tomahawks and Spanish F-18s and French Mirages carried out the odd mission. French Marines (RIMA) were left to kick their heels in neighbouring Uzbekistan. An advance party of British Paratroops was abandoned to embarrassing and almost threatening isolation at Bagram air base north of Kabul and forces available from other countries were not even requested. The invasion of Afghanistan was to mark a radical departure from traditional US policy. Allies no longer mattered, but neither did the announced policy goals of the US.

In late 2002 the US Department of Defense's office of Special Operations and Low Intensity Conflict (SOLIC) asked Colonel Hy Rothestein, a leading US military expert on unconventional warfare, to study and report on the planning and execution of the US war in Afghanistan.

His report was devastatingly critical of the Bush administration's strategy. He commented that the dependence on aerial bombardment was the wrong approach to hunting down Osama bin Laden. He argued that the US had failed to translate early tactical successes into a strategic victory, and in the words of the US military expert, the proclaimed US victory in Afghanistan was not a victory at all.[38]

This contrasts starkly with the claims advanced by a leading neoconservative writer, Norman Podhoretz, in September 2004 that

> the B-52's and the 15,000-pound 'Daisy Cutter' bombs exerted a terrifying psychological impact as they exploded

just above ground, wiping out everything for hundreds of yards...our 'smart bomb' technology...satellite drones and other systems...were incredibly precise in avoiding civilian casualties and absolutely lethal in destroying the enemy...'battle-hardened' troops of the Taliban regime in less than three months, and with the loss of very few American troops.[39]

The counter-terrorism and military experts describe the invasion of Afghanistan as a failure, whereas the neoconservatives paint it as a stunning success – 'Afghanistan showed that the military option was open, available for use, and lethally effective.'[40] Who do you believe? Who do you choose to believe? Tellingly, one's interpretation of reality when it comes to US policies and achievements has become a matter of choice.

US *Guardian* correspondent Gary Younge identified this in describing the Alice-in-Wonderland role of reality in the 2004 US presidential campaign: 'On these rare occasions when people are presented with the same raw data, the two camps have managed to fashion conclusions that are not just different but almost entirely contradictory. So rather than partisan arguments adjusting to take account of reality, reality is altered to suit the argument.'[41]

To quote the then chairman of the US Joint Chiefs of Staff, General Richard Myers, the US has not only 'lost momentum'[42] in Afghanistan, it seems to have lost the plot. *The Boston Globe* pointed out that the 2002 Afghan opium crop was 3,700 tons and that 'the United States has a strategic interest in helping build a sound and stable Afghanistan.'[43] In its 2003 report, the United Nations Office on Drugs and Crime noted that Afghan opium production had increased twentyfold during 2001 to 2003.[44] In 2003, US aid to Afghanistan was just over $1.2 billion. The US military operation in the country costs just under $1 billion a month.[45]

By the spring of 2002 Kabul was no longer centre stage in Washington. It vanished from its brief starring role as President Karzai's interim government installed itself and Washington's attention shifted to Baghdad. There was a quite literal sense of amnesia about a country in which the US had invaded a few months before. In the 2003 budget that the White House submitted to Congress, there was no request for any money for the reconstruction of Afghanistan, even though Bush had earlier talked of a 'Marshall Plan' for the devastated country. Congress itself had to cobble together $300 million to save America's blushes.

As former US Secretary of State Warren Christopher warned, 'In foreign affairs, Washington is chronically unable to deal with more than one crisis at a time.'[46] When Washington switched its focus to Kabul, concentration on the incremental and difficult War on Terrorism inevitably decreased. Arabic-speaking US Special Forces and some CIA paramilitary teams were pulled out of the hunt for Arabic-speaking Al Quaida terrorists in Afghanistan in early 2003.[47] They were needed in Iraq. The only Al Quaida presence in Iraq in the spring of 2002 was a small group which had fled Afghanistan to install itself in northern Iraq, where the US Air Force and the British RAF protected it from Saddam's government forces.

The neoconservatives were not overly interested in Al Quaida, apart from hyping it into an existential threat. US security was not to be achieved by pursuing, attacking and destroying those who had attacked the US. US security was to be achieved by attacking where the neoconservatives believed a threat to US security might come from.

There are two possible conclusions from US operations in Afghanistan in late 2001 and early 2002. One is that the political leadership at the Pentagon is seriously incompetent. The other is that Al Quaida was not seen as a military priority in Washington.

The George W. Bush administration was about to clearly demonstrate that these two possible conclusions are by no means mutually exclusive.

11

Baghdad or Bust

'Does Saddam now have weapons of mass destruction? Sure he does.'

— Richard Perle, Senate Testimony 2001[1]

'We believe he has, in fact, reconstituted nuclear weapons.'

— Dick Cheney[2]

'The regime has long-standing and continuing ties to terrorist organisations and there are al-Qaeda terrorists inside Iraq.'

— George W. Bush[3]

'I'm the commander – see, I don't need to explain.'

— George W. Bush[4]

'He beamed satisfaction and confidence. His great plan was prospering. The whole atmosphere of this secluded little community reeked of that sycophantic optimism.'

—British Prime Minister David Lloyd George,
World War One[5]

'Invade Brazil...'

Some of those protesting outside the Republican Convention in New York during September 2004 wore T-shirts proclaiming 'If Dubya had been in office in December 1941, the United States would have invaded...Brazil'. If the slogan, referring to the Japanese pre-emptive attack on Pearl Harbor, was not all that snappy, the message was crystal clear – September 11th had been hijacked by the neoconservatives for the war they had wanted for years.

During the eleven months between September 2001 and July 2002, they set to work deploying their considerable skills of argument, lobbying and intimidation to drive home their message within the US administration. The administration used similar methods to sell that message globally – and failed. Nevertheless, with UK and Australian participation, the US would invade Iraq in March 2003.

The neoconservatives came to power determined to refurbish and reinforce the standing and power of the US in the world. A student using their approach, not so much a failure of reasoning as a reversal of reasoning – first determining the outcome, then finding the arguments to support it – would have failed any exam. But they were not students; they had become the US government. The prime tool at their disposal, the one thing the US government controlled that nobody else on the planet could duplicate, their unique selling point, their ace in the hole, was their ability to project military power. They took their sole ace, bet it on a high-stakes Iraqi gamble – and lost.

'Can't You Get These Guys Back in Their Box?'

By the early afternoon of 11 September 2001, the CIA was able to confirm that known Al Quaida operatives had been on board American Airlines flight 77, which had hit the Pentagon.[6] Al Quaida became the immediate focus of US security, intelligence and defence professionals.

At the US National Security Council meeting on the afternoon of 12 September 2001, however, Donald Rumsfeld raised the question of attacking Iraq.[7] At the Pentagon press briefing on 13 September, Paul

Wolfowitz talked of 'ending the states who sponsor terrorism.'[8] At the Camp David War Cabinet brainstorming session on 15 September, Rumsfeld suggested that they needed a fallback position if things did not work out in Afghanistan. Wolfowitz seized the moment to propose attacking Iraq.[9]

The State Department, the intelligence community and the military high command were all primarily concerned with developing a plan to tackle Al Quaida and remove the Taliban regime in Afghanistan. The leaders and professionals in these bodies saw the neoconservative preoccupation with Iraq as a diversion. When Paul Wolfowitz first talked of ending the 'states who sponsor terrorism' on 13 September, Colin Powell publicly distanced himself, saying, 'Ending terrorism is where I would like to leave it, and let Mr. Wolfowitz speak for himself.'[10]

Powell asked General Hugh Shelton, the then chairman of the Joint Chiefs, 'What the hell, what are these guys thinking about? Can't you get these guys back in their box?'[11] Shelton was opposed to including Iraq in the War on Terrorism unless there was clear evidence that Baghdad had been involved in the September 11th attacks, and that evidence simply did not exist.

The neoconservatives had their mission – to topple Saddam Hussein – and they now had an opportunity to realise it. In the winter of 2001 and spring of 2002, Washington was buzzing with ideas and proposals for executing the War on Terrorism. This unique combination of mission and opportunity might never present itself again. Al Quaida did not interest the neoconservatives all that much. Its shadowy menace had not featured in their out-of-office seminars through the 1990s. They are extraordinarily old-fashioned and out of date in their perverted Straussian reasoning – all they can get their heads around in terms of threat are states; terrorist groups do not fit their ideological arguments and so they are ignored. Their favourite threatening state in late 2001 was, as it had been since 1991, Saddam Hussein's Iraq.

They had to sell their mission to one man, President George W. Bush. President Bush expressed his view of presidential power quite clearly: 'I'm the commander – see, I don't need to explain – I do not need to explain why I say things. That's the interesting thing about being the president. Maybe somebody needs to explain to me when they say something, but I don't feel like I owe anybody an explanation.'[12]

In July 2002 the State Department's Richard N. Haass had one of his regular meetings with Condoleezza Rice. Haass suggested they might use some time to look at the pros and cons of attacking Iraq. Rice told him not to bother as the President had already made his decision – the US was going to attack Iraq.[13] It was now just a question of getting the pieces into place.

'The Fucking Crazies': Arguments within the Administration[14]

President Bush had secretly authorised contingency military planning for Iraq in September 2001. In his 29 January 2002 State of the Union address, Bush declared Iran, Iraq and North Korea to be an 'axis of evil' and warned that he would not 'wait on events' while these countries developed WMD and shared them with terrorist organisations.

Speaking to the annual graduation ceremony at West Point on 1 June 2002, Bush said,

> The gravest danger to freedom lies at the crossroads of radicalism and technology. When the spread of chemical and biological and nuclear weapons, along with ballistic missile technology – when that occurs, even weak states and small groups could attain a catastrophic power to strike great nations. Our enemies have declared this very intention, and have been caught seeking these terrible weapons. They want the capability to blackmail us – and we will oppose them with all our power.[15]

In strategic terms, for the US Saddam Hussein was what the former Defense Secretary and Assistant

Defense Secretary Bill Perry and Ashton Carter had defined in 1999 as a B-list threat: a problem that 'may threaten vital US interests, but not America's survival.'[16] They saw the danger posed by Iraq even to US regional interests as more theoretical than real for the obvious and clearly demonstrated reason that 'the US military is capable of inflicting a decisive defeat' on Iraq: 'Saddam Hussein's Iraq is militarily weaker today than it was in 1990, while US forces are better positioned to repel Iraqi aggression.' If anything, between 1999, when this uncontroversial assessment was published, and 2003, the military balance had tilted even further in favour of the US because of the continuing effect of sanctions on Iraq.

Colin Powell, Condoleezza Rice and President Bush met on the evening of 5 August 2002 in the White House residence. The meeting stretched into dinner and then adjourned to the President's office. Over two hours Powell, accepting that the decision to go to war with Iraq had already been made, argued, with Rice's support, that there was a need to build an international coalition and to work with the United Nations. Bush agreed.[17] A 16 August National Security Council meeting confirmed the decision: Bush's 12 September speech to the UN would be about Iraq.

The neoconservatives set out to force the President into a corner over what he could say at the UN. In a 27 August speech, Dick Cheney was to say, 'The Iraqi regime has in fact been very busy enhancing its capabilities in the field of chemical and biological agents. And they continue to pursue the nuclear program they began so many years ago...Simply stated, there is no doubt that Saddam Hussein now has weapons of mass destruction.' Cheney also questioned how useful the 1991–1998 UN weapons inspections in Iraq had been and said, 'A return of weapons inspectors would provide no assurance whatsoever of his [Saddam's] compliance with U.N. resolutions.'[18]

On 28 August Rumsfeld addressed US Marines at

Camp Pendleton in California, saying in connection with Iraq that 'I don't know how many countries will participate in the event the president does decide that the risks of not acting are greater than the risk of acting...at the onset it may be lonesome.'[19]

At a meeting in Camp David on 6 September, Powell and Cheney clashed over the issue of a resolution. Cheney said it would tie the US down while Powell argued it was essential. The battle raged on in Washington in the run-up to the speech. Draft No. 21 of Bush's speech on 10 September did not contain the request for a resolution. Finally Powell carried the day, although the vital sentence was left out of the TelePrompter text Bush read to the UN – he ad libbed it in.[20]

On several occasions, different administration figures clearly spelled out their belief that Iraq retained and was developing significant WMDs. Speaking of Saddam Hussein, Dick Cheney said on 16 March 2003, 'We believe he has, in fact, reconstituted nuclear weapons.'[21] The Vice-President told the Saudi Foreign Minister that the reason for attacking Iraq was that it was 'do-able'.[22] That is probably the most honest statement he has made about the war. Another way of expressing Cheney's explanation is that power was exercised for its own sake. Like the mountaineers who climb Everest because they can, the US invaded Iraq because it could.

The statements on an established link with Al Quaida were even clearer. In September 2002 President Bush stated, 'The regime has long-standing and continuing ties to terrorist organisations and there are Al Qaeda terrorists inside Iraq.' Secretary of Defense Donald Rumsfeld said that Baghdad had discussed giving haven to officials of Al Quaida and training them in the use of chemical weapons. He reported 'increasing contacts' between Al Quaida and Iraq. Condoleezza Rice added that 'we clearly know that there were in the past and have been contacts between senior Iraqi officials and members of Al Qaeda going back for actually quite a long time.'[23] In March 2003, the President was to affirm that he knew Baghdad had 'trained and financed...Al Qaida'.[24] Rand Beers, the senior director for counter-terrorism at the US National Security Council, who resigned in early 2003, said that on the basis of the intelligence he saw, he did not believe there was a significant relationship between Saddam Hussein and Al Quaida.[25]

With so many incoherent war aims, the war itself became a simplifying force for the administration. It took a multiplicity of motives and agendas and gave them an apparently simple outcome: invade Iraq. Instead of arising from a hard-won agreement, the war itself was the source of agreement among the administration's major players. And since that agreement had little to do with the announced reasons for the war, no argument was going to make any impression. Essentially, this nexus of ideologically driven goals had the character of a system of religious belief. And as with any religion, those who try to test its claims against reality are missing the point. In the very effrontery of the attempt, they merely prove themselves infidels. When US military, intelligence and diplomatic professionals and US allies sounded notes of caution, or even asked why, they were ignored, muzzled, dismissed, rubbished, retired or vilified.

The Case for War: Rest of the World

The process of negotiating what would become UN Security Council Resolution 1441 began following Bush's UN General Assembly speech. Washington had a genuine security concern about Iraq and its possible links with Al Quaida, but everybody, including the US, lacked hard intelligence. The US military build-up in the Gulf was putting pressure on Baghdad. Using that leverage, the Security Council challenge was to get the UN inspectors back into Iraq and find out what was really happening.

It was clear that if Iraq refused inspections or if the inspectors found solid, even circumstantial, evidence that Iraq had reactivated its WMD programmes, then military action would have to be taken. This was clear even to countries that were reluctant to use force. In the autumn of 2002 France began to plan for its contingent in a putative war with Iraq, something along the lines of what it had contributed to the 1991 Gulf War – a reinforced armoured division of 15,000 troops backed by naval forces and 100 combat aircraft.[26]

However, Washington was making it clear that Saddam Hussein, rather than Iraqi weaponry, was the problem. The administration issued an open invitation to Iraqi dissidents, or even to rivals within the Baath Party hierarchy, to assassinate Saddam. White House spokesman Ari Fleischer said, 'The cost of a one-way ticket is substantially less than the cost of war; the cost of one bullet, if the Iraqi people take it on themselves, is substantially less than that.'[27]

Following difficult, and occasionally animated, negotiations, the 15 members of the UN Security Council unanimously adopted Resolution 1441 on 8 November 2002.

There were three central aspects to the resolution: inspectors would return to Iraq, Iraq had a month to produce a full inventory of its relevant weapons and the inspectors would report back to the Security Council in January 2003. The Security Council would then decide whether or not the use of force was necessary. This last element was fudged since the US wanted an automatic use of force if Iraq was found to be in 'material breach' of its obligations.

Saddam capitulated and the inspectors returned. On 7 December 2002, General Hassam Mohamed Amin, head of Iraq's National Monitoring Directorate, handed over the Iraqi report of 12,159 pages written in English and comprising 43 spiral-bound volumes of documents, six folders and 12 CD-ROMs. General Amin said, 'I reiterate here Iraq has no weapons of mass destruction.

I think if the United States has the minimum level of fairness and braveness, it should accept the report and say this is the truth.' The Chief UN Inspector, Hans Blix, not unreasonably said that it would take several weeks to work through the report. Washington was furious.[28]

International opinion tended to agree with Hans Blix that Saddam Hussein was now less dangerous than he had been before because he was trapped 'in a box with the inspectors inside the box.'[29] Colin Powell probably concurred but understood there was no way he could sell that position within the Bush administration. Powell was not overly discomfited by the delays. The US armed forces wanted more time to get their troops into position and there were persistent stories of clashes between General Tommy Franks, who would have to lead any invasion of Iraq, and Donald Rumsfeld over the number of troops the mission would require.

By any normal standards, this was a triumph both of US power and US influence. The threat of overwhelming military force made the Iraqi regime change its behaviour. American influence produced an international consensus that backed that threat.

During December 2002 the US informed France that the nature of France's military participation needed to be nailed down. Paris remained willing to participate, but refused to commit itself until after a UN decision had been taken following the inspectors' scheduled report to the UN Security Council on 27 January 2003. Rumsfeld's Pentagon replied that January would be too late. President Chirac now fully understood that Washington was not genuinely looking for a solution other than military action to the Iraq crisis.[30]

It became clear to all that Washington had decided to invade Iraq sometime in the late spring or early summer of 2002. Between that decision and the US attack of 20 March 2003, it also became clear that Washington wanted war for war's sake. In the beginning of 2003 there was a flurry of offers from Baghdad, including access for US forces to Iraq and even the holding of elections to replace Saddam Hussein. Traces of some of these contacts by Hassan al-Obeidi, chief of foreign operations of the Iraqi Intelligence Service, and Tahir Jalil Habbush, the director of the Iraqi Intelligence Service, have surfaced.[31] Offers at that level could only have been made with the approval of Saddam Hussein himself. Washington was not interested.

'I'm Not Reading This': Colin Powell and the UN Security Council

Colin Powell was a man caught in the middle, uneasily straddling the fault lines between what he had come to understand of international relations and military facts (the Powell Doctrine), his duty to his President and his devotion to his country. He was losing the Washington battle, with the Pentagon eclipsing his State Department. In mid-2002, Rumsfeld had virtually unlimited access to President Bush, but Powell was restricted to 20 minutes a week, audiences he had to share with Condoleezza Rice.[32] Powell decided to make the US case at the UN Security Council to present it, US and global public opinion with solid arguments in a dramatic 75-minute speech on 5 February 2003. As a former general and chairman of the US Joint Chiefs of Staff, Powell had the necessary expertise to evaluate intelligence reports.

It is perhaps a sign of how charged relations within Washington had become that Powell, rather than asking for a briefing from the State Department's own Bureau of Intelligence and Research or from the CIA, took the unprecedented step of personally visiting CIA headquarters and going through the allegations one at a time. On 1 February 2003, during a rehearsal of his speech, Powell is reported to have thrown several pages into the air, shouting, 'I'm not reading this, this is bullshit.' Powell's vetting procedure involved CIA director George Tenet and his deputy, John McLaughlin. Powell would ask what the sources for different allegations were and then decide what he would include. He refused to include specific elements which the White House tried to insist on (just six pages out of 38 supplied by Vice-President Dick Cheney were to survive the vetting). Powell finally insisted that Tenet accompany him to the UN – a physical statement that the CIA stood behind his assertions.[33]

Colin Powell did his very best with what he had, but what he had did not amount to very much, not even to convincing circumstantial evidence. A satellite photo here, an artist's impression of a mobile laboratory there, a photograph of a drone that had not been taken in Iraq – this was not the kind of evidence on which the rest of the world could base a decision to sanction a war with wildly unpredictable consequences. There was nothing new, nothing that the French DGSE, the German BND or the Chinese or Russian intelligence services had not already briefed their governments on. Powell himself is reported to have shared similar concerns with UK Foreign Secretary Jack Straw just before his Security Council address. He reportedly said he was 'apprehensive' about the material and worried that it would 'explode in their faces' after the invasion of Iraq.[34]

For example, the issue of Iraq's supposed deployment of mobile labs in which terrible weapons were being secretly developed had already been investigated in Britain. The British knew rather a lot about them, not least because the systems had been sold to Baghdad by Britain in 1987. The late Dr David Kelly, who was the UK's leading expert on Iraqi weapons programmes, had an overview of the official British investigation into the vehicles which had decided they were facilities for the production of hydrogen. Those findings were passed to the Ministry of Defence and the Foreign Office and David Kelly made them available to trusted journalists.[35]

Taji, near Baghdad, was the only specific location singled out by Colin Powell. He said, 'This is one of 65 such facilities in Iraq, we know this one has housed chemical weapons.' When US forces searched Taji in late April 2003, no traces of such weapons were found.[36]

In February 2002 the inspections were continuing,

and if the Iraqis were not actively co-operating, then they were not obstructing either. Several members of the Security Council offered to assist the inspectors with equipment. French Mirage F-4P photo reconnaissance aircraft were deployed, along with Russian Antonov 30Bs to support the US U-2 spy planes which had begun missions over Iraq on 17 February 2003.[37]

The inspectors investigated sites such as the Baghdad hospital where the Pentagon's Office of Special Plans said there were secret underground laboratories. They used ground-penetrating radar equipment and found nothing.[38]

At the end of the Security Council process the US could not convince the rest of the world of its case. Eleven of the 15 members of the Security Council were prepared to vote against a war resolution. Three of the five permanent members of the Council – China, Russia and France – had indicated that they would veto any resolution authorising force. The final Chilean attempt at a compromise was to allow another 45 days for the inspectors to carry out their work. The US rejected it.

Around the world, people across dinner tables, in bars, intelligence services and foreign ministries struggled and failed to understand why Washington so desperately wanted to go to war. There were worrisome echoes of the syndrome US Vice-President Walter Mondale had described when people tried to figure out the USSR's invasion of Afghanistan in 1981: 'I don't know if fear is the right word to describe our reaction, but what unnerved everyone was the suspicion that Brezhnev's inner circle might not be rational.'[39]

Patriotic Fervour and Propaganda

This kind of situation, in which crucial policy decisions are being made on the basis of blind faith, is precisely why democratic systems of governance have checks and balances. If one branch of government is mal-functioning, the other will step in to restore order.

The co-equal branch of the US government, the Congress, completely failed to either check or balance the Bush administration. The US media, with a few notable exceptions, failed to challenge the White House line, to cover the differing opinions within the intelligence community and even to report what little debate took place in Congress.

The administration managed to sell the Iraq War through a rather crude word association game: Terrorism – Al Quaida – WMD – Iraq – Saddam Hussein. It succeeded to the point where, according to a *New York Times*/CBS News poll, 42 per cent believed Saddam Hussein was directly responsible for the September 11th attacks. An ABC News poll showed 55 per cent believing Saddam Hussein directly supported Al Quaida.[40] Professor Paul Krugman was to ask,

> What is it about today's right that lets it bully the press so easily, that creates such an effective machine of propaganda, intimidation, and base mobilization? Money is surely part of the story. Religion is also part of the story…And 9/11 was, of course, the best gift the right could have wished for: a perfect occasion to shift politics to a permanent war footing, in which criticism of our leaders could be shouted down as unpatriotic.[41]

When US senator Robert Byrd, at 85 the oldest and longest-serving man in the US Congress, denounced his nation's march to war in March 2003, his speech went virtually unreported until a supporter paid to have it printed as an advertisement in *The New York Times*. It is worth quoting at some length because it said many of the things that a functioning superpower should have wanted to hear:

> I believe in this beautiful country. I have studied its roots and gloried in the wisdom of its magnificent Constitution. I have marvelled at the wisdom of its founders and framers. Generation after generation of Americans has understood the lofty ideals that underlie our great republic. I have been inspired by the story of their sacrifice and their strength.
>
> But, today, I weep for my country. I have watched the

events of recent months with a heavy, heavy heart. No more is the image of America one of strong yet benevolent peacekeeper. The image of America has changed. Around the globe, our friends mistrust us, our word is disputed, our intentions are questioned.

Instead of reasoning with those with whom we disagree, we demand obedience or threaten recrimination.

Instead of isolating Saddam Hussein, we seem to have isolated ourselves. We proclaim a new doctrine of preemption which is understood by few and feared by many. We say that the United States has the right to turn its firepower on any corner of the globe which might be suspect in the war on terrorism.

We assert that right without the sanction of any international body. As a result, the world has become a much more dangerous place.

We flaunt our superpower status with arrogance. We treat UN Security Council members like ingrates who offend our princely dignity by lifting their heads from the carpet. Valuable alliances are split.

After war has ended, the United States will have to rebuild much more than the country of Iraq. We will have to rebuild America's image around the globe.

The case this administration tries to make to justify its fixation with war is tainted by charges of falsified documents and circumstantial evidence. We cannot convince the world of the necessity of this war for one simple reason. This is a war of choice.

There is no credible information to connect Saddam Hussein to 9/11. The Twin Towers fell because a worldwide terrorist group, al-Qaeda, with cells in over 60 nations, struck at our wealth and our influence by turning our own planes into missiles, one of which would likely have slammed into the dome of this beautiful Capitol except for the brave sacrifice of the passengers on board.

The brutality seen on September 11th and in other terrorist attacks we have witnessed around the globe are the violent and desperate efforts by extremists to stop the daily encroachment of Western values upon their cultures. That is what we fight. It is a force not confined to borders. It is a shadowy entity with many faces, many names and many addresses.

But this administration has directed all of the anger, fear

and grief which emerged from the ashes of the Twin Towers and the twisted metal of the Pentagon towards a tangible villain, one we can see and hate and attack. And villain he is. But he is the wrong villain. And this is the wrong war. We will probably drive Saddam Hussein from power. But the zeal of our friends to assist our global war on terrorism may have already taken flight.

The general unease surrounding this war is not just due to 'orange alert'. There is a pervasive sense of rush and risk and too many questions unanswered. How long will we be in Iraq? What will be the cost? What is the ultimate mission? How great is the danger at home?

What is happening to this country? When did we become a nation which ignores and berates our friends? When did we decide to risk undermining international order by adopting a radical and doctrinaire approach to using our awesome military might? How can we abandon diplomatic efforts when the turmoil in the world cries out for diplomacy?

Why can this President not seem to see that America's true power lies not in its will to intimidate, but in its ability to inspire?

I along with millions of Americans will pray for the safety of our troops, for the innocent civilians in Iraq, and for the security of our homeland. May god continue to bless the United States of America in the troubled days ahead, and may we somehow recapture the vision which for the present eludes us.[42]

Byrd's questions, however, were no match for George W. Bush's certainty. He was listening to a veteran even more grizzled and monumental than the senator from West Virginia. As he later told the Palestinian Prime Minister Abu Mazen, 'god told me to strike at al-Qaida and I struck them; then he instructed me to strike at Saddam, which I did.'[43]

The Case for War

The Bush administration offered a confusing, and often conflicting, mixture of at least six main policy objectives to be achieved by invading Iraq:

- This defeated, down-at-heel, contained, bankrupt country with no navy, no operational air force and a poorly equipped, inadequately trained and badly led conscript army posed a clear and present military danger, most particularly because it was packed with concealed chemical and biological weapons of mass destruction (WMD) and racing to develop nuclear ones.
- This secular, mock-socialist failed dictatorship, ruled by a 65-year-old megalomaniac and former US ally, was working hand-in-glove with fundamentalist religious fanatics dedicated to establishing an Islamic caliphate. Furthermore, Iraq was going to supply Saddam Hussein's sworn enemies with the very WMDs he saw as being vital for his political and physical survival.
- The road to peace in Jerusalem passed through Baghdad. Once Iraqi support was removed, Palestinian demands for self-determination would evaporate.
- Toppling Saddam Hussein's regime would lead to a flowering of democracy on the banks of the Tigris, and the entire Middle East would quietly yet radically be transformed by this shining example.
- The US alliance with Saudi Arabia spectacularly failed on 11 September 2001. The US needed a new secure base from which to stabilise this sensitive yet vital region. The new Iraq would provide the key to securing US oil supplies.
- The international community, under US leadership, had a moral duty to use its military leverage to remove totalitarian regimes and secure human rights worldwide, and this sacred quest had to begin in Baghdad.

None of it made much sense to anybody, largely because most of it was nonsense.

261

'War Based on Lies and Misinterpretations': President Jimmy Carter[44]

Washington's case rested on two main assertions. Firstly, that Iraq, in contravention of UN Security Council resolutions, had retained significant quantities of WMD. Secondly, that Baghdad was actively co-operating with Al Quaida.

The term WMD was carelessly bandied about and never challenged. In reality the only real weapon of mass destruction is an air-detonated thermonuclear device. Detonating such a device a kilometre above a target can cause up to 50 per cent casualties. Thermonuclear weapons and the ballistic missile systems needed to deliver them cannot be manufactured in secret. They require significant industrial plants, easily detectable by satellite and other means. Much of the highly sophisticated and specialised technology and machinery needed to produce such weapons and systems can only be obtained from a handful of state and state-dependent suppliers. Iraq had no such systems.

The primary concerns expressed were about chemical and biological weapons (CBW). Many experts would argue that such weapons cannot be considered as WMD for the simple reason that they are not overly effective at killing people. This is why the world's armies have all gradually abandoned the production and deployment of such weapons. As a zone needs to be saturated with CBW for them to be lethal, an attacker needs both significant quantities and time to disperse them. This makes CBW particularly unattractive for terrorist groups which need fast-acting weapons that can be deployed before the security forces can intervene.

The Japanese Aum Shinrikyo dispersed Sarin, one of the most deadly nerve agents known to man, on five rush-hour trains arriving at Tokyo's Kasmagaseki Central Metro station in March 1995. Almost 6,000 people were contaminated, 493 admitted to hospital and 12 died.[45] On 11 March 2003 an Islamic fundamentalist terror group, largely composed of Moroccans, attacked Madrid commuter trains using commercial explosives packed with screws, nails and metal fragments. Just under 200 people were killed and almost 1,500 injured.[46] Conventional weapons are more effective for terrorists.

The Iraqi air force attacked the town of Halabjeh in March 1988 using a cocktail of Sarin, Tabun and VX, flying almost 400 missions in three days to saturate that defenceless town of at least 80,000 inhabitants with limited medical services. Iranian government sources put the death toll at 6,000, or less than 7 per cent. Conventional weapons would have achieved a similar or greater kill ratio.[47]

When the US armed forces abandoned their chemical and biological programmes, US policy warned that any CBW attack on US personnel would be treated as a WMD attack and the US would retaliate with nuclear weapons. This led to CBW being included in the WMD category.

Producing CBW involves no great scientific challenge. Any country capable of producing chlorine products for water purification or insecticides, weed-killers and vaccines has the industrial capacity to make chemical and biological weapons. Massachusetts Institute of Technology's Owen R. Coté summed it up thus: 'essentially all states are capable of producing them [CBW].'[48]

Two particular nuggets of nuclear intelligence were serially reiterated. One was that Iraqi purchases of aluminium tubes were for centrifuges for uranium enrichment, the other that Iraq had sought to acquire uranium yellowcake ore from Niger.

President Bush referred to these tubes in his speech to the UN General Assembly, despite the fact that intelligence experts at the US Department of Energy, the State Department's Bureau of Intelligence and Research and the UN's International Atomic Energy Agency (IAEA) were all arguing that these precision-engineered tubes were for standard artillery rockets and not suitable for centrifuge use.[49]

The Niger yellowcake story is even more informative, revealing sloppy intelligence, rejection of information that does not fit with the pre-established and desired result and a degree of personal vindictiveness leading some Bush officials to break the law and undermine US intelligence operations when their official version is challenged.

In 2002 Italian intelligence services received crude forgeries which purported to show that Iraq was seeking to purchase yellowcake from Niger. Even a cursory glance at the documents showed they were forgeries (wrong titles, poor notepaper and signatures by out-of-office officials). The most cursory investigation would have shown that a French corporation controls the uranium mines in that former French colony. In other words, Iraq would have had to buy Niger yellowcake in Paris, not Niamey.

The CIA decided to check it out by sending a retired US ambassador, James Wilson, to Niger (where he had previously been stationed). Wilson, who had acted to protect US lives when stationed in Baghdad during the 1991 Gulf War, had been described by President Bush, Sr. as a 'truly inspiring diplomat'. Ambassador Wilson duly travelled to Niger and reported back to the CIA that there was no basis to the story.

President Bush referred to the Niger yellowcake in his January 2003 State of the Union address. Wilson went public following the invasion of Iraq with a story in *The New York Times* entitled 'What I did not find in Africa'. White House staff counter-attacked, seeking to smear and discredit Wilson. In his 14 July *Washington Post* column, conservative columnist Robert Novak named Ambassador Wilson's wife, an undercover CIA operative charged with tracking WMD proliferation. The suggestion was that Wilson had only been sent by the CIA at his wife's insistence, although Wilson had in fact been responsible for African questions at the US National Security Council. Naming Wilson's wife destroyed a CIA operation, possibly placing the lives of several people at risk and was in direct contravention of US law. Novak's information came from a White House official. In the eyes of at least some staffers there, criticism of the Bush White House had become the equivalent of treason.[50]

There was no evidence of any operational links between Saddam Hussein's Iraq and Al Quaida. The US 9/11 Commission examined this question, both in terms of general links and with reference to the alleged meeting between Mohammed Atta and the Iraqi intelligence officer Ahmad Khalil Ibrahim Samir al Ani at the Iraqi embassy in Prague at 11.00 on 9 April 2001. US counter-terrorism staff reported to Condoleezza Rice in late September 2001 that they could find no evidence of Iraqi involvement in the 9/11 attacks. The Commission closely examined the alleged April meeting in Prague and concluded that it had not, in fact, taken place.[51]

The White House's best efforts fell far short of building a solid case for a war. Hans Blix told the BBC on 22 April 2003, 'I think it's been one of the disturbing elements that so much of the intelligence on which the capitals built their case seemed to have been so shaky.'[52]

The reality was that this was both a very new and a very old form or war. It was what President Bush called a pre-emptive war, one where you struck your potential enemy before he had even begun to organise to strike you. This smacks of ancient 'might is right' reasoning coupled with some of the most modern weapons on our planet. It is a form of warfare which under the UN Charter must be sanctioned by the Security Council, as it is patently not a question of self-defence. It was this which led UN Secretary General Koffi Annan to agree with a BBC interviewer that the 2003 Iraq War could be classified as illegal.[53] The very essence of the pre-emptive war concept is that one has access to sufficient, and sufficiently clear, intelligence to determine the potential enemy's status, power and intentions.

Intelligence

One commentator described this dramatic shift in the status of intelligence as follows:

> Now, the Bush administration's doctrine of pre-emption has given this iffy, imprecise art grave new responsibilities. It presumes that American intelligence can ferret out the most secret of foreign science with near infallibility, doing so not only to inform policy makers but potentially to build a case for war. In effect, it posits a crystal ball.[54]

Hard intelligence, e.g. how many tanks a particular nation has, is relatively easy. Soft intelligence is more difficult. The target nation moves its tanks for an exercise. Is this the usual exercise, or is it a pre-invasion movement? Here you enter the realm of intentions. What is the target government intending to do? As anybody who has ever shared their life with another human will quickly tell you, human intentions are extraordinarily difficult to decipher. The official US term for documents presenting the intelligence community's take on a given subject is National Intelligence Estimates (NIE). The term 'estimate' goes to the heart of intelligence. Professional intelligence organisations gather as much information as possible, analyse and distil it and arrive, at best, at something a little better than a very educated guess. Above all, intelligence is about identifying patterns.

Intelligence comes in many forms. Much is publicly available, even in totalitarian states, through newspapers, broadcasts and specialist publications. Communications intelligence, sometimes known as COMINT or SIGINT, involves the interception of telecommunications, coded transmissions, etc.

Using film, radar and other means, overhead imaging provides a great deal of physical information. This imaging can be taken from aircraft or satellites, but specialist knowledge is required for the interpretation of these images. A layperson would find it impossible to distinguish between a fertilizer factory and a clandestine chemical weapons operation. Similarly, a construction engineer could easily determine if a piece of roadway was being built as a hidden runway or not.

There are two golden rules of image interpretation. One is to report what the image actually shows separately from what it might be interpreted as indicating. The other is that such imaging is only valid if the whole cycle is identifiable – control over the flight, downloading and processing of the images. It is simply too easy to 'add' features to a computer image.

These functions are separated within US and other intelligence services. Image interpreters describe what the images show them and analysts take that interpretation and seek to integrate it into overall intelligence reports. Description and analysis must be totally separated, otherwise you wind up seeing what you want to see.

In the run-up to the Iraq War, however, the rules were reversed. With an acquiescent London in tow, Washington needed to establish certain 'realities': Iraq had retained WMD in defiance of the UN and Iraq was co-operating with Al Quaida. By means of a simple accountancy exercise, it was claimed that Iraq had 500 tons of mustard gas and nerve gas, 25,000 litres of anthrax, 38,000 litres of botulinum toxin, 29,984 prohibited munitions capable of delivering chemical agents, several dozen Scud missiles, gas centrifuges to enrich uranium, 18 mobile biological warfare factories, long-range unmanned aerial vehicles to dispense anthrax and close ties with Al Quaida.[55]

A great deal was in fact known about Iraq. It had been extensively observed by satellite and other means since 1990. The mountainous northern Kurdish areas had been autonomous since 1992, protected by patrols of USAF, RAF and initially French aircraft. Most of the rest of Iraq is flat and open and the weather is generally clear, creating near-perfect conditions for overhead imagery.

The 1991 Gulf War coalition had devoted considerable

intelligence efforts to tracking Iraqi purchases of weapons and related technologies and equipment, a task rendered considerably easier by the fact that the members of that coalition were the countries which had sold most of the equipment and technology in the first place.

From 1992 to 1998, Iraq had been criss-crossed by teams of UN weapons inspectors from UNSCOM and the IAEA Iraq Action Team operating under UN Security Council Resolution 687. These inspectors were nearly all national officials from military, intelligence and weapons research laboratories such as the late Dr David Kelly of the UK Ministry of Defence and Dick Spertzel, former US Army biological warfare officer, who headed up the UNSCOM biological inspections.

The inspectors were highly successful. 'Inspections were maintained from 1991 to 1998, in which period the U.N. destroyed far more Iraqi weaponry than the U.S. had during the Gulf War.'[56] The British Foreign Office stated that 'UNSCOM has destroyed more weapons than were destroyed during the whole of the Gulf War.'[57]

The inspectors were a major source of intelligence information, both directly by what they found and indirectly through the Iraqi reactions they triggered. The 2003 internal CIA review of intelligence on Iraq is reported to have 'made it clear just how dependent American intelligence agencies were on the United Nations weapons inspection process.'[58] Information primarily flowed from the inspectors to US and other intelligence agencies rather than the other way around.

The generally held view by the summer of 2002 was that Iraq probably retained some minor chemical and biological warfare abilities, but had no serious delivery or production capacities. That view was well summed up by Robin Cook, the former UK Foreign Minister, when he wrote:

Iraq probably has no weapons of mass destruction in the commonly understood sense of that term – namely, a credible device capable of being delivered against strategic city targets. It probably does still have biological toxins and battlefield chemical munitions. But it has had them since the 1980s when the US sold Saddam the anthrax agents and the then British government built his chemical and munitions factories.[59]

The International Institute for Strategic Studies (IISS, London) took a similar view in September 2002: 'The regime is capable of resuming BW [bacteriological warfare] production on short notice (in weeks)'[60] and 'It is capable of resuming CW [chemical warfare] production on short notice (months).'[61] On the subject of whether Iraq might have the delivery systems necessary to deploy any such weapons, it was thought to be possible that Iraq might have retained a handful of its unreliable and inaccurate SCUD missiles. The IISS suggested that 'Iraq has probably retained a small force of about a dozen 650km range al-Hussein missiles.'[62]

If most qualified observers doubted Iraq's WMD capabilities, there was an even broader consensus that Baghdad was not actively co-operating with Al Quaida. The CIA stated in October 2002 that Iraq would only consider arming Al Quaida if Iraq itself was attacked.[63]

This general picture of a down-at-heel Iraq unlikely to supply whatever obsolete remains of WMD it had to Al Quaida did not fit with Washington's decision to go to war. The Bush administration set about finding the 'facts' it needed, and since the intelligence expertise the US had developed at enormous cost was unable to supply these 'facts', the administration created a more compliant fact factory.

Donald Rumsfeld created the Office of Special Plans at the Pentagon, known as The Cabal, in the days after the September 11th attacks. The Cabal's director was Abram Shulsky, a Straussian neoconservative academic who had worked for Richard Perle during the Reagan administration. Shulsky had a staff of eight or nine temporary contractors. The Cabal was 'created in order to find evidence...that Saddam Hussein had close ties to

Al Quaeda, and that Iraq had an enormous arsenal of chemical, biological, and possibly even nuclear weapons.'[64]

These operatives used single-source material, ignored intelligence which contradicted the administration's case and consistently repeated claims such as Iraq's alleged attempts to buy uranium in Niger or aluminium tubes for nuclear centrifuges even after they had been discredited. They also used the testimony of Iraqi exiles, even when the exiles in question had been shown to be less than reliable. Little of this material met professional intelligence standards, but it became the main source of information for the White House, displacing reports from the established US intelligence community.[65]

W. Patrick Lang, a former director of Middle East analyses at the Defense Intelligence Agency (DIA), said Pentagon officials 'started picking out things that supported their thesis and stringing them into arguments that they could use with the president. It's not intel, it's political propaganda.'[66]

In the run-up to the Iraq War, a new intelligence term emerged in Washington: RUMINT. Some suggested that the title stood for Rumour Intelligence, others that it was an abbreviation of Rumsfeld Intelligence. Either way, the White House needed RUMINT because classic intelligence estimates did not, and could not, supply either the information or the pattern the administration was looking for.

In the confusion of claims and counterclaims between the White House, the State Department, the Pentagon and other elements of the US government, it is impossible to determine who knowingly advanced statements they knew to be false and who was taken in by such statements. As Bill Keller wrote in *The New York Times* in June 2003, 'The president either believed what he wanted to believe or was given a stacked deck of information, and it's a close call which of those possibilities is scarier.'[67]

Scariest of all, perhaps, is the strong likelihood that many of the key people around Bush could at times no longer differentiate between what was true, what they genuinely believed to be true and what they had at some moment known to be false. The golden rule of distinguishing between image and interpretation, evidence and belief, had been broken, rendering the whole concept of an intelligence-based war deeply problematic. Yet in the new Bush doctrine of pre-emptive war, intelligence itself was supposed to be crucial. Thus, not just the Powell Doctrine but its replacement had been effectively abandoned.

'We Should Not March into Baghdad...Assigning Young Soldiers to Fight...an Unwinnable Urban Guerrilla War': President George H. Bush (1991)

Why did intelligent, experienced people get themselves into this kind of mess? One reason is that as well as the rather confusing range of publicly stated justifications for invading Iraq, they also had less explicit agendas. Different individuals were motivated by different desires. Two broad categories, imperial and domestic, are identifiable.

The New York Times columnist Maureen Dowd articulated this cacophony when she wrote:

> Mr. Rumsfeld thought the war could showcase his transformation of the military to be leaner and more agile. Paul Wolfowitz thought the war could showcase his transformation of Iraq into a democracy. Dick Cheney thought the war could showcase his transformation of America into a dominatrix superpower. Karl Rove thought the war could showcase his transformation of W. into conquering hero. And Mr. Bush thought the war could showcase his transformation from family black sheep into historic white hat.[68]

A powerful aspect of the 2002–2003 Washington agenda was a lingering notion that there was unfinished business in Iraq. While the Powell Doctrine largely assumed that the best use of military force was as a fast, temporary intervention in which getting out was as important as getting in, the neoconservative mindset was drawn towards epoch-making, once-and-for-all events. The neoconservatives, like the revolutionary Marxists that many of them had once been, saw history in terms of great turning points. The ambivalent outcome of the 1991 Gulf War, with the immediate objective of getting Iraq out of Kuwait achieved but Saddam left in power, was for them deeply un-satisfactory. They despised ambivalence.

The 1991 decision not to pursue the collapsing Iraqi forces to Baghdad and topple Saddam Hussein (together with the US abandoning the insurgent Iraqi Kurds and Shiites it had called upon to revolt) angered many neoconservatives. Paul Wolfowitz was one of the most ardent critics of that 'failure of US nerve'. However, this was a difficult critique to push since that decision had been taken by the administration of the 41st President, George H. Bush, where Wolfowitz had been Under Secretary of Defense to Dick Cheney. In September 2000, during the presidential campaign, Cheney had defended the 1991 decision not to attack Baghdad because he said the US should not act as though 'we were an imperialist power, willy-nilly moving into capitals in that part of the world, taking down governments.'[69] Colin Powell had observed that occupying Baghdad in 1991 would have involved an 'unpardonable expense in terms of money, lives lost and ruined regional relationships.'[70] President Bush, Sr. had written:

> We should not march into Baghdad...To occupy Iraq would instantly shatter our coalition, turning the whole Arab world against us, and make a broken tyrant into a latter-day Arab hero...assigning young soldiers to a fruitless hunt for a securely entrenched dictator and condemning them to fight in what would be an unwinnable urban guerrilla war. It could only plunge that part of the world into even greater instability.[71]

Amongst the imperial arguments we find the desire to affirm Washington as the centre of world power through its creation of a new Middle Eastern settlement, securing US power in the region, and with it US oil supplies, strengthening Israel, toppling Saddam Hussein, as his survival showed US weakness, and destabilising or destroying the UN and the whole concept of a multilateral international order.

The Middle East became more and more important as the world's dependence on oil grew. The UN decision to partition Palestine in 1948 was meant to be the final chapter in a story which began with the Anglo-French 1922 Sykes-Picot agreement. But these imperial arrangements had not, in fact, brought stability. The region that produced most of the world's oil was still beset by the Palestinian conflict, and even its old Arab tyrants were at risk from burgeoning and increasingly radicalised populations. The old imperial settlements having failed, it fell to today's imperial hyperpower to create a new one, not through twentieth, much less twenty-first, century negotiation, but by nineteenth-century force of arms.

Effectively uncritical support for Israel spans the US political spectrum, although the strategic reasons for such support have become steadily less evident since the end of the Cold War. The neoconservatives take this support even further, with a significant core being known in Washington as Likudniks, ardent supporters of the hardest possible Israeli line.

The Likudniks, led by Richard Perle, have staunchly opposed the Middle East peace process. In 1996 they produced *A Clean Break: A New Strategy for Securing the Realm for Israeli Prime Minister Binyamin Netanyahu*. This document rejected the peace agreements and called for war on Iraq.[72]

Only as the dominant imperial power could the US hope to impose a solution:

> the United States'…status as the dominant power in the region as a whole…hinges on maintaining an unassailable

American predominance in the Persian Gulf...defeating Saddam would offer the United States a golden opportunity to show the Arab and Muslim worlds that Arab aspirations are best achieved by working in co-operation with Washington. If an American road to a calmer situation in Palestine does in fact exist, it runs through Baghdad.[73]

This idea of imperial liberation is central to the neoconservative belief that the US is a mighty Gulliver tied down during the long post-war sleep of dreamy liberalism by the puny Lilliputians of international order. A fundamental article of faith for the neo-conservatives is the failure and irrelevance of all multilateral institutions and treaties, particularly the UN.

Richard Perle liked to call the UN 'the chatterbox on the Hudson', showing his contempt by not even noticing that its headquarters is in fact on the East River. By quickly and cleanly dealing with the Iraq and Middle East problems, the US imperium would also demolish the whole UN and multilateral approach to ordering our world. John Bolton, Under Secretary at the US State Department, spelled it out: 'the goal of those who think that international law really means anything are those who want to constrict the US.'[74] Richard Perle wrote in March 2003: 'What will die [in the US triumph in Iraq] is the fantasy of the UN as the foundation of a new world order.'[75]

Domestic reasons included the transformation of the US armed forces into a leaner, more cost-effective tool for projecting power, enhancing US security both in terms of possible terrorist attacks and cheap oil supplies, victory in the ongoing turf war between the Pentagon and the State Department over control of US foreign policy and guaranteeing President Bush a second term.

These various aims, all of them epic in scale but rather abstract in conception, formed a barely coherent ideological nexus in which the one real binding force was the agreement to attack Iraq.

A Bowling 'Strike'

In March 2003 the United States of America invaded Iraq. In the ten-pin bowling language beloved of Middle America, this new military adventure was a strike. It achieved the considerable feat of knocking down all of the Powell Doctrine criteria at once. There was no clear risk to the US from Iraq. Invasion was patently not a last resort: the stated aims of preventing Iraq from developing weapons of mass destruction were being met by a restored UN weapons inspection team. The force used, though certainly adequate to the task of defeating the bedraggled Iraqi army, was not strong enough to actually control the territory invaded. Domestic support was shaky and ambivalent, never likely to withstand any serious military reversals. And the exit strategy, in so far as it existed, was based on a vague fantasy of quick victory, huge Iraqi enthusiasm for the invaders and a smooth transition to a strong and gratefully pro-American democracy. It is doubtful that any great power has ever embarked on a military campaign with such a clear understanding that its own conditions for success were so starkly absent.

How did this happen? Vietnam had taught America the limits of power. The experience of defeat had provided a lesson in the reality that vast wealth and military superiority do not in themselves generate unlimited power. The US undoubtedly had the ability, in open conflict, to kill many more of the enemy's troops than they could kill of the US's. But Vietnam had made it clear that this ability was useful only up to a point. Its meaning depended on other factors: the reactions of other countries and of the civilian populations both of the country where the fighting was taking place and of the US itself.

Politics, both global and local, turned might into power, and politics are always subtle and complex. In the political domain, the means and the end are intertwined. Troops, ships, tanks, planes and helicopters can help to shape the political context, but they are, at best, the scalpel. They can never be the surgeon.

Learning this had cost the US oceans of blood, tons of treasure and an abyss of lost innocence. How could something so hard won be so quickly discarded?

The Politics of Arrogance

The US, the most militarily powerful nation the world has ever known, projected the bulk of its offensive capacity halfway around the world to attack a country which posed no real threat in March 2003.

The Prussian strategist Karl Von Clausewitz famously wrote, 'War is nothing but a continuation of politics (or policies) with the admixture of other means.'[76] In 2003 Von Clausewitz would have asked what policy objectives the US was pursuing. The question was crushingly obvious: how do you know you have succeeded if you do not know what your aims are?

Whatever the aims of those in Washington who so wanted this war, who invested so much of their political capital, risked their nation's future and possibly the stability of the world to provoke this war, were, they had little, if anything, to do with the aims they announced. In their myopic arrogance they did not even bother to subsequently defend those aims. They had merely been advanced as dross to satisfy us little ill-informed people.

In May 2003 Jack Straw told the BBC that 'it's not crucially important' whether the US and British occupation forces found WMD in Iraq.[77] In the same month Paul Wolfowitz, perhaps the prime architect of the war, would admit to *Vanity Fair*: 'For bureaucratic reasons we settled on one issue, weapons of mass destruction, because it was the one reason everyone could agree on.'[78] The bureaucratic reasons referred to here cover international law and much of what most people might regard as norms of civilised human behaviour at the beginning of our twenty-first century.

Donald Rumsfeld told a Senate committee in July 2003 that the US and Britain had not invaded Iraq 'because we had discovered dramatic new evidence of

Iraq's pursuit of weapons of mass murder.' The US acted because it saw 'existing evidence in a new light, through the prism of our experience on September 11th.'[79] Such comments would have been unthinkable just two months earlier, in March 2003, for then we were being warned of an imminent threat from Iraq, one that only a pre-emptive war could save us from.

Colin Powell's concerns that the thin arguments in support of such a war might explode in the faces of those who advanced them had come to pass. But much more had already exploded by then, including Iraq itself.

12

Baghdad and Bust: Catastrophic Success and Hillbilly Armour

'Had we had to do it over again we would look at the consequences of catastrophic success.'

– George W. Bush[1]

'And I just realised – we're on top. Rome fell, and Greece fell, and I thought, I like being an American.'

– Captain John Prior, US Sixth Infantry, Baghdad[2]

'It's hard to conceive that it would take more forces to provide stability in post-Saddam Iraq than it would take to conduct the war itself...hard to imagine.'

– Paul Wolfowitz[3]

'I have to deal with the fucking stupidest guy on the face of the earth almost every day.'

– General Tommy Franks, on Douglas Feith[4]

'Why do we soldiers have to dig through...the best of this scrap to put on our vehicles...Hillbilly armor?'

– Specialist Thomas Wilson, Tennessee National Guard[5]

Back to Babel: Case Studies Past, Present and Future

On 20 March 2003 the US, the UK and Australia invaded Iraq – ancient Mesopotamia, one of the cradles of our civilisation. Baghdad fell on 9 April and the occupation of Iraq followed.

There are few human activities older than one group seeking to impose its will on another by force. Yet in two essential ways this was a new war. Not since World War Two had democratic states initiated a war of choice against another sovereign state. Iraq had not attacked its aggressors, nor did it have any capacity to do so. The US and the UK had failed to convince the UN Security Council that Iraq posed a threat to world peace, and the Council had not authorised their invasion. They were operating beyond international law, or more simply, in violation of it.

In just three weeks the aggressors would topple the Iraqi government in a rapid war that challenged established military doctrines. They would succeed almost completely in their revolutionary blending of traditional firepower and innovative electronics, writing a new strategic doctrine in the sands, ruins and blood of Iraq. This novel success would be followed by one of the oldest challenges facing an aggressor, that of governing the territory and peoples they had conquered.

Their stunning success at the new would be matched by their abysmal failure at the old. Synthesising the two extremes into a single story is impossible, for they are linked only by the revolutionary ideology that now seeks to transform our world from the banks of another historic river, Washington's Potomac.

'If We Run Out of Batteries, This War is Screwed'

Donald Rumsfeld's primary mission is to transform the US military from a force designed to fight heavy armoured battles against the USSR into a light, lethal force capable of rapidly deploying and winning almost anywhere in the world. Out with the Powell Doctrine of overwhelming force, in with Rumsfeld's industry-inspired one of just enough, just-in-time. If the US intervention in Afghanistan had provided for some limited feasibility trials, the invasion of Iraq offered a complete laboratory.

In 1991 the US had provided almost 600,000 of the 1.2 million troops assembled to eject Iraqi forces from Kuwait. In 2002, Rumsfeld's Pentagon planned to conquer the whole of Iraq with a force eight to 10 times smaller, and one which would be almost exclusively American. Two developments made this (just) possible.

One was the decline of Iraq's armed forces. The defeat of 1991 had significantly weakened them, and the ensuing sanctions had prevented Iraq from replacing lost materiel. While Baghdad's various ground forces remained relatively impressive on paper, much of their equipment was not fully operational. During the 1991 war most of Iraq's modern fighter aircraft had been flown to Iran, where they had been interned. While the Iraqi air force continued to exist, many of its planes lacked vital parts and most of its pilots were under-trained.

More importantly, Iraq's air defence system was a shadow of its former self. By late 2002 the USAF and the RAF had flown almost 300,000 missions over Iraq to enforce the no-fly zones. These missions had destroyed many Iraqi anti-aircraft units and located most of the rest.[6] The invasion forces could count on complete air superiority. This meant that Iraqi ground forces, however powerful, could not manoeuvre to support each other. They had to fight more or less where they were positioned when their country was attacked.

The single greatest change in US forces during 1991 to 2003 was their integration of modern electronics and communications into their order of battle. US forces were able to communicate with and identify each other, to locate their positions, to operate at night or in poor visibility and to identify regular Iraqi units with ease. US air-dropped ordnance was infinitely more lethal – almost 70 per cent of the approximately 30,000 air-dropped weapons were precision guided.[7]

None of this was quite as smooth as Hollywood or the Pentagon might have us believe. Joshua Davis of *Wired* described the reality he found:

> I discovered...something entirely different from the shiny picture of techno-supremacy touted by the proponents of the Rumsfeld doctrine. I found an unsung corps of geeks improvising as they went, cobbling together a remarkable system from a hodgepodge of military-built networking technology, off-the-shelf gear, miles of Ethernet cable, and commercial software. And during two weeks in the war zone, I never heard anyone mention the revolution in military affairs.[8]

'Rumsfeld...You Just Get Tired Arguing with Him'

1003 Victor was the military codename for the US invasion of Iraq. Planning began in late 2001 for the first of Rumsfeld's transformed wars.

Much has been written about this planning process, but little is really known about it. The inner secrets are held by a handful of people, senior military figures and those close to the Office of the Secretary of Defense (OSD). While none of them have yet chosen to talk in any detail, two realities seem to have been confirmed by events and the limited insights we have been granted: 1) the level of dispute between the military and their masters has probably been exaggerated, and 2) the centre of foreign policy power in Washington, DC has shifted dramatically.

There were undoubtedly serious differences of opinion between senior officers and their political bosses. Such clashes are a normal part of any military planning exercise. Every soldier would prefer to assault an enemy position with 3,000 troops and 50 tanks rather than 300 troops and five tanks. Given the revolutionary approach Rumsfeld favoured, the 2001–2003 disputes were probably more acute. However, if the senior officers involved, and in particular the CENTCOM commander General Tommy Franks, had believed they were being tasked with war while being denied essential resources, we would have known about it in great detail.

General Franks may not have been overly content with what he was given, but he had to believe that he had been given nearly enough. Thomas E. White, US Secretary of the Army 2001–2002, said Rumsfeld just ground Franks down: 'If you grind away at the military guys long enough, they will finally say "Screw it, I'll do the best I can with what I have." The nature of Rumsfeld is that you just get tired arguing with him.'[9]

The shift of political power in Washington was away from the State Department and the National Security Council to the Department of Defense. This trend has been apparent for some years, but under the Bush administration it went into overdrive. The personal and ideological Rumsfeld–Cheney–Bush links played a major part, as did the role National Security Adviser Condoleezza Rice assigned herself.

In the absence of a collegiate government system where Cabinet ministers collectively tackle questions, either in full Cabinet or in sub-committee, Washington's National Security Council has partly fulfilled that role, allowing serving military officers, intelligence specialists, State Department diplomats and the political leadership to debate issues and approaches. Ms Rice saw her role as more of a conduit to the President, and under her stewardship the National Security Council became less of a forum. The consequent reduction in debate, and in particular the absence of professional military, intelligence and diplomatic input, was to impact negatively on war planning, US allies and above all on the post-war situation.

The plan that finally emerged involved beginning hostilities with relatively few troops in-theatre, with reinforcements either en route or ready to be dispatched who could be fed into the conflict as required.

The major thrust would come from Kuwait (once Saudi Arabia had made it clear its territory would not be available) to the south. This would comprise the equivalent of four heavy divisions, or around 120,000 troops supplied by the US 3rd Infantry Division, 101st Airborne Division and 1st Marine Division, together with the UK's reinforced 1st Armoured Division.

The secondary thrust would come via Turkey and the autonomous Kurdish areas of northern Iraq. Here the US 4th Infantry and the 3rd Armoured Cavalry Divisions (around 40,000 troops) would seize the northern oilfields around Kirkuk and Mosul before pushing south to secure the Sunni Arab heartland north of Baghdad.

Something of the order of 100 Special Forces teams (1,200–1,500 troops) from the US, UK and Australia would enter Iraqi territory from the south, the north and from Jordan to the west. These teams would largely act as spotters, calling air strikes on specific targets.

An essential element of the military plan recognised that not all Iraqi soldiers necessarily dreamed of dying to defend Saddam Hussein. An extensive psychological warfare campaign was planned, with telephone calls to Iraqi commanders asking them to surrender, combined with leaflet drops and broadcasts instructing unit commanders how their troops should be marshalled to indicate surrender. There would be no major pre-invasion air campaign as it was not felt to be necessary; the air and ground attacks would happen in tandem.

US military reinforcements were designated, but in the words of Douglas Feith, Under Secretary for Defense Policy, there would be numerous 'off ramps', or motorway exits, so that units which were not needed could be stood down before they arrived in-theatre.

Many senior officers were worried about how unrealistic some of the reinforcement scenarios appeared to be. Moving an army division is a daunting task. In February 2003 it had taken the US rail company CSX two weeks and 1,900 railway wagons to move the 101st Airborne to Jacksonville, Florida, where its materiel was loaded on ships for transport to Kuwait.[10] An airborne division, it should be noted, is a considerably lighter and easier entity to move than an armoured or mechanised infantry one.

The campaign was to be Baghdad centric, its purpose to capture, kill or depose Saddam Hussein. Planners understood that Iraq's government had been effectively reduced to one man, and that as long as he appeared to be in power, conventional hostilities would continue.

This was the plan. While it is understood that no military plan survives the first shot, this one began to come seriously unstuck before it was ever activated. On 1 March 2003 the Turkish parliament voted to refuse US forces the use of Turkish territory for an invasion of Iraq. This defeat, by a narrow margin, has been laid squarely at the door of inadequate and heavy-handed action by Washington.[11]

Gambling from Dora Farms to San Diego

The CIA assured the White House on 19 March that Saddam Hussein and his family were staying in concrete bunkers at a specific location at Dora Farms near Baghdad. The President decided it was too good an opportunity to miss. He ordered a strike using F-117 stealth aircraft armed with satellite-guided bombs, followed by Cruise missiles. It is a mark of the exponential progress of US military communications that the air war commander, Lieutenant General Michael Moseley, was able to quickly mount a mission from Saudi Arabia. The Dora Farms target was hit – only Saddam was not there. After the war US forces found there were not any bunkers there either.[12] Iraqi forces replied to the raid by firing short-range missiles into Kuwait and torching some southern oil wells. US forces invaded. The actual start of the war was triggered 24 hours early by a failed gamble.

The opening land war was largely successful. US and UK forces secured many of the key oil installations in the Rumayla field and the vital Faw peninsula. UK forces, with US Marines in support, quickly 'captured' the Iraqi port of Umm Quasr. With hindsight, the Umm Quasr experience would illustrate a key weakness of the campaign. Although troops took the harbour, it would take them several days to secure the area, and even longer to clear the port for use. Iraqi resistance was tougher, and different, from what had been anticipated.

The degree of Iraqi resistance came as a surprise to many. US military planning anticipated up to 64,000 Iraqi prisoners of war. After the fall of Baghdad, the Occupying Powers held just 6,200 Iraqi POWs.[13] Some had fought and many had fallen, but the majority had just gone home to wait. US Lieutenant General William Wallace was the victim of a media stampede when he told *The New York Times* that enemy tactics had been 'a bit' different from what had been war-gamed against. Most accounts lost the 'a bit', exaggerating General Wallace's degree of concern.[14]

A column of Iraqi T-55 tanks, probably from the 51st Division, whose surrender had been so often announced, charged the UK's 7th Armoured – the Desert Rats – from Basra. These 50-year-old tanks, with an effective range of around 1,000 metres and no air cover, took on British Challengers which have a range of 4,000 metres. This was either foolhardy or the stuff of heroics, as in the charge of the British Light Brigade at Balaclava in 1854, or Polish cavalry on horseback attacking German Panzers with drawn sabres in September 1939.

Over 30 Apache AH-64D attack helicopters of the US 11th Aviation Regiment lifted off into the pre-dawn darkness of 24 March to attack Iraqi Republican Guard units. US intelligence logged 50 calls from mobile phones along the choppers' route. As they approached a small town, somebody cut the electricity supply. This was the signal for everybody to fire into the air as the Apaches swept invisibly overhead. One chopper was shot down and 33 others were hit. The 11th Aviation Regiment was no longer battle worthy. Lieutenant General Wallace was to observe: 'We're dealing with a country in which everybody has a weapon, and when they fire them all into the air at the same time, it's tough.'[15]

Appalling weather, sandstorms and rain reduced the effectiveness of US air power between 24–26 March. The 101st Airborne's helicopters were grounded and its trucks had yet to arrive from Kuwait. The 3rd Infantry Division had not been resupplied with food, water or ammunition since it had left Kuwait and was now down to a couple of days' supplies.[16] It was during these difficult days that Jessica Lynch's 507th Maintenance Battalion strayed into Nasiriya.

As the weather improved, the US dash north to Baghdad regained its pace, although it became obvious that it was stretched perilously thin. The only in-theatre reserves, US and British airborne troops had to be committed between Baghdad and the Kuwaiti border to secure supply lines. The US 4th Infantry Division was still at sea, en route from Turkey.

The other reality that became clear was that for a variety of reasons, most Iraqis were sitting the war out. The GIs were not receiving the kind of welcome they had been led to expect. Kanan Makiya, whose brilliant 1989 book, *Republic of Fear*, had done so much to awaken the outside world to Saddam's monstrosity at a time when most of the Western world was supporting him, had predicted, with the wishful thinking for which refugees from hideous regimes can be forgiven, that invading forces would be greeted with 'sweets and flowers'. Professor Fouad Ajami, a Middle East scholar at the Johns Hopkins School of Advanced International Studies, coined the oft-quoted 'kites and boom boxes'[17] phrase to describe the tumultuous greetings that awaited British and US Forces in Iraq. US Deputy Secretary of Defense Paul Wolfowitz promised that 'an explosion of joy will greet our soldiers.'[18] They were wrong, as post-Saddam Baghdad would show.

On 9 April 2003 US Marines attached a tow rope to the Saddam statue in Firdos Square, Baghdad. The world watched as the Marine track took up the slack and Saddam's effigy buckled, then crashed to the ground. Baghdad had fallen. The Western media devoted a lot of coverage to the understandable, if not over-diplomatic, gesture in which a young Marine hung the US flag over Saddam's face, but largely ignored a much more significant image.

At least two cameras were filming the event – one close in with the Marines, the other overlooking the square. The close-in camera provided familiar images of a popular revolutionary mob during the fall of a dictatorship. The camera overlooking the square showed less than a thousand Iraqi spectators watching US Marines topple a statue.

When Iraqis did flood onto their streets it was for the predicted frenzy of chaos and looting. Captain David G. Fivecoat of the 101st Airborne was to record the process as he searched for a building in Baghdad to serve as divisional headquarters: 'First they removed the furniture; then the doors, windows and light fixtures; then banisters, light switches and wires; and then, finally, they would take the building down, brick by brick.' On the evening of 11 April, Donald Rumsfeld was to dismiss reports of looting in Baghdad as wildly exaggerated, arguing, 'The images you are seeing on television you are seeing over and over and over, and it's the same picture of some person walking out of some building with a vase.'[19] US troops in Iraq could only conclude that the Secretary was either very poorly informed or was lying.

The fall of Baghdad signalled the end of what President Bush was to later term 'major combat operations', but it would not be until 24 April, two weeks after the fall of Baghdad, that the first US troops arrived in Falluja. The US had toppled Saddam, but was far from having conquered Iraq.

Probably something close to 20,000 people died during the 'active' phase of the war, up to the end of April 2003, and maybe as many as 50,000. The dead included 159 US and UK troops and 13 journalists.[20] The figures for Iraqi casualties are less precise. The best estimates for civilian casualties range from 5,425 to 7,041. Iraqi military casualties are even more difficult, with estimates ranging from 13,500 to 45,000 dead. Most observers agree that a figure closer to the lower end is the more likely. That there should be such a massive imbalance in the death toll between the invaders and the invaded was not, in the twenty-first-century world, a shock to anyone. In that very limited sense, the neoconservatives' faith in the might of the US armed forces was justified. Among the dead, things turned out exactly as they thought they would. For the living it was a different question.

General Tommy Franks, using fewer troops than he would have liked, ran a high-risk campaign, exposing his supply lines – and won. High-risk strategies that work are defined as brilliant improvisations. Ones that do not go down in history as disasters.

The outcome of the war was never really in question – the US Army would crush its dilapidated Iraqi counterpart. What was in question was what the US would do next. Part of the answer would come from its Commander-in-Chief.

On 1 May 2003 President Bush landed on the aircraft carrier USS *Abraham Lincoln* off the California coast. He would declare victory, that 'major combat operations' in Iraq were over. The *Lincoln*'s superstructure was draped with a banner proclaiming 'Mission Accomplished'. The White House would first suggest that Bush had been flown in on a S-3B Viking jet 'because the *Lincoln* was too far off the California coast for a helicopter.'[21] Later, according to the Associated Press, administration officials 'acknowledged positioning the massive ship to provide the best TV angle for Bush's speech, with the sea as his background instead of the San Diego coastline.'[22]

Was the President as ill informed as his Secretary of Defense had been three weeks earlier? Was he lying? Or worse, was he telling the truth? That the US had no real interest in or responsibility for Iraq now that the Baghdad regime had been toppled?

Bush began the war with a gamble on killing Saddam. Now he was gambling that having embarked on a war of choice, Washington could also choose when and how to end it. The difference was that before the war nobody outside the Washington decision-making circuit had much of a say – now the Oval Office had invited 24 million Iraqis into the loop.

'China Shop Rules – You Break It, You Own It' – Colin Powell[23]

General Tommy Franks flew into the broken Baghdad he now owned on 16 April 2003. The worst of the looting was over. He met with his senior commanders in Abu Ghraib North Palace and told them their job was to prepare for a steady drawing down of US troops in Iraq. The first departures would be in 60 days, and by September US forces would be down from 140,000 to a reinforced division, some 20,000–30,000 troops. President Bush joined them for a teleconference and congratulated them on a job well done. The then Secretary of the Army, Thomas White, confirmed this approach: 'Our working budgetary assumption was that 90 days after completion of the operation, we would withdraw the first 50,000 and then every 30 days we'd take out another 50,000 until everybody was back.'[24]

The day before in Washington at a meeting of the US National Security Council, the Pentagon had briefed the President on replacing US troops with four divisions of peacekeeping troops from other countries. One of these would be British, essentially the British forces already present around Basra. The second would be a NATO division, the third a division composed of troops from Arab countries and the final would be an international division under Polish command. A NATO division, as distinct from a British one, given the German deployment in Afghanistan and the Balkans, essentially meant a French division.

It was truly surreal to suggest that France or the Arab states, without having been consulted, would be willing to commit troops to a US-led and directed occupation of Iraq, having so strongly opposed the invasion. On this basis, Donald Rumsfeld cancelled the deployment of the US Army's 1st Cavalry Division on 21 April.

The US would eventually seek to persuade India to commit a division. New Delhi declined in July 2003, saying that India would only consider sending troops as part of a UN force.[25] By July the wheels had already come off in Iraq, and the US invitation to commit troops to a failing policy into which the troop-supplying nation could have no input was one that was all too easy to decline.

Condoleezza Rice was to spell out what passed for the Bush administration's post-war planning: 'The concept was that we would defeat the army, but the institutions would hold, everything from ministries to police forces.'[26] That was not planning, it was wishful thinking.

The mess of post-Saddam Iraq was largely Washington's making. The administration had been warned and warned and warned again, but had chosen to ignore what it did not wish to hear.

'Facts Are Fine So Long as They Bolster the President's Case'[27]

In late October 2001 the State Department, traditionally responsible for post-war administration within the US government, began the process of preparing for 'transition' in Iraq. It announced its Future of Iraq Project in March 2002. In May 2002 Congress provided $5 million to fund it. The Project was headed by State Department official Thomas Warrick, who organised several conferences and seminars, eventually assembling 200 Iraqi exiles into 17 working groups with US officials and consultants. These exiles came from widely different backgrounds and included the exiled Iraqi intellectual Kanan Makiya.[28]

These groups covered a wide range of issues –

Democratic Principles Procedures (Makiya wrote most of its report), Transitional Justice, Public Finance, Oil and Energy, Water, Agriculture and Environment, Preserving Iraq's Cultural Heritage, Education, Free Media, etc. Three themes ran through many of the reports: the importance of infrastructure (electricity and water in particular – 'Stressed importance of getting electrical grid up and running immediately – key to water system, jobs. Could go a long way to determining Iraqis' attitudes toward Coalition forces'), the need to retain and restructure the army and how anarchic and disorderly Iraq would be immediately after Saddam was toppled.

In March 2003 the Project published its 2,500-page, 13-volume report, which the CIA endorsed.[29] *The Future of Iraq Report* sought more to describe conditions and priorities rather than precise steps. It laid a basis for those whose job it was to plan such steps.

In May 2002 the CIA began a series of war-game exercises to develop best- and worst-case scenarios for Iraq post-Saddam. A recurring theme of these was the likelihood of civil disorder in Baghdad. Representatives of the Defense Department participated in these until Rumsfeld's office (OSD) reprimanded them and ordered them not to join future meetings.[30] One practical and one ideological reason for the Pentagon's attitude suggest themselves. The practical reason was that the OSD did not want anything which suggested a war in Iraq might be difficult or expensive to circulate while it was seeking to persuade the US that toppling Saddam would be easy. The ideological reason was that the neoconservatives simply did not trust US diplomats, or spooks, to stay 'on-message'. Iraq was going to be an OSD affair, and nobody else's.

The Senate Foreign Relations Committee invited an expert panel to address it on 31 July 2002 on the implications of war with Iraq. Phebe Marr from the US National Defense University warned that the US 'should assume that it cannot get the results it wants on the cheap.' Rend Rahim Francke, then an Iraqi exile serving on the Future of Iraq Project and later Iraqi ambassador to the US, was more specific: 'the system of public security will break down, because there will be no functioning police force, no civil service and no justice system.'

In September 2002 the US Agency for International Development (USAID) brought together some of its officials and representatives of various humanitarian NGOs to begin contingency planning for post-war Iraq. One of their early priorities was to ask for a directive exempting US NGO representatives from the ban on US citizens travelling to Iraq. Sandra Mitchell of the International Rescue Committee explained that 'the reason we were so insistent in this case was the precarious situation that already existed in Iraq. The internal infrastructure was shot, and you could not easily swing resources in from neighboring countries.' The NGOs never got a response, despite repeated requests.

They warned about looting and anarchy in the immediate aftermath of the war, but were told this war would be different. The NGOs also tried to draw officials' attention to the responsibilities of an Occupying Power under the Fourth Geneva Convention. US officials responded that since US forces would be liberators rather than occupiers, the convention did not apply. On 30 January 2003 the International Rescue Committee publicly warned that law and order in Iraq would break down post-war unless US forces acted immediately. Refugees International issued a similar warning a week later.

When the US Senate authorised President Bush to go to war in mid-October 2002, the Strategic Studies Institute of the US War College began a post-war planning exercise. The draft report of this exercise, *Reconstructing Iraq: Insights, Challenges, and Missions for Military Forces in a Post-Conflict Scenario*, was finished by late December. The report warned of chaos following regime change and on the need to retain the Iraqi army:

'To tear apart the Army in the war's aftermath could lead to the destruction of one of the only forces for unity within the society.'

The Council on Foreign Relations issued a report in late January 2003 on *Guiding Principles for U.S. Post-war Conflict Policy in Iraq*. The report warned that 'U.S. and Coalition military units will need to pivot quickly from combat to peacekeeping operation in order to prevent post-conflict Iraq from descending into anarchy.'

Secretary of the Army, US General Eric K. Shineski, told a hearing of the US Senate's Armed Services Committee in February 2003 that 'something of the order of several hundred thousand soldiers' would be needed to successfully occupy Iraq.[31] Defense Secretary Donald Rumsfeld dismissed Shineski's estimate as being grossly inflated. Civilian Defense Department officials suggested that General Shineski did not understand the Bush administration's plan for Iraq and was ill informed.[32] Shineski was effectively fired by having his successor named over a year before he was due to retire.

A broad spectrum of US foreign policy experts were all warning the Pentagon and the White House of the uphill job Iraq might prove post-Saddam. Not only was nobody listening, but some were working hard in the opposite direction. Military aides at the National Security Council prepared a briefing called *Force Security in Seven Recent Stability Operations* for Condoleezza Rice and her then deputy, Stephen J. Hadley, on forces needed for occupation duties. If the Kosovo model was used, the US would need 480,000 troops in Iraq. If Bosnia was the model, it would need 364,000. If Afghanistan was picked as the model, only 13,900 troops would be needed. The Afghan model was selected. The White House's special envoy for Afghanistan, James F. Dobbins, commented, 'They preferred to find a successful nation building model that was not associated with the previous administration, and Afghanistan offered a much more congenial answer in terms of what would be required in terms of inputs, including troops.'[33]

In December 2002 President Bush decided that the

Pentagon, not the State Department, would be responsible for administering occupied Iraq. The Pentagon established its Office of Reconstruction and Humanitarian Assistance (ORHA) under General Jay Garner on 20 January 2003, just eight weeks before the invasion of Iraq. General Garner had distinguished himself in organising humanitarian aid for Kurdish refugees in Iraq after the 1991 Gulf War. Initially the creation of the ORHA was seen as just another skirmish in the turf war between the State and Defense Departments.

However, it soon became clear that something deeper was involved when Garner sought to recuperate some of the State Department's work, and in particular hired Tom Warrick for his team. Rumsfeld and Wolfowitz threw out both the work and the personnel of the Future of Iraq Project. Tom Warrick, who knew much more about Iraq than virtually anyone else in the administration, was removed from Garner's team on the personal instructions of Donald Rumsfeld. Garner and his planners had to start more or less from scratch. Judith Yaphe, a former CIA analyst and a leading expert on Iraqi history, pointed out that 'even the Messiah couldn't have organized a program in that short a time.'[34] In the beginning of February 2003, the ORHA had a staff of four.

The ORHA did make some contingency plans for post-war chaos. An ORHA document was sent to senior US generals on 26 March, listing 16 Baghdad institutions that 'merit securing as soon as possible to prevent further damage, destruction and or pilferage of records and assets.' The Iraqi National Bank was first on the list, the National Museum came second and the Oil Ministry came last, sixteenth out of 16. In the event, the Oil Ministry was the only Iraqi institution US troops guarded.[35]

The combat forces of the US 3rd Infantry Division and the US Marines which took Baghdad were ill trained and ill equipped to administer the city. The decision to deploy vital peace-enforcement military police units was not made until late April 2003, and those units then had to deploy from the continental US.[36] This was a fatal consequence of Rumsfeld's obsession with a lean 'war on the cheap'. The US had barely enough troops to win its Iraq War and far too few to win its Iraq peace. General Franks was to comment on Mr Feith's (limited) intellectual abilities as he argued for more, and more appropriate, troops. He was concerned that not only did he not have enough troops, he had the wrong kind of troops. He lacked civil affairs and military police units in particular.

Garner Tries His Hand

The still-emerging ORHA staff flew to Kuwait during the US invasion. Getting from there to Baghdad illustrated a weakness that would bedevil US efforts in Iraq. Former US Ambassador Timothy Carney, of Garner's staff, recalled, 'I should have had an inkling of the trouble ahead for our reconstruction team in Iraq from the hassle we had just trying to get there.'[37] On 24 April, 15 days after Baghdad had fallen, the core ORHA team still could not get priority on US military flights from Kuwait. The US political entities in Iraq, first ORHA and later the Coalition Provisional Authority (CPA), never exercised any authority over US forces. They would have to beg for every helicopter and vehicle they needed. The line of command ran from Baghdad to the Pentagon, then from the Pentagon back to the military. It was not a recipe for speedy action.

In its short life the ORHA had given priority to preparing for a refugee crisis. As the Iraqis had not used the chemical weapons they did not have and as there had been relatively little fighting in the cities, the refugee crisis never materialised.

The other two priorities of the ORHA were organising reconstruction efforts and recycling the Iraqi army. Garner is a 'can do' pragmatist, as his largely unsung efforts in Iraq testify. The ORHA plan was to retain at least three divisions of the Iraqi army, which was in large part made up of some 275,000 conscripts who were by definition largely untainted by the former regime. An initial $650,000 contract was awarded by the ORHA to the US MPRI company headed by retired General Carl Vuono, former US Army Chief of Staff, to retrain the Iraqi army. Another US consultancy, RONCO, developed a screening programme to remove officers who were too closely identified with Saddam.

General Josh P. Abizaid, then Franks's deputy, endorsed the proposals in March. In early May 2003 Lieutenant General David McKiernan met with Faris Naima, the former head of Iraq's Al Bakr Military College and a returned exile. Mr Naima had already elaborated a plan for three Iraqi divisions, a new Defence Ministry and a reformed police force. Colonel Hughes from the ORHA staff also met a group of Iraqi officers who called themselves the Independent Military Group. They had removed the computers containing personnel records from the Iraqi Ministry of Defence before the war and were able to offer the ORHA a list of 70,000 names, including the military police.[38] The US could have had a functioning Iraqi force in place by the end of June 2003. It might not have been perfect, but it would have existed, but Washington was about to compound its errors in Iraq, driving the final nail into the coffin of any hope of a smooth transition.

Coalition Provisional Authority (CPA)

Out of the blue the White House announced that the ORHA was dissolved, replaced by the CPA. General Garner was out, Paul Bremer was in. Bremer, a former diplomat, had no nation-building experience, but he was close to the neoconservatives. He arrived in Baghdad with an ideological mission. He saw his task not as a 'can do' one of getting Iraq more or less ticking over again, but as one of transforming it into an ultra free market, US-style democracy.

Within a month of his arrival, Bremer was to issue three vice-regal decrees – disbanding the Iraqi army, announcing a sweeping de-Baathification process[39] and finally a ban on state-owned Iraqi companies bidding for reconstruction contracts.[40] This meant that the US Army and less than 20,000 troops from other nations now had to police the whole of Iraq – alone. Their task would be somewhat complicated by the fact that there were now over 350,000 unemployed, angry and humiliated Iraqi soldiers rattling around a country awash with arms. It meant that civil servants, school principals, university professors and local and regional authority officials, all of whom had been obliged to become members of the Baath Party during its 30-plus years of dictatorship, could not play a part in running or rebuilding their country. It also meant that upwards of 400,000 workers in around 200 Iraqi state-owned companies, the ones who ran the oil industry and the electricity, water, telecoms and sewage utilities, could not bid for contracts to repair or maintain those services.

'Give Me Security, and I'll Give You Electricity'

Dr Karim W. Kassam, director general of Iraq's electricity commission, summed up the feelings of many Iraqis with the statement 'Give me security, and I'll give you electricity', made after looters had pilfered underground cables and then carted off the computers that regulate power distribution. Thieves then stole 25 of Dr Kassam's guards' 30 patrol cars, emptied warehouses of spare parts, ransacked substations and shot up transmission lines. Armed bandits stole the only cable splicer in central Iraq, and then, to add insult to injury, another group of gunmen stole Dr Kassam's own car.[41]

During the US invasion, Baghdad's main telephone exchange was twice hit by cruise missiles. Following the US arrival, the exchange's director inspected the premises, found that most of the equipment had survived and that it could be made operational within months. He duly informed the Coalition authorities, who did precisely nothing while the exchange was ransacked and burned under the noses of US troops. Such stupidity led *The Daily Telegraph*'s Con Coughlin to write in May 2003, a little more than a month after the fall of Baghdad, that 'US troops in Iraq are no longer being seen as liberators, but as occupiers – and incompetent ones at that. The goodwill gained from ousting Saddam has turned to resentment.'[42]

Sabah Al-Ani has 40 years of experience with the Iraqi General Company for Water Projects and is one of Iraq's top experts in water treatment, having kept the country's systems working through droughts, floods and three wars. His company was working on the reconstruction of the Sharkh Dijlah, or East Tigris, water treatment plant before the CPA ordered them off. The CPA subsequently awarded a $16 million contact to the Bechtel Corporation for the work. Bechtel spent four months checking Mr Al-Ani's plans, found they were adequate and then ordered parts from the same suppliers the General Company for Water Projects had selected. Mr Al-Ani, as a state employee, is still paid. He spends his days sitting in his office, reading, playing video games and chatting with his colleagues. Work on the Sharkh Dijlah project stopped when foreign subcontractors left the site for security reasons. According to the Iraqi Health Ministry, 40 per cent of child hospital admissions in Baghdad are for gastrointestinal problems related to poorly treated water.[43]

CPA specialists inspected the Daura electricity station in southern Baghdad in the summer of 2003. They decided to refurbish and develop it to achieve an output of 500 megawatts by 1 June 2004. The CPA hired German and Russian specialists and placed Daura at the head of their priority list. The German contractors fled in May 2004 and the Russians followed a month later after two of their engineers had been killed. In the summer of 2004 Daura was generating 100 megawatts, half of what it had managed a year before. In its turbine room a slogan is painted on the wall – 'Long Live the Resistance'.[44]

In the Best of Cases: 'We Blatantly Failed to Get It Right'

Exploring the successes and failures of the US occupation of Iraq and touching on some of the historic and ethnic realities of that country merits a book of its own. The following illustrations of the CPA's approach should provide a flavour.

There is the story of Andrew Erdmann, a 36-year-old former postgraduate history student at Harvard who had just finished his thesis on 'Americans' Search for Victory in the Twentieth Century'. When working for the State Department's accomplished Director of Policy Planning, Richard Haass, Dr Erdmann had prepared a memo on successful post-war reconstructions with an eye to a likely invasion of Iraq. His memo, stressing the importance of international support and of having enough troops on the ground to guarantee security, was circulated to Secretary of State Colin Powell, Vice-President Dick Cheney, Secretary of Defense Donald Rumsfeld and National Security Adviser Condoleezza Rice.

A year after Erdmann spelled out the lessons of history for his bosses, he was installed as Iraq's new Minister for Higher Education and Scientific Research. When the journalist George Packer interviewed Erdmann for *The New Yorker* in late 2003, he found that the Minister for Higher Education could barely remember yesterday. He was shell shocked, not least by the murder of one of his own American guards, a 22-year-old soldier who was waiting for Erdmann to come out of a meeting at Baghdad University. 'I can't think historically,' Erdmann told Packer. 'There've been times when I don't even know what I did forty-eight hours before. I try. It's like a test for myself. Can I remember what I did the day before? I eventually can, but it takes effort. That's not a good situation. You should be able to remember what you did in the last twenty-four hours.'[45] Memory had collapsed into amnesia.

Most of the CPA hiring was done by White House and Pentagon personnel offices with posts going to people with connections with the Bush administration or the Republican Party. A 24-year-old who had sought a job at the White House found himself in Baghdad with responsibility for reorganising the Baghdad Stock Exchange. It never opened.[46]

Congress voted for $18.4 billion for reconstruction aid for Iraq. When the CPA disbanded itself, transferring power to the interim Iraqi government 48 hours early for security reasons, it emerged that only $400 million of that money had been disbursed. For over a year, the CPA had spent Iraqi money, almost $20 billion of it, from oil sales. KPMG auditors were hired to oversee this expenditure in April 2004, almost a year after the CPA had been created. The auditors found that accounting consisted of 'spreadsheets and pivot tables maintained by a single accountant.' KPMG was also denied access to records on 'sole-source contracts', contracts awarded without tenders, like the $1.4 billion one Halliburton received.[47]

Larry Diamond, Senior Fellow at the Hoover Institution of Stanford University, who served as an adviser to the CPA, summed up the sorry tale: 'We blatantly failed to get it right. When you look at the record, it's impossible to escape the conclusion that we squandered an unprecedented opportunity.'[48]

Perhaps the most stunning reality is the fact that even in the best of cases the US could not have invaded and transformed Iraq on its own. If the State Department's planning exercise had been allowed to continue, an interim Iraqi authority could possibly have emerged following the fall of Baghdad. This would most likely have been a relatively pragmatic structure bringing together the best, or the least unacceptable, elements of the old Iraqi state (civil servants, state companies and armed forces) with political parties, returning exiles, ethnic and religious representatives, intellectuals, etc. Whether it would have led to a flowering of democracy is another question. Kanan Makiya condemned the drift towards a new authoritarian regime in Baghdad.[49] Achieving even this modest result could have quickly furnished up to 200,000 Iraqi soldiers and police.

Alternatively, if the US was determined to administer and rehabilitate Iraq, guaranteeing security and economic development while democratic institutions were encouraged (the German or Japanese post-World War Two models often cited by the neoconservatives), it would have required a security force of around 300,000, together with teams of civil administrators in every province of Iraq. The US was, and remains, incapable of fielding such an effort. Washington would have needed significant inputs from NATO, its Asian allies, geographically removed Arab countries (Algeria, Egypt, Morocco, Tunisia) and others to provide the 150,000 necessary troops, police and civil affairs specialists. Such an effort could only have been mounted on the basis of a UN Security Council resolution. For such a resolution to be conceivable, there would have had to have been a clearly demonstrated need or threat, which there was not.[50]

Even the traditional imperialist role of first invading and then presenting the conquered populace with their new ruler (as the British had done in Iraq post-World War One, and which the neoconservatives toyed with with Ahmad Chalabi before denouncing him as an Iranian spy) would have required more troops than the US could deploy. In March 2004 the US Army had 5,000 troops in its 25 civil affairs battalions (the units which provide interim military government services), but only 200 of these were full-time professionals; the rest were reserves. There were a mere 1,500 full-time military police, with a further 2,500 in the reserves. The Pentagon had mobilised 2,000 'weekend soldiers' from National Guard artillery units and was urgently retraining them to serve as military police. All 13,000 peacekeeping troops would only have been a drop, however useful a drop, in the Iraqi bucket.[51]

In short, whatever the neoconservative bluster from Washington, the US, our sole surviving superpower, simply does not have the means to realise its foreign ambitions. There are echoes here of our other recently deceased and unlamented superpower.

Back in the USSA?

There are ways in which the United States of America today resembles its former rival superpower, the Union of Soviet Socialist Republics, just before the latter imploded. While one should be careful about pushing historical comparisons too far, this one is valid in three key respects.

Firstly, both powers were committed to maintaining armed forces which their respective economies could not afford. Secondly, both powers launched foreign adventures of choice – the USSR in Afghanistan and the US in Iraq – for which there was no obvious rationale. Thirdly, the political systems in both powers had become ossified to a degree that all but precluded meaningful reform.

Fifteen years before the US invasion of Iraq, the Reagan administration understood the folly of the Soviet invasion of Afghanistan. In 1988, the official Department of Defense publication *Soviet Military Power: An Assessment of the Threat* noted 'the unacceptability of [the Soviet] attempt to dictate to another sovereign nation through the introduction of Soviet troops.' It also offered an incisive analysis of the reasons why the Soviets had 'seriously miscalculated' in undertaking the invasion in 1979:

- 'It assumed that its client government in Kabul could establish sufficient domestic support to sustain its power and eventually take on the military burden of defending itself.'

- 'It expected US and worldwide condemnation for the Soviet invasion to subside quickly.'
- 'It miscalculated the ability of the Afghan nationalist resistance to defend its country.'[52]

Change the locations and the names, and the 'serious miscalculations' could apply to Iraq in 2005.

The Iraq adventure parallels the reasons for these miscalculations, and indeed for the ultimate collapse of Soviet power. The communist set-up withered from within because it had become a faith-based system in which whenever the facts did not conform with the governing ideology, it was the facts that were deemed to be problematic. Apparatchiks and experts had learned over time that it was pure folly to do one's job competently and to raise problems so that they could be addressed. They had been taught that doubt was not a professional duty but a symptom of unbelief and thus a disqualification for office. Americans had looked at the consequences of this self-delusion and smiled, secure in the knowledge that in their open democracy such a culture could never take root.

Yet precisely this process had unfolded in the run-up to the Iraq War. Both of the thought systems that were meant to govern big decisions on the use of military power — the Powell Doctrine and the Bush doctrine of pre-emptive wars based on intelligence — had been abandoned in favour of an act of faith. Conscientious officials who told the truth as they honestly understood it were punished as heretics.[53]

Limping into the Future

If the US lacked the means to realise its Iraqi ambitions when it invaded in March 2003, the consequences of that ill-conceived action have significantly weakened US military power. With around 150,000 troops deployed to Iraq and other deployments, something close to 90 per cent of its military capacity is deployed outside the US, or is recovering from the effects of such deployment. The

US Army is stretched to the limit to even maintain the inadequate numbers of the wrong kind of troops it has in Iraq. Almost all its main strike capacity is committed there and is being stationed there for longer and longer stretches of duty. General Abizaid has reintroduced 12-month tours of duty for US troops, the system used in Vietnam, commenting, 'We've done it before, we can do it again.'[54] Upwards of 50,000 reservists and National Guard soldiers have been mobilised.

In 2003 the US Army had to cancel almost a third of its scheduled training exercises.[55] At the end of that year Lieutenant General Ricardo Sanchez had warned that Army units in Iraq were 'struggling just to maintain...relatively low readiness rates' on their main combat systems, M-1 Abrams tanks, Bradley fighting vehicles, anti-mortar radars and helicopters.[56] In December 2004 House Armed Services Committee figures showed that only 10 per cent of medium trucks and 15 per cent of heavy ones in Iraq were armoured.[57] The situation on Iraq's roads had become so dangerous by December 2004 that the US Air Force stepped in to replace road convoys with flights, moving 450 tons of cargo a day.[58]

The Army is reeling from the consequences of fighting a much longer war than it anticipated. The US armoured fist is breaking down. In peacetime armoured vehicles are normally transported by truck and spend relatively little time travelling on their own tracks. The main US tank, the M-1 Abrams, normally averages 809 miles a year, but Abrams in Iraq are clocking up 3,600. The Bradley AFVs, designed for 872 miles, are hitting a similar figure. The ubiquitous Humvees, accustomed to 2,640 miles a year, are clocking up 7,400.

As soldiers weld pieces of Hillbilly armour to their vehicles, their chassis, springs, shock absorbers and engines struggle with weight they were never designed to handle. The Army has ordered 12,500 armour kits for its still unarmoured Humvees. The Red River Army Depot at Texarkana, Texas is now struggling to launch an urgent project to refit Humvees with heavier suspensions, shock absorbers and 6.5 litre engines. Dennis L. Lewis, chief of the business office at the Red River Depot, admitted his frustration, saying, 'We'd like to produce them all today so the soldiers have their equipment, but…the reality is, there isn't the funding.'[59] The Army is still seeking 373,000 sets of personal body armour from its suppliers.

US military operations in Iraq are costing around $4.5 billion a month, while the monthly Afghan bill is running at just under $1 billion.[60] Defence and security expenditure is costing US taxpayers $42 million an hour. In Iraq, a Kalashnikov rifle sells for as little as $12 and an anti-tank rocket-propelled grenade (RPG) for around $800.[61]

Weakened with No Exit in Sight

Wishful thinking about the garden of delightful consequences that would bloom after the earth of Iraq had been watered with a little blood had taken the place of planning and foresight. The checks and balances of an independent legislature and a free media had failed. Ends and means had been hopelessly confused. To most people outside the US and to an increasing number within, this looked like a demonstration not of awesome power, but of a fundamental weakness.

The US showed what it could do — defeat an already degraded Middle Eastern army in a matter of weeks. The value of that demonstration was limited by the fact that it showed intelligent observers nothing they did not already know. In the process, the US also showed, rather more surprisingly to many of its allies but apparently not yet to itself, what it could not do. It could not turn dictatorship into democracy with a single wave of its military wand. It could not provide a quick fix to the historical problems of the Middle East. It could not control post-war Iraq. It could not install a friendly government, even with its troops on the streets. It could not stop terrorism.

The more grandiose ambitions that drove the war were in fact just as nebulous and distant in its aftermath. Israel was no closer to making a final settlement with the Palestinians. The supply of oil was no more secure and Islamic fundamentalists have a whole new failed state, awash with arms and US targets, where they can train and fight alongside an indigenous resistance which the interim Iraqi government estimates at 200,000 active members.

In the spring of 2003 the White House wanted to dazzle the world with a demonstration of US might. It failed. Two years later the US Army is tied down and weakened. Occupation force casualties have increased over tenfold since the fall of Baghdad, from 139 to almost 1,500, and recruitment is falling. Iraqi casualties are heading towards the 150,000 mark according to one US study.[62]

The US government invaded Iraq to prove that international institutions, weapons inspectors and policies of containment did not work and that the US offered the only available instrument capable of creating a world order. Washington convincingly proved the opposite – that it is incapable of establishing a Pax Americana. As it prepares to attack Iranian targets,[63] the second Bush administration is incapable of recognising reality, even the realities it has created. That leaves the rest of the world with a challenge.

13

A Post Washington World

'We don't just disagree on what America should be doing;
we disagree on what America is.'
                                        – Thomas L. Friedman[1]

'There is a Tide in the Affairs of Men.'
                                        – William Shakespeare[2]

'Dost thou not know, my son, with how little wisdom the world
is governed?'
                                        – Count Oxenstierna[3]

'History teaches us that men and nations behave wisely once they
have exhausted all other alternatives.'
                                        – Abba Eban[4]

The *USS Titanic*?

Had the *RMS Titanic* sailed serenely into New York on
16 April 1912, she would be a little-remembered
footnote in specialist naval histories. However, she
sank, largely due to the hubris-driven recklessness of
her owners, and became a legend. Will the US come to
be remembered for its many achievements in its first 225
years or for a spectacular wreck in the not-too-distant
future?

In *Post Washington* we have outlined many of the major weaknesses and challenges affecting the United States of America at the beginning our third millennium. The US has the capacity, the skills and the resources to address those challenges, some alone and some co-operatively with the rest of the world. The first step in such a process has to be a recognition that those weaknesses and challenges exist. For the moment, there are precious few signs of such recognition in Washington.

The second administration of George W. Bush seems not only determined to continue the errors of the first, but to compound them while maintaining its ostrich posture on problems – Problems? What problems?

Problems often begin as minor difficulties, but if consistently ignored they steadily grow to become major challenges. Over time, the unfixed loose roof tile allows water to rot the roof timbers to the point where the house collapses.

If the US does not act to correct its federal and trade deficits, the dollar will lose its position as the world's primary currency. There are already signs of central banks reducing their dollar holdings.[5]

If the US fails to invest in public education, it will find itself starved of the scientific and other skills its economy so desperately needs. A US government study has identified the increasing shortage of trained scientists as the second biggest threat facing the US.[6]

Most stark of all is the absence of any internal debate over its disastrous invasion of Iraq and the structural fault lines in its system of government which made such a disaster possible. President Bush awarded the Presidential Medal of Freedom, America's highest civil honour, to both the former US viceroy to Iraq, Paul Bremer, and the former CIA director George Tenet in December 2004. When governments start decorating the architects of their worst failures, it's time to worry.[7]

The US fled its Vietnam fiasco 35 years ago. America's rulers today are of that generation, yet the lessons of Vietnam remain unlearned or distorted. Those who articulate them are pilloried as traitors or fools. Worse, in this orchestrated ignorance, the US plans to invest more and more borrowed money in ever more sophisticated weaponry. Iraq is a horrifying failure of US 'hard power', yet the White House's response is to make the US better and better equipped to carry out similar missions. All the friends of the US can do is warn, but until the US itself wakes up to its dangerous realities, those friends remain essentially powerless, unable to affect systems and events that will profoundly affect them.

In the meantime, the world continues to turn, and how we manage it is a task that falls to what Washington newspeak refers to as ROW – the Rest of the World, us.

The Mindset Challenge

Our first challenge is to change our inherited assumption that the organisation of our planet and of our futures is largely determined by the US and our relations with it.

Since World War Two, and in particular since its final failed imperial fling of invading Egypt in the coyly named 'Suez Crisis' of 1956, the UK's political mindset has been fixed on the principle that the best interests of the UK are served by being as close as possible to the US. This has not always been a completely blank cheque – witness Harold Wilson's refusal to send troops to Vietnam or Margaret Thatcher's perceptive observation in a BBC radio interview that 'I am totally and utterly against communism and terrorism, but if you are going to pronounce a new law that wherever communism reigns against the will of their people, the United States shall enter – then we are going to have really terrible wars in the world.'[8] Yet Tony Blair, whatever his reasoning, could not have taken the UK to war against Iraq in 2003 if the belief that Britain could not afford to get out of step with the US had not permeated the British political, diplomatic, military and intelligence cultures.

So we need to purge our minds of 'there's a problem, what will the Americans do?' reasoning and replace it with 'there's a problem, what needs to be done?'.

The US currently supplies three major components of our world order – its reserve currency, military power projection capabilities and money. We need to replace these three components.

Dollar, Carriers and Dues

Most of our very young global institutions were created at the end of World War Two. The 1944 Bretton Woods conference led to the World Bank and International Monetary Fund, all anchored on a gold-based US dollar. While that arguably made sense in 1944, it makes none at all in 2005. Nor does it make sense to substitute another existing currency, euro, yen or renimbi. Our global economy needs a global currency unit to balance trade fluctuations and to act as an international reserve. The proposal, developed by John Maynard Keynes, for an International Clearing Union is as good a place as any to start.[9]

The US currently has a unique capacity to project military power almost anywhere in the world. The level of technical development of US systems in what the military call C[4]ISR (command, control, communications, computers, intelligence, surveillance and reconnaissance) means that US forces are less exposed to danger and better able to identify and destroy targets while inflicting less collateral damage than any of their counterparts. This has meant that any major intervention, such as would have been required to prevent the 1994 Rwandan genocide in which 800,000–1,000,000 people were slaughtered,[10] required active US participation. This, together with the 'what will America do?' mindset, has often provided an excuse for others, Europeans in particular, not to act.

One example of this is military heavy-lift aircraft. At the moment the US has 250 such planes and European states have 11.[11] This allowed some European capitals to assert that they were ready to intervene in Rwanda but could not do so without US aircraft. The decision to order 180 heavy-lift A400M transport aircraft from Airbus Military through the European Joint Armaments Co-operation Agency (OCCAR) removes this dependency, and with it the excuse.[12] Europe as an entity and its member states are acting to reduce dependency on US technical means across a range of military areas.

The US, largely for historical reasons, contributes a disproportionate amount to many world bodies, including the UN and its agencies. If we want our global organisations to work, they must be adequately funded, and if we want them to really work, they need to become less dependent on national state contributions. Some system of global taxation is required to fund our institutions, their development programmes and what the EU has begun to refer to as Human Security Policy (see below).

The Tobin tax's[13] time has come – as President Chirac and Chancellor Schroeder advocated at the 2005 Davos World Economic Forum, our world needs a form of global taxation. James Tobin proposed a minuscule levy of 0.01 per cent on speculative international capital transfers. Others have suggested a euro-a-ticket tax on international airline tickets. One or both of these proposals needs to be implemented if vital international institutions are to develop the independent capacities they need.

Certainties and Uncertainties

Our world faces many uncertainties, and sometimes we overlook established certainties. We actually have a rather good idea of what works and a common history bloodily over-stocked with very clear examples of what does not.

Democracy, in its various forms, works. Undemocratic regimes do not, and usually end up causing untoward suffering to their own and other peoples. Democracy is not necessarily efficient, but it's not meant to be; it's just meant to be democratic.

Private enterprise has shown itself to be the most efficient method of producing wealth in most sectors of the economy and relatively hopeless at distributing it, either nationally or globally.

These two success stories need to be harnessed together in constant and constructive conflict. The ultra free market US system does not work; derivatives of the European social market economy do. Societies that devote less than 40 per cent of their GDP to their public requirements wind up with massive and destabilising injustices and creaky infrastructures.

Whether the relationship between free market economies and democracy is symbiotic or dialectical is a matter of opinion. What is clear is that both do so much better in the presence of the other and that in the long run they are essential to each other. It is impossible for a free market to flourish where there is no rule of law based on clear texts and an independent judiciary. If who owns what is determined by the Generalissimo's nephew or the cousin of the local party secretary, investors will be few and far between. Who's going to build a factory on land they cannot establish title to? It was this necessity of title which drove the US and the UK to seek recognition as Occupying Powers in Iraq from the UN.

It is difficult for democracy to thrive where there is no free market, not just because there is no free market, but because if there is no market freedom, then there will probably be precious few other freedoms either. Markets chafe at democratic constraints, while the state views market operations with more than a hint of suspicion. The art of regulating the constantly moving boundaries between the two is one of the primary political functions of today's largely consensual societies.

This (almost) global consensus of the desirability of

the social market economy finds many different expressions in different countries. Where debate was once concentrated on ownership, it has now become more concerned with delivery. Is the UK's state-run health system necessarily better or worse than France's state-guaranteed, social partner-managed and significantly privately delivered one? Does it really matter as long as patients receive effective and timely treatment?

Apart from a handful of 'dustbin dictatorships', this consensus is global and growing. One of the few ideological exceptions is the US, where the very idea of public intervention is derided to the extent that the second Bush administration wants to more than triple its deficit to dismantle an essentially sound Social Security system (the US system that deals with pensions and disability benefits).

We know that this century will see the end of our oil-based economies. We also know that the transition from oil to a new energy mix will need to be both managed and organised. One element of this will probably include measures to replace oil with electricity wherever possible since we can produce electricity from a variety of non-fossil fuel sources.

This will require tax incentives, clear national energy strategies and significant public investment in infrastructure such as electricity grids. Infrastructure investment is less and less attractive to the US free market model, as the return on investment occurs over too long a period. Former US Energy Secretary Bill Richardson commented that the US had become 'a major superpower with a third-world electrical grid.'[14] Part of the explanation for the surge in crude oil prices in late 2004 was the absence of refining capacity in the US. It has become more commercially attractive to trade oil than it is to refine it.[15]

China and India have become the industrial workshops of the world in a classic Fordist approach. One of the key factors is a large supply of cheap labour. As in the original English Industrial Revolution, this is

313

supplied by rural populations migrating to cities (unlike the nineteenth-century US model, where immigrants supplied the cheap labour). The classic Fordist model means that as these workers prosper they become consumers, and the numbers are impressive. The Chinese middle class is estimated at 200 million and the tourism industry expects 100 million Chinese tourists to be travelling abroad each year by 2010. All Chinese workers already have a minimum of two weeks' paid annual leave. There will be far more Chinese than US tourists by the end of the decade. Within the same timeframe Chinese and Indian domestic markets will become at least as economically determinant as their export ones.

As Chinese and Indian prices and incomes rise, some of their activities will migrate to neighbouring lower-wage countries such as Vietnam and Indonesia. Globally, however, that will be more or less the end of the Fordist chain – there simply are not huge reserves of poor peasants anywhere else in the world where the Chinese and Indian approaches can be duplicated.

Which leads us to another certainty – our planet's population is stabilising. The rate of population increase has fallen by over 40 per cent since the late 1960s and experts now predict that it will plateau at 9 billion by 2070 and shrink dramatically thereafter.[16]

The number of UN member states more or less quadrupled in the 50 years between the organisation's founding and the end of the last century, from around 50 to almost 200. While it is likely that some new states may emerge in the coming decades, there will probably not be more than 20 of them.

One major challenge is global climate change. There is almost a global consensus that human consumption of fossil fuels makes a significant contribution to global warming. One has to insert the 'almost' since the US government obstinately insists, in the face of evidence to the contrary, that human activities are not central to the question of global warming. Curiously, while the

White House denies global warming, the Pentagon is reported to be looking closely at how the US military will need to react as the world's climate goes awry.[17]

We know many of the challenges we face and have a fairly clear picture of their scale. How we tackle them is up to us, and that too will involve questioning some of our mindsets.

Security and Threats

Inter-state war is no longer a real security concern for most of the world's population. If you have a problem with that statement, try the following exercise. Create two columns, one labelled 'defence' and the other 'offence', placing all the countries you feel might attack yours in the first column and all the countries your country might conceivably attack in the second. Most of us would draw a blank.

If we leave aside the continuing tensions between India and Pakistan and the essentially intra-Chinese dispute between Beijing and Taipei, it becomes difficult to construct a plausible scenario for inter-state war. Such a war on the American continents is unthinkable. Is the US likely to invade Canada or Mexico? Does Brazil plan to attack Ecuador, or Argentina to annex Uruguay? The possibility of inter-state war in Europe is equally far-fetched. Can anyone make a serious case for a German invasion of France in 2009? Or will Denmark thrust into southern Sweden to recover Skåne?

Terrorism poses a discernible threat to our societies, but not an existential one. Over-reaction to terrorism can easily become more dangerous than terrorism itself. The terrorist threat must be fought on several fronts, of which the military response is only a minor one. Listening to some of the advocates of the US Global War on Terrorism (GWOT), it is all too easy to forget that Osama bin Laden's announced desire to return a thousand years into the past and recreate the Baghdad caliphate is distinctly unattractive to the majority of his fellow Arabs. It is also easy to overlook the fact that Islam today is predominantly an Asian religion within which Arab believers are a minority – a large minority, but a minority nonetheless. Dick Cheney's desire to have the world return to some mythical US golden age, a fantasy cocktail of 1950s *Saturday Evening Post* with the American West of the 1880s, is equally unattractive.

The essence of our security today is to be found in what has begun to be referred to as Human Security:

> contemporary conflicts are characterised by circumstances of lawlessness, impoverishment, exclusivist ideologies, and the daily use of violence. This makes them fertile ground for a combination of human rights violations, criminal networks, and terrorism, which spill over and cause insecurity beyond the area itself...sources of insecurity are no longer most likely to come in the form of border incursions by foreign armies.[18]

Europe: Actor and Catalyst

We face new threats that require new kinds of collective response. For some, especially in the US, the whole notion that new kinds of international institutions, sharing sovereignty, using international political structures to address problems that cannot be addressed on a national level and operating through the building of a perpetually negotiated consensus, is mere pious fantasy. For the neoconservatives in particular, the world is shaped by the simple pursuit of national interests, and anyone who pretends otherwise is a fool or a liar.

Yet the most successful political institution on the planet operates precisely in the way that the neoconservatives deride. The EU is a wildly imperfect creation, dogged by the tedious complexity of its decision-making and the constant difficulty of connecting its bureaucracy to the people it represents, but its fundamental success can by measured by two simple criteria. How many of those who joined want to leave? How many of those who are not yet members want to join? The answers are obvious. In each of the current 25 member states of the EU, there are some political forces more sceptical of the EU than others, but in none are those who want to withdraw altogether more than a small minority. On the other hand, almost every state that is not a member but may be eligible to become one wishes to join. Even in the exceptions, like Iceland, Norway and Switzerland, there is a growing sense that the issue is not whether to join the EU but when. In a continent notorious for its violent history and its cultural and linguistic diversity, the EU has become simply a fact of life. Even its greatest critics would find it hard to imagine Europe without it.

The EU has succeeded because it has expanded peacefully and voluntarily. It has spread its ethic – legality, democracy and the global market – much more effectively than the neoconservatives in the US have spread their. It underpinned the evolution of democracy in Spain, Portugal and Greece. It has allowed former Warsaw Pact states – Poland, the Czech Republic, Hungary, Estonia, Latvia, Lithuania, Slovakia, Slovenia and the current candidate countries Bulgaria, Romania and Croatia – to make the transition from communism to market democracy. Even the prospect of future membership has driven the greatest advances for human rights in Turkish history. Stack up the states transformed to democracy by aggressive American action against those transformed to democracy by the EU's law-bound, consensual approach and there is simply no contest. Moreover, the EU has chalked up these achievements without firing a shot. It may have bored the life out of its own citizens, but the EU has not asked anyone to die for its democratising project.

Indeed, part of the EU's charm has been its relative passivity on the international stage. But as it expands almost willy-nilly into a global power and as the consequences of global dependence on American power become ever clearer, passivity is a luxury that Europe can no longer afford. The EU needs to develop its potential, both as a direct actor and as a catalyst, to help shape our future global management systems. There is a broad consensus across much of Europe on the need to undertake such a role, but it is a passive consensus, an agreement that 'something needs to be done'. We urgently need to move on to a set of active policy objectives. The EU Constitutional Treaty provides one vital tool in terms of establishing a treaty basis for an operational European foreign and security policy. This is an area tailor-made for the EU principle of subsidiarity – that the Union should primarily concern itself with actions the member states cannot individually undertake.

The EU has already taken several key concrete decisions. It is in the process of creating its European Rapid Reaction Force (ERRF) of 60,000 troops for major classical interventions. It is also working on its poorly named Battle Groups of 1,500 troops each, capable of deployment within days. It is considering what it has labelled a Human Security Response Force, a modular entity mixing troops with civil administrators, humanitarian assistance, development specialists, police and judges, etc. In other words, a form of a mobile ad hoc governmental entity whose composition would change in relation to the crisis it was being deployed to meet.[19] As Turkey and the Ukraine move towards EU membership, these capacities can only be enhanced.

The EU as an international catalyst can play a much more effective role. The EU can reach out to other countries and regional organisations, engaging them in a security and co-operation dialogue. This will involve a mixture of bilateral discussions with individual states such as Argentina, Brazil, China, India, Indonesia, Japan, Nigeria and South Africa and active co-operation with regional bodies like the African Union, Merocsur and ASEAN.

The EU could assist the African Union with the

creation, training and equipment of an African Rapid Deployment Force. African peacekeeping missions have often been bedevilled by the absence of suitable logistics and even by shortages of convertible currency to pay soldiers posted abroad. The EU could easily assist with such problems, furnishing necessary equipment, developing an African training centre and providing vital start-up assistance. Training support could be provided by those EU member states which did not have colonial empires in Africa and therefore carry less baggage with them now.

Brazilian and Chilean troops are already providing the international stability force in Haiti. The EU should develop its security co-operation with Latin America's leading democracies, thus creating greater global capacity to react to emergencies. Similar co-operative ventures could be developed with ASEAN and with Asia's main military powers.

Such initiatives might have to begin on a fairly small scale, but could quickly lead towards a reality where our world would gradually develop an ability to respond to crises, natural or man-made, with military and civil forces used to training and working together – without having to await Washington's pleasure. This would not involve any significant increase in expenditure, more a reallocation of existing funds.

A common security policy involving partners across the world can only develop when the priorities of all partners are addressed. Brazilian President Luiz Ignacio Lula da Silva has called for 'a new kind of foreign policy to help build a new world order that is both fairer and more democratic.'[20]

If physical security is a European concern, economic security is a more pressing one in much of Africa and Latin America. Energy policy, trade and environmental challenges are likely to be more and more at the centre of much of Asia's concerns. It is through addressing these different, but far from exclusive, priorities that we can help to create true global security.

Failures: Ours or the System's?

Advocates of US-style 'hard power' often argue that UN-style soft power simply does not work. They have a wealth of material to draw on in support of that argument, with the UN's failures in Rwanda and ex-Yugoslavia being the most obvious.

In April 1993 the UN Security Council passed a resolution establishing the UN's first-ever 'safe areas', places in the midst of a horrifically violent civil war where Muslims and others opposed to the aggressive campaign for a greater Serbia could be protected as non-combatants. The then Secretary General Boutros Boutros-Ghali asked for 34,000 peacekeepers to put the new policy into effect. He was given 7,600. Seven hundred and fifty lightly armed UN soldiers were given the task of disarming the Srebrenica's defenders and deterring Serb attacks. Two years later, a Serb flag flew over Srebrenica and 7,079 Muslim men were missing, presumed dead.[21] A year earlier, UN troops and the international community had stood aside while around 800,000 civilians were butchered in Rwanda.

These grotesque failures discredited the UN, but the largest part of the responsibility for them lies not with the UN, but with its members – us. We talked the talk, but when push came to shove we declined to walk the walk, and those we proclaimed our intention to defend were left to their defenceless fate.

We need not only to honour the peacekeeping commitments we make and to equip ourselves to honour those commitments, but also to prepare ourselves to go beyond such missions into uncharted waters. The argument that our young international institutions should be scrapped because they have sometimes failed is rather like calling for the abolition of the fire brigade following a dramatic blaze in which several people died. The real question to be discussed is how to improve our global fire-fighting and fire-prevention systems.

There is a need for a mechanism to provide for

international or internationally supported regional interventions to guarantee the stability of a state or region. Such a mechanism is not reconcilable with a purely Westphalian world model of completely independent nation-states. The UN Secretary General, Kofi Annan, put the question in the following terms to the UN General Assembly in 2000: 'if humanitarian intervention is, indeed, an unacceptable assault on sovereignty, how should we respond to a Rwanda, to a Srebenica – to gross and systematic violations of human rights that affect every precept of our common humanity?'[22]

We have yet to find the answer, but we know we have to try. That process will involve us progressively recognising international standards and duties and transferring some of our precious sovereignty to the institutions we create, or reform, to monitor those standards and carry out those duties.

'Up Down!': Sovereignty and Identity

Supporters of County Down teams must enjoy their cry of 'Up Down!', rejoicing as many of us do in a sense of identity, or to be more accurate, identities, for we all enjoy several identities. Coming from County Down, being a woman, a smoker, a mother, a model railway enthusiast, a nudist and a neurosurgeon are all compatible within one individual. At different times of the day and different times within a life, different identities naturally enjoy different levels of priority. They only conflict when tried simultaneously – smoking in the operating theatre is not a good idea, and while running a model railway layout in the nude is entirely possible, it's probably unusual. All of the above are about identity, not sovereignty, and the two should not be confused.

An inordinate degree of introverted nationalism continues to inform many of our political debates. For many, any pooling of sovereignty is seen as a form of treason, diminishing their control over their own lives. We would argue the opposite.

Before the American and French revolutions, sovereignty was, as the word suggests, invested in the monarch, or sovereign. The sovereign received that power from god or the gods – the divine right of kings. Revolutionaries stood that idea on its head, vesting sovereignty in the individual, who transfers some of that sovereignty to local authorities, national governments and increasingly to international bodies.

One problem with the latter is that much of the transfer is indirect. You vote for a government and that government then participates in the nomination of the President of the European Commission or the UN Secretary General. It is time to seriously consider systems for the direct transfer of sovereignty from individuals to international bodies. Should EU citizens elect the European Commission? Should the UN Secretary General be directly elected? What about a bicameral UN Security Council mixing state-appointed representatives with those elected by global suffrage?

There are obvious practical difficulties, but on closer examination they are considerably less daunting than they might appear to be.[23] Such a development would also begin to move us away from the amateur organisation of our world.

Our international bodies actually resemble semi-professional theatre groups or sports clubs. The technical staff are full-time professionals (EU or UN officials), some of the players are semi-professionals on fixed contracts (European Commissioners, UN Secretary General), but the Committee or Board are amateurs (national ministers). Like the Boards of many clubs, their members may be successful professionals in their primary functions, but their service on the Board is not their main job. If we want our global bodies to work properly we will need to elect professionals to do the job, rather as we elect prime ministers and presidents today.

'Good King Wenceslas Looked Out': St Stephen's Day 2004

Public opinion changes slowly, steadily, but often imperceptibly. These constant imperceptible changes are frequently difficult to observe and can pass unnoticed until a particular event dramatically marks them. Historians subsequently identify the moment after which these imperceptible changes have become obvious.

We would argue that public opinion has digested our global reality more quickly than our political systems and institutions. Millions of people marched around the world to demonstrate their opposition to the US invasion of Iraq. It was one of the biggest marches London has ever seen and probably the biggest march on an international question Ireland has ever seen. The UN debate reflected global opinion more accurately than did those of the national parliaments in Canberra, London or Washington.

Through the end of 2004 we had all watched and admired the Orange Revolution in Ukraine, as hundreds of thousands of Ukrainians braved bitter temperatures, Russian disapproval and potentially hostile security forces to defend their infant democracy. Ukraine had changed, something Kiev's semi-reformed apparatchiks could not grasp. The people resisted and the security forces made it clear they would not interfere while the Ukrainian Supreme Court asserted its independence in defending the constitution and the rule of law.

It was a revolution without a single shot being fired and without a single fatality, and around the world it became our revolution. Which of us was not moved by the peaceful determination of the crowds on the streets of Kiev? Those orange banners became our flags, our rejection of corruption and autocratic rule, our bastions of democracy.

On 26 December 2004 Ukraine voted, again. All around the world foreign ministries and newsrooms had organised themselves to cover the event. Through our Christmas-befuddled brains we waited for the first exit polls.

Then at 07.59 (local time) 30 kilometres below the Indian Ocean a 1,200-kilometre long rupture occurred where the Indo-Australian and Burmese tectonic plates collide, provoking an earthquake measured at 9.0 on the Moment Magnitude Scale. The earthquake devastated large areas of the Indonesian island of Sumatra and much more lethally generated a violent tsunami. Probably something around 300,000 people died within hours, from Sumatra to the coast of Somalia, 7,000 kilometres away. The Ukrainian revolution became a footnote to the day's news.

Our world's peoples responded to the Indian Ocean disaster as never before, with their governments playing catch-up. It was as if the disaster had struck people around the corner, in the next county, rather than half a world away. In tragedy, humanity had perhaps come of age.

The US had no policy on disaster relief for tsunamis in the Indian Ocean because the President had not determined what that policy should be. President Bush was at home in Crawford, Texas. As he struggled to put together a response in the absence of serious input from the State Department or USAID, he fluffed it. The initial offer of support was tiny, the subsequent one larger but mixed with a US decision that the US, Australia, India and Japan would form a coalition to administer aid in the Indian Ocean. There was no mention of the UN or its specialised agencies, no reference to Europe nor to China. History will doubtless reveal whether Canberra, Delhi and Tokyo were consulted about their willingness to form such a coalition. In the end the coalition idea faded away and the President pledged the whole of the US Federal Disaster Fund for fiscal 2004.

In one sense the US effort in the Indian Ocean encapsulates the whole thesis of *Post Washington*. The US aid pledge of $350 million is something less than 10 per cent of the $4 billion in public aid which has been offered, but the dispatch of US military forces was of inestimable help in bringing relief supplies to shattered and isolated communities.

The US sent an aircraft carrier to the coast of Sumatra, with elements of a Marine Amphibious Group deploying in both Sumatra and Sri Lanka. Marine hovercraft, landing craft and helicopters roared ashore, bringing supplies, equipment, medical aid and unarmed troops. The *USS Abraham Lincoln* (she of the 'Mission Accomplished' San Diego stunt) cruised off Banda Aceh. Her F-14, F-18 and A6 strike aircraft were pushed aside to free her flight deck for the incessant shuttle of 80 desperately needed helicopters. It would be over two weeks before the German naval hospital ship *Berlin* and the French helicopter carrier *Jeanne d'Arc* would reach Sumatra to share the load.

This image of a US with her heart in the right place, a governmental system that acts as a block to her interaction with the rest of the world, a political elite that cannot even begin to understand that world, empty coffers and largely irrelevant military might perfectly illustrates our *Post Washington* argument.

We are one, one species on one planet, responsible for our actions and their consequences. We know that our world produces more than enough food to feed its inhabitants, so we also understand that when people somewhere are starving to death, the problem is one of political will, not resources, much less divine inter-vention.

There is no doubt in our minds that the amazing, vibrant country that is the United States of America will either eventually recognise and address the challenges it faces or be forced to do so in extremis; when and how remains to be seen. When the US emerges from that transition it will undoubtedly re-engage with the world it has done so much to shape.

The world cannot wait on the US to wake from its slumber. We must move on, building our *Post*

Washington world with the US where possible, but without it where necessary. In doing so, we can, rather paradoxically, help the US to look away from the distorting mirror of hyperpower mythology and see itself for what it can be – a vibrant part of a global community in which survival increasingly depends on a recognition of mutual dependence.

Notes

1 Superman and the Krypton Factor

[1] Marshall McLuhan, *The Mechanical Bride*, New York: Vanguard Press, 1951, pp. 102–103.

[2] Eric Hobsbawm, *Nations and Nationalism since 1780: Programme, Myth, Reality*, New York: Cambridge University Press, 1990, p. 44.

[3] George Santayana (Jorge Augustín Nicolás Ruiz de Santayana), *The Life of Reason*, vol. 1, ch. 12, 1905, from *The Oxford Dictionary of Quotations*, New York: Oxford University Press, 1999, p. 644.

[4] The *Toledo Blade* investigation was published over four days from 22 October 2003. The text of this deposition is from *Harper's*, February 2004, pp. 24–5.

[5] *Atlas Obs*, Paris: Le Nouvel Observateur, 1999 figures.

[6] *GDP per Capita 2001 at Current Prices in US Dollars*, Paris: OECD, April 2003.

[7] Tim Allen, *Statistics in Focus, An Enlarged EU – A Trade Heavyweight*, Luxembourg: Eurostat, 2001.

[8] Michael Fishpool/European Defence 2002, *NATO and EU Forces Guide 2002–2003*, www.european-defence.co.uk. Defence budgets detailed in this guide are gathered and estimated from a number of sources, including NATO and the International Institute of Strategic Studies (IISS) Military Balance.

[9] *Military Spending: U.S. vs. the World, FY'03*, Washington, DC: Center for Defense Information, 4 February 2002.

[10] 'An Analysis of the President's Budgetary Proposals for Fiscal Year 2006', Washington, DC: Congresssional Budget Office, March 2005, table 1.5. The CBO puts 2005 spending at $497 billion, but this may well increase if further supplementary appropriations are sought for Iraq and Afghanistan. It also estimates a further $5,154 billion in military spending between 2006 and 2015.

[11] Francis Fukuyama, *The End of History and the Last Man*, New York: Penguin, 1992.

[12] *The National Security Strategy of the United States of America*, Washington, DC: The White House, 17 September 2002.

2 Jingle All the Way

[1] 'IMF Says Rise in US Debts is Threat to World Economy', *The New York Times*, 8 January 2004.

[2] Desmond Lachman, 'As the Dollar Declines', *The Washington Post*, 29 May 2003.

[3] Unless otherwise attributed, these figures and the subsequently quoted historical figures were compiled by the US Congressional Trade Deficit Review Commission.

[4] Will Hutton, 'When America Sneezes…', *The Observer*, 14 November 2004.

5 US Congressional Trade Deficit Review Commission, op cit.; Congressional Budget Office, Baseline Projections of Federal Debt, 25 January 2005.

6 Peronet Despeignes, 'US Faces Future of Chronic Deficits', *The Financial Times*, 28 May 2003.

7 Edmund L. Andrews, 'Deficits and Tax System Changes in Bush's Second-Term Economy', *The New York Times*, 4 November 2004.

8 Stephen S. Roach, 'When Weakness is Strength', *The New York Times*, 26 November 2004.

9 Patrick McGeehan, 'The Plastic Trap', *The New York Times*, 21 November 2004.

10 Ibid.

11 US Congressional Trade Deficit Review Commission, op. cit.

12 US Department of Commerce, Bureau of Economic Analysis, 30 June 2003.

13 Allen Sinai, *Macroeconomic Consequences and Implications of the U.S. Trade and Current Account Deficits*, New York, Boston, London: Decision Economics, Inc., December 2000.

14 *Macroeconomic Consequences and Implications of the U.S. Trade and Current Account Deficits*, op. cit.

15 Jane D'Arista, *Flow of Funds, Review and Analysis*, Financial Markets Center, 2nd quarter, 2003.

16 'As the Dollar Declines', op. cit.

17 Abdellazziz Al-Nasser, Djeddah businessman, quoted in *Le Nouvel Observateur*, Paris, 8–14 May 2003, p. 65.

18 Cited in David J. Rothkopf, 'Just as Scary as Terror – Anyone Seen Our Economic Policy?', *The Washington Post*, 25 July 2004.

19 David Streitfeld, 'Dollar's Decline is Reverberating', *The Los Angeles Times*, 14 November 2004.

20 Ibid.

21 Larry Elliott, 'US Risks a Downhill Dollar Disaster', *The Guardian*, 22 November 2004.

22 Edmund L. Andrews, 'Greenspan Shifts Views on Deficits', *The New York Times*, 16 March 2004.

23 Charlotte Denny, 'Who's Bush Going to War With? The Poor', *The Guardian*, 13 January 2003.

24 *The Defense Monitor*, vol. XXXII, no. 2, November/December 2003, p. 5.

25 *Mid-Session Review, Fiscal Year 2004*, Washington, DC: Office of Budget and Management, 15 July 2003.

26 David S. Broder, 'Tipping the Republicans' Hand?' *The Washington Post*, 18 June 2003.

27 Cited in Paul Krugman, 'Stating the Obvious', *The New York Times*, 27 May 2003.

28 Ibid.

29 Jodi Wilgoren, 'With Deadline Near, States are in Budget Discord', *The New York Times*, 27 June 2003.

30 Lis McNichol, *The State Fiscal Crisis: Extent, Causes and Responses*, Washington, DC: Center on Budget and Policy Priorities, 24 April 2003.

31 Quoted in Julian Borger, 'Long Queue at Drive-in Soup Kitchen', *The Guardian*, 3 November 2003.

32 David Teather, 'Greenspan Does Down the Dollar', *The Guardian*, 20 November 2004.

33 'When America Sneezes...', op. cit.

[34] Paul Krugman, 'Rubin Gets Shrill', *The New York Times*, 6 January 2004.

[35] 'Greenspan Shifts Views on Deficits', op. cit.

[36] See Armand Van Dormael, *Bretton Woods: Birth of a Monetary System*, London: Macmillan, 1978.

3 THE PRE-RICH: CLASS AND POVERTY IN TODAY'S US

[1] See the Horatio Alger Society website, www.ihot.com/~has/.

[2] David Brooks, 'The Triumph of Hope over Self-Interest', *The New York Times*, 12 January 2003.

[3] Jeremy Rifkin, 'Daring to Dream', *The Guardian*, 1 September 2004.

[4] Alan Greenspan keynote speech to the US Federal Reserve Annual Jackson Hole Economic Conference, 1998.

[5] Paul Krugman, 'For Richer', *The New York Times Magazine*, 20 October 2002.

[6] Paul Krugman, 'Our So-Called Boom', *The New York Times*, 30 December 2003.

[7] Cited in Paul Krugman, 'For Richer', op. cit.

[8] Cited in David Leonhardt, 'Who are the Truly Rich?', *The New York Times Magazine*, 12 January 2003.

[9] Cited in Paul Krugman, 'For Richer', op. cit. See also Thomas Piketty and Emmanuel Saez, *Income Inequality in the United States, 1913–1998*, Paris: CEPREMAP Centre d'Etudes Prospectives d'Economie Mathématique Appliquées a La Planification (Ecole Normale Supérieure), 1999.

[10] Will Hutton, *The World We're In*, London: Little, Brown (Time Warner Books UK), 2002, p. 149.

[11] Cited in David Leonhardt, 'Who are the Truly Rich?', op. cit.

[12] Bernadette D. Proctor and Joseph Dalaker, US Census Bureau, Current Population Reports, pp. 60–219, 'Poverty in the United States: 2001', Washington, DC, September 2002, pp. 1–4.

[13] Julian Borger, 'Long Queue at Drive-In Soup Kitchen', *The Guardian*, 3 November 2003.

[14] 'Census Data Shows Increases in Extent and Severity of Poverty and Decline in Household Income', Washington, DC: Center on Budget and Policy Priorities, 24 September 2002.

[15] 'Help for the City's Neediest', 3 November 2002 and 'The Smallest and the Neediest', *The New York Times*, 25 November 2002.

[16] Business Leaders for Sensible Priorities (website) citing US Census Bureau figures.

[17] US Census Bureau, 30 September 2003.

[18] US Census Bureau, Low Income Uninsured Children by State 1999, 2000, 2001.

[19] US Office of Budget and Management estimates cited in Paul Krugman, 'Hey, Lucky Duckies!', *The New York Times*, 3 December 2002.

[20] 'Passport to Health', *The Observer*, 25 May 2003.

[21] 'Daring to Dream', op. cit.

[22] Julian Borger, 'Land Where Calling an Ambulance is the First Step to Bankruptcy', *The Guardian*, 4 November 2003.

[23] Katherine Barrett *et al.*, *A Case of Neglect: Why Health Care is Getting Worse Even Though Medicine is Getting Better*, Governing, February 2004, pp. 22–4 and Rodger Doyle, *Getting Sicker*, *Scientific American*, November 2004.

[24] 'For Richer', op. cit.

25 Michael Moore, *Stupid White Men*, New York: Harper Collins, 2001, pp. 107–108.

26 David J. Rothkopf, 'Just as Scary as Terror – Anyone Seen our Economic Policy?', *The Washington Post*, 25 July 2004.

27 Jared Bernstein, Chauna Brocht and Maggie Spade-Aguilar, *How Much is Enough? Basic Family Budgets for Working Families*, Washington, DC: Economic Policy Institute, 2000, p. 14.

28 National Housing Trust Fund Campaign, *The Affordable Housing Crisis is Not Just a State and Local Problem*, Washington, DC: National Housing Trust Fund Campaign Fact Sheet, August 2002.

29 *Myths and Facts about Homelessness*, 1997 Report by the US National Coalition for the Homeless, cited in Barbara Ehrenreich, *Nickel and Dimed*, New York: Henry Holt and Company, 2001, p. 26.

30 Amy Goldstein and Jonathan Weisman, 'Bush Seeks to Recast Federal Ties to the Poor', *The Washington Post*, 9 February 2003.

31 *The Affordable Housing Crisis is Not Just a State and Local Problem*, op. cit.

32 Barbara Ehrenreich, *Nickel and Dimed*, New York: Henry Holt and Company, 2001, p. 3.

33 Andrew Gumbel, 'America's Rich Get Richer Thanks to Tax-Cutting Bush', *The Independent*, 20 September 2003.

34 Bob Herbert, 'Working for a Pittance', *The New York Times*, 8 October 2004.

35 *Nickel and Dimed*, op. cit., p. 199.

36 'For Richer', op. cit.

37 *Nickel and Dimed*, op. cit., p. 22.

38 *Stupid White Men*, op. cit., pp. 47–9.

39 Ibid., p. 102.

40 Bob Herbert, 'Out the Door', *The New York Times*, 1 January 2003.

41 Michael Moore, *Downsize This!*, London: Pan Books, 2002, p. 137.

42 US Census Bureau, 26 September 2003.

43 Richard Sennett, *The Corrosion of Character*, New York: Norton, 1998, p. 50.

44 *The World We're In*, op. cit., p. 169.

45 *OECD Employment Outlook*, Paris: OECD, 2000.

46 David Friedman, 'Trouble at Home – The Housing Boom Helped Us Out of the Recession, But It May Be a New Financial Bubble', *Los Angeles Times*, 19 May 2002.

47 *The World We're In*, op. cit., p. 169.

48 Cited in Albert B. Crenshaw, 'A Tax Cut of Varied Proportions', *The Washington Post*, 25 May 2003.

49 'A Closer Look – How Stocks Are Held, New York Stock Exchange Based on the Federal Reserve's Survey of Consumer Finances', *The New York Times* graphic, December 2002.

50 Lawrence Mishel, Jared Bernstein and John Schmitt, *The State of Working America 2000-2001*, New York: Cornell University Press, 2001, p. 386.

51 *OECD Employment Outlook*, op.cit., Ch. 2.

52 US Census Bureau's 2001 American Housing Survey.

53 Edward J. Blakely and Mary Gail Snyder, *Fortress America: Gated Communities in the United States*, Washington, DC: Brookings Institutions Press, 1997.

54 Haya El Nasser, 'Gated Communities', *USA Today*, 15 December 2002.

55 David Brooks, 'The Triumph of Hope over Self-Interest', *The New York Times*, 12 January 2003.

[56] 'Trouble at Home – The Housing Boom Helped Us Out of the Recession, But It May Be a New Financial Bubble', op. cit.

[57] Ibid.

[58] *Nickel and Dimed*, op. cit., pp. 25–7.

[59] *Writing of Thomas Jefferson (1899)*, vol. 10, in a letter to William Charles Jarvis, 28 September 1820, from *The Oxford Dictionary of Quotations*, New York: Oxford University Press, 1999, p. 21, 405.

[60] Speech in the House of Commons, 15 June 1874.

[61] Prof. Robert Maddox of Penn State University, quoted in Christina Davenport, 'The Middle Class Rose – As Did Expectations', *The Washington Post*, 27 May 2004.

[62] *The World We're In*, op. cit., p. 156.

[63] *Education at a Glance: OECD Indicators*, Paris: OECD, 2000.

[64] Greg Winter and Jennifer Medina, 'More Students Line Up at Financial Aid Office', *The New York Times*, 10 March 2003.

[65] *Business Week*, 27 August 2001, p. 75.

[66] US College Board survey of 2,700 colleges and universities, cited in Greg Winter, 'Public University Tuition Rises Sharply Again for '04', *The New York Times*, 20 October 2004.

[67] US Department of Education, National Center for Education Statistics (NCES) Digest of Education Statistics, 2001.

[68] Ted C. Fishman, 'The Chinese Century', *The New York Times Magazine*, 4 July 2004.

[69] Thomas L. Friedman, 'Losing Our Edge?', *The New York Times*, 22 April 2004.

[70] Thomas L. Friedman, 'Oops, I Told the Truth', *The New York Times*, 17 October 2004.

[71] V.S. Mullis *et al.*, *Mathematics and Science Achievement in the Final Year of Secondary School: IEA's Third International Mathematics and Science Study, 1998*, Chestnut Hill, MA: International Association for the Evaluation of Educational Achievement, October 1998.

[72] Donald Kaul, 'America's Best and Brightest are Clueless About Our History', *Des Moines Register*, 7 July 2000.

[73] US Department of Education, National Center for Education Statistics (NCES) Digest of Education Statistics, 2001.

[74] Kathleen Kennedy Manzo, 'Era of Neglect in Evidence at Libraries', *Education Week*, 1 December 1999.

[75] Peter T. Kilborn, 'As State Budgets Break, Pain Trickles Down', *The New York Times*, 15 December 2002.

[76] Lois Romano, 'Tulsa's Desperate Times and Measures', *The Washington Post*, 29 December 2002.

[77] Sam Dillon, 'Schools Ending Year Early to Cut Costs', *The New York Times*, 12 January 2003.

[78] Timothy Egan, 'States Facing Budget Shortfalls, Cut the Major and the Mundane', *The New York Times*, 21 April 2003.

[79] *Stupid White Men*, op. cit., pp. 113–14.

[80] Elizabeth Becker and Marian Burros, 'Eat Your Vegetables? Only at a Few Schools', *The New York Times*, 13 January 2003.

[81] Ibid.

[82] 'More Students Line Up at Financial Aid Office', op. cit.

[83] James Ryan, 'Sit In for School Equality', *The Washington Post*, 19 May 2003.

[84] 'When a College Scholarship Buys a Car', *The New York Times* editorial, 4 November 2002.

[85] Study by the Center for Labor Market Studies at Boston's Northeast University, cited in 'Greatest Wave of Migrants Drives US Engine', *The Guardian*, 3 December 2002.

[86] Krissah Williams, 'Salvadorans Buying Up Stakes in Homeland', *The Washington Post*, 28 November 2004.

[87] 'As Billions Flow South, Governments Play Catch Up', special to www.washingtonpost.com, *The Washington Post*, 21 November 2002.

[88] Larry Elliott, 'The Atkins-diet Approach to Economic Management: Loading Up on Debt Will Do Nothing to Avert Another Crash', *The Guardian*, 26 September 2003.

4 FROM FORDISM TO FANTASY: THE HOLLOWING OF AMERICAN INDUSTRY

[1] Paul Kennedy, *The Rise and Fall of the Great Powers*, New York: Vintage Books, 1987, pp. 242–9.

[2] President Franklin D. Roosevelt, 'We must be the great arsenal of democracy' Fireside Chat, radio broadcast 29 December 1940, in *Public Papers*, 141, vol. 9.

[3] *MIA: Encyclopedia of Marxism*, Glossary of Terms, www.marxists.org, May 2003.

[4] Will Hutton, *The World We're In*, London: Little, Brown, 2002, p. 120.

[5] Mary O'Sullivan, *Contests for Corporate Control: Corporate Governance and Economic Performance in the United States and Germany*, New York: Oxford University Press, 2000, p. 156.

[6] *The World We're In*, op. cit., p. 145.

[7] Ibid., p. 24.

[8] Alan Kennedy, *The End of Shareholder Value: The Real Effects of the Shareholder Value Phenomenon and the Crisis it is Bringing to Business*, London: Orion Business, 2000, general account of the Welch phenomenon, pp. 50–7.

[9] R. Gourvish, *Railways and the British Economy 1830-1914*, London: Macmillan for the Economic History Society, 1980, p. 33.

[10] Arthur Beesley, 'Divorce Case Reveals Pampering on a Scale Likely to Cause Widespread Executive Envy', *The Irish Times*, 7 September 2002.

[11] Mr Jeffrey Swensen, a senior trader at John Hancock Advisers, cited in Claudia H. Deutsch, 'GE Earnings Decline 11%; Key Product Lines Sluggish', *The New York Times*, 11 October 2003.

[12] *The World We're In*, op. cit., p. 130.

[13] Gary A. Dymski, *The Bank Merger Wave: The Economic Causes and Social Consequences of Financial Consolidation*, New York: M.E. Sharpe, 1999.

[14] Stephen Nickell, *The Performance of Companies*, Oxford: Blackwell, 1995, p. 23.

[15] George Draffan, *Profile of The Boeing Company*, 2005, www.endgame.org/boeing.html.

[16] *Business Week*, 7 April 1998.

[17] *The World We're In*, op. cit., p. 132.

[18] Rick Anderson, 'McBoeing [McDonnell Douglas] Will Have Two-Thirds of the Pentagon's Annual $100 Billion in Contracts', *Seattle Weekly*, 2 April 1997, pp. 14–15.

[19] Peter Almond and Sean Rayment, 'Biggest-ever Plane Will Carry an Army', *The Sunday Telegraph*, 6 October 2002.

20 'L'incroyable saga des avions brésiliens', *Le Nouvel Observateur*, Paris, no. 2032, 16–22 October 2003.

21 Greg Schneider, 'Lockheed, Boeing Spar in a Battle of Rivals', *The Washington Post*, 16 June 2003.

22 'Bad Company – Pipe Dreams', extract from Robert Bryce's book *Pipe Dreams* published in *The Guardian*, 4 November 2002. Unless otherwise attributed, figures and elements in this Enron section are taken from that extract.

23 Greg Palast, *The Best Democracy Money Can Buy*, London: Constable & Robinson, 2003, p. 117.

24 Ibid., p. 119.

25 Pat Regnier, 'American Pie – The US Economy Wasn't All That It Seemed', *Time*, 8 July 2002, p. 8.

26 *Pipe Dreams*, op. cit.

27 *Time*, 8 July 2002, p. 25.

28 Ibid., p. 90.

29 'List of the 12 Largest US Bankruptcies', *The New York Times*, 18 December 2002.

30 'WorldCom', *Time*, 8 July 2002, p. 24.

31 Ed Vulliamy and Faisal Islam, 'And Now for the Really Big Guns', *The Observer*, 29 June 2003.

32 Brian Whitaker, 'Network Error', *The Guardian*, 29 September 2003.

33 'L'incroyable train de vie de Dennis le Magnifique', *Le Nouvel Observateur*, Paris, no. 1973, 29 August 2002, p. 72.

34 *Business Week*, 28 May 2001.

35 *Le Nouvel Observateur*, Paris, no. 1973, 29 August 2002, p. 74.

36 Ien Cheng, 'Barons of Bankruptcy', *The Financial Times*, 31 July 2002.

37 'The Fruits of Irrationality', book extract from Joseph Stiglitz, *The Roaring Nineties*, *The Guardian*, 24 September 2003.

38 Chalmers Johnson, *Blowback: The Costs and Consequences of American Empire*, New York: Henry Holt & Co., 2000, p. 201.

39 Tom Burke, 'Profit Must Be Seen to Have a Purpose', *The Guardian Weekly (Observer)*, 17–23 April 2003, p. 12.

40 Quoted in Felix G. Rohatyn, *The Betrayal of Capitalism*, *The New York Review of Books*, 28 February 2002.

41 Felix G. Rohatyn, 'From New York to Baghdad', *The New York Review of Books*, 21 November 2002.

42 Cited in Brian Whitaker, 'Spoils of War', *The Guardian*, 13 October 2003.

43 Joseph P. Quinlan, *Drifting Apart or Growing Together? The Primacy of the Transatlantic Economy*, Washington, DC: Center for Transatlantic Relations, 2003.

44 Ibid., p. 3.

45 Ibid., p. 4.

46 Ibid., p. 10.

47 Ibid., p. 6.

48 US Bureau of Economic Analysis, cited in *Drifting Apart or Growing Together? The Primacy of the Transatlantic Economy*, op. cit., p. 6.

49 www.telegeography.com, cited in *Drifting Apart or Growing Together? The Primacy of the Transatlantic Economy*, op. cit., p. 34.

50 'From New York to Baghdad', op. cit.

51 Cited in Paul Krugman, 'The Sweet Spot', *The New York Times*, 17 October 2003.

5 THE MILITARY-INDUSTRIAL COMPLEX

[1] President Dwight D. Eisenhower, *Farewell Address to the Nation*, 17 January 1961, Public Papers of the Presidents, Dwight D. Eisenhower, 1960, p. 1035–40, www.coursesa.matrix.msu.edu/.

[2] William D. Hartnung, 'Eisenhower's Warning: The Military-Industrial Complex Forty Years Later', *World Policy Journal*, vol. XVII, no. 1, Spring 2001.

[3] Chalmers Johnson, 'The War Business', *Harper's*, November 2003, p. 54.

[4] *The New York Times*, 18 January 1925.

[5] 'The 30 Leading Suppliers of Conventional Weapons', Stockholm International Peace Research Institute (www.sipri.se) and Thom Shanker, 'US and Russia Still Dominate Arms Markets', *The New York Times*, 30 August 2004.

[6] Marcus Corbin and Olga Levitsky, 'Vital Statistics: The U.S. Militlary', *The Defense Monitor*, vol. XXXII, no. 5, November/December 2003 and Winslow T. Wheeler, 'Don't Mind if I Do', *The Washington Post*, 22 August 2004.

[7] Lawrence J. Korb, Director of National Security Studies, US Council on Foreign Relations, former US Assistant Secretary of Defense under US President Ronald Reagan (1981–1985), testimony to the US House of Representatives Budget Committee, 12 February 2002.

[8] Center for Defense Information, *Military Spending: US vs the World, FY'03*, Washington, DC: Center for Defense Information Factsheet, 4 February 2002.

[9] Center for Defense Information, *Military Almanac 2001–2002*, Washington, DC: Center for Defense Information, 2002, p. 40.

[10] Tim Weiner, 'Lockheed and the Future of Warfare', *The New York Times*, 28 November 2004.

[11] 'Eisenhower's Warning: The Military-Industrial Complex Forty Years Later', op. cit.

[12] Center for Responsive Politics, *The Arms Lobby: A Profile*, Washington, DC: Center for Responsive Politics, 1998.

[13] 'Eisenhower's Warning: The Military-Industrial Complex Forty Years Later', op. cit.

[14] Greg Schneider, 'Lockheed, Boeing Spar in a Battle of Rivals,' *The Washington Post*, 16 June 2003.

[15] Center for Defense Information, *Fiscal Year 2004 Budget: Request for Selected Weapons Systems*, Washington, DC: Center for Defense Information (www.cdi.org), 3 February 2003.

[16] Leslie Wayne, 'Pentagon Says It Plans to Kill Copter Program', *The New York Times*, 24 February 2004.

[17] 'Lockheed and the Future of Warfare', op. cit.

[18] Ibid.

[19] Ibid. and Tim Weiner, 'Pentagon Envisioning a Costly Internet for War', *The New York Times*, 13 November 2004.

[20] Leslie Wayne, 'Unusual Pentagon-Boeing Deal is Attacked', *The New York Times*, 10 June 2003.

[21] Renae Merle, 'Boeing Loses Out on Air Force Tanker Deal', *The Washington Post*, 10 October 2004 and 'Boeing Competitors Protest', *The Washington Post*, 13 October 2004.

[22] Patrick E. Tyler, 'US Strategy Plan Calls for Insuring No Rivals Develop', *The New York Times*, 13 February 1992.

[23] The White House, *The National Security Strategy of the United States of America*, Washington, DC: The White House, September 2002, p. 30.

24 John Koster, 'Columbian Tragedy', *War Monthly*, Issue 44, 1977, p. 35.

25 *Military Almanac 2001–2002*, op. cit., p. 21.

26 'Columbian Tragedy', op. cit., p. 40.

27 *Military Almanac 2001–2002*, op cit., p. 21 and N.8.

28 'US, History of: Madison as President and the War of 1812' and 'New Orleans, Battle of', *Encyclopaedia Britannica* CD-ROM, 2001.

29 'Seminole Wars', *Encyclopaedia Britannica* CD-ROM, 2001.

30 'Cherokee', 'Indian Removal Act' and 'Trail of Tears', *Encyclopaedia Britannica* CD-ROM, 2001.

31 'Mexican War', *Encyclopaedia Britannica* CD-ROM, 2001.

32 'US, History of: The Cost and Significance of the Civil War', *Encyclopaedia Britannica* CD-ROM, 2001.

33 *Military Almanac 2001–2002*, op. cit., p. 21 and N.8.

34 'Wounded Knee', *Encyclopaedia Britannica* CD-ROM, 2001.

35 *The United States and Canada 1865–1920*, The Times Concise Atlas of World History, London: Times Books, 1992, p. 111.

36 Jasen Castillo, Julia Lowell, Ashley J. Tellis, Jorge Muñoz and Benjamin Zycher, *Military Expenditures and Economic Growth*, MR–1112–A, CA: The Rand Corporation, 2001, p. 90.

37 Paul Kennedy, *The Rise and Fall of the Great Powers*, New York: Vintage Books, 1987, pp. 242–9.

38 *Military Expenditures and Economic Growth*, op. cit., p. 88.

39 Nelson Blake, 'Background of Cleveland's Venezuela Policy', *American Historical Review*, vol. 47, no. 2, January 1942, pp. 259–76.

40 'Spanish-American War', 'Maine Destruction of' and 'US, History of: Imperialism, the Progressive Era and the rise to world power 1896–1920', *Encyclopaedia Britannica* CD-ROM, 2001.

41 *Military Expenditures and Economic Growth*, op. cit., p. 90.

42 Speech in Chicago, 3 April 1903, reported in *The New York Times*, 4 April 1903.

43 *The United States and Canada 1865–1920*, op. cit.

44 Peter Duus, *The Rise of Modern Japan*, Boston, MA: Houghton Mifflin, 1976, pp. 52–78.

45 See Robert Art, 'A Defensible Defense: America's Grand Strategy After the Cold War', *International Security*, vol. 15, no. 4, Spring 1991, pp. 5–53. See also Nicholas Spykman, *America's Strategy in World Politics: The United States and the Balance of Power*, New York: Harcourt Brace and Co., 1942.

46 *The First World War*, The Times Concise Atlas of World History, London: Times Books, 1992, p.118.

47 Walter Lippmann, 'Security Not Sentiment', in Herbet J. Bass (ed.), *America's Entry into World War 1*, New York: Holt, Reinhart and Winston, 1964.

48 *Military Expenditures and Economic Growth*, op. cit., p. 92.

49 *Military Almanac 2001–2002*, op. cit., p. 21.

50 *Military Expenditures and Economic Growth*, op. cit., p. 93.

51 *Military Almanac 2001–2002*, op. cit., p. 21 and N.3.

52 AFIO (US Association of Former Intelligence Officers) website June 2003 citing letter in *The Washington Post*, 16 December 1999, p. A38.

53 *Military Almanac 2001–2002*, op. cit., p. 21.

54 *Military Expenditures and Economic Growth*, op. cit., p. 94.

55 *Military Almanac 2001–2002*, op. cit., p. 35.

56 *Farewell Address to the Nation*, op. cit.

[57] Martin Woollacott, 'The Greatest Risk to the US is Its Own Imagination', *The Guardian*, 21 February 2003.

[58] Carl Sagan, *Billions and Billions*, London: Headline Book Publishing, 1999, p. 200.

[59] Max Boot, 'Waging Modern War', *Foreign Affairs*, July–August 2003.

[60] Bob Woodward, *Bush at War*, London: Pocket Books, 2003, p. 55.

[61] 'Waging Modern War', op. cit.

[62] Philip Smucker in Cairo and Toby Harnden in Washington, 'CIA Missile Team Stalked Bin Laden's Top Man for Months', *The Daily Telegraph*, 6 November 2002.

[63] Matthew Brezinski, 'The Unmanned Army', *The New York Times Magazine*, 20 April 2003.

[64] Ibid.

[65] Julian Borger, 'US-Based Missiles to Haye Global Reach', *The Guardian*, 1 July 2003.

[66] Julian Colman, 'Pentagon Wants "Mini-Nukes" to Fight Terrorists', *The Sunday Telegraph*, 26 October 2003.

[67] 'US-Based Missiles to Have Global Reach', op. cit.

[68] 'The Unmanned Army', op. cit.

[69] Yves Eudes, 'Le Soldat du Futur', *Le Monde*, 6 March 2003.

[70] Ibid.

[71] 'Waging Modern War', op. cit.

[72] 'Le Soldat du Futur', op. cit.

[73] 'The Unmanned Army', op. cit.

[74] Tim Weiner, 'Pentagon Envisioning a Costly Internet for War', *The New York Times*, 13 November 2004.

[75] See Bruce Berkowitz, *The New Face of War*, New York: Free Press, 2003 for more details.

[76] Francis Fukuyama, *The End of History and the Last Man*, New York: Penguin, 1992.

[77] Donald Rumsfeld, 'Thoughts from the Business World on Downsizing Government', Heartland Policy Study No. 67, Policy Studies, The Heartland Institute, Chicago, IL, 1995.

[78] Ian Traynor, 'The Privatisation of War', *The Guardian*, 10 December 2003.

[79] Ibid.

[80] Conor O'Clery, 'Iraq War Contracts Dispute Rebounds on Bush', *The Irish Times*, 13 December 2003.

[81] 'The Privatisation of War', op. cit.

[82] 'President Bush makes a point about the economy during the first meeting with his Cabinet since the war in Iraq began. At left are Interior Secretary Gale A. Norton and Treasury Secretary John W. Snow.' (Kevin Lamarque - Reuters), photo caption, *The Washington Post*, 10 June 2003.

6 WHIZZARDS AND WIDE OPEN SPACES: US AGRIBUSINESS

[1] Larry Elliott, 'What WTO Needs is a New Reformation', *The Guardian*, 2 August 2004.

[2] Victor Davis Hanson, 'A Secretary for Farmland Security', *The New York Times*, 9 December 2004.

[3] RTI International news release, 21 January 2004.

[4] Jonathan D. Salant, 'U.S. Opposes U.N. Obesity Report', Associated Press, 16 January 2004.

[5] Sarah Boseley, 'Sugar Industry Threatens to Scupper WHO', *The Guardian*, 21 April 2003.

[6] Anthelme Brillat-Savarin, 'Tell me what you eat and I will tell you what you are', Physologie du Goût (1825), aphorism no. 4, from *The Oxford Dictionary of Quotations*, New York: Oxford University Press, 1999, p. 148, 17.

[7] Upton Sinclair, *The Jungle*, a startling description of Chicago stockyards working life first published in 1906. Complete edition published Tuscon, AZ: Sharp Press, 2003.

[8] Eric Schlosser, *Fast Food Nation*, New York: Penguin, 2002, pp. 150, 151.

[9] Dan Barber, 'Food without Fear', *The New York Times*, 23 November 2004.

[10] Larry Rohter, 'South America Seeks to Fill the World's Table', *The New York Times*, 12 December 2004.

[11] Alessandro Bonanno, Lawrence Busch, William H. Friedland, Lourdes Gouveia and Enzo Mingione (eds.), *From Columbus to ConAgra: Transnational Corporations and the Globalization of the Food System*, Lawrence, KS: University Press of Kansas, 1994, pp. 32, 33.

[12] *Fast Food Nation*, op. cit., Ruben Ramirez's story, pp. 154, 155.

[13] Ibid., p. 164.

[14] 'The Slaughter of Meatpacking Wages', *Business Week*, 27 June 1983.

[15] *Fast Food Nation*, op. cit., p. 154.

[16] Lourdes Gouvela, 'Global Strategies and Local Linkages', in *From Columbus to ConAgra*, op. cit., p. 129. See also Iowa Beef Processors Annual Report, Dakota City, Nebraska, 1987 and 1991.

[17] James M. MacDonald, Michael E. Ollinger, Kenneth E. Nelson and Charles R. Handy, *Consolidation in U.S. Meatpacking*, Washington, DC: Economic Research Service, US Department of Agriculture, February 2000, p. 9.

[18] Ibid., p. 8.

[19] *From Columbus to ConAgra*, op. cit., Table 1.2, p. 36.

[20] *Fast Food Nation*, op. cit., p. 117.

[21] Grain Inspection, Packers and Stockyards Administration (GIPSA), US Department of Agriculture, 1195 Reporting Year, SR-97-1, September 1997, p. 49.

[22] *From Columbus to ConAgra*, op. cit., p. 37.

[23] *Consolidation in U.S. Meatpacking*, op. cit., p. iii.

[24] *Fast Food Nation*, op. cit., p. 137.

[25] Ibid., p. 138.

[26] USDA Advisory Committee on Agricultural Concentration, *Report 1996*, Executive Summary citing USDA Red Meat Packing Industry study, p. 3.

[27] *Critical Issues - Critical Choices*, 1999 Annual Report, Washington, DC: US Farm Foundation.

[28] Center for Public Integrity, Washington, DC.

[29] McDonald's corporate press release, Oak Brook, IL, 5 December 2002.

[30] *Fast Food Nation*, op. cit., p. 71.

[31] Barbara Ehrenreich, *Nickel and Dimed*, New York: Owl Books, 2002, p. 16.

[32] Ibid., p. 14.

[33] *Fast Food Nation*, op. cit., p. 4.

[34] Ibid., p. 136.

[35] Ibid., p. 115.

[36] Nancy Helmich, 'Six in 10 Are Overweight; Health Fall Out Feared', *USA Today*, 9 October 2002.

[37] US Center for Disease Control, 'Obesity Epidemic Increase Dramatically in the United States', press release citing CDC research published in the 27 October 1999 *Journal of the American Medical Association* (JAMA).

[38] Elizabeth Becker and Marian Burros, 'Eat Your Vegetables? Only at a Few Schools', *The New York Times*, 13 January 2003.

[39] 'Obesity Epidemic Increase Dramatically in the United States', op. cit.

[40] 'Food without Fear', op. cit.

[41] *Fast Food Nation*, op. cit., p. 173.

[42] Ibid., p. 203.

[43] USDA Agricultural Research Service, 'Study Urges Pre-Processed Beef Test for *E. coli*', cited in CDC Health Letter, 13 March 2000.

[44] *The Denver Post*, 26 July 2002.

[45] See *Fast Food Nation*, op. cit., Hudson p. 211 and Bauer p. 219.

[46] Government Executive, 'Beefing Up Inspection', February 1999.

[47] Robert H. Frank, *Luxury Fever*, New York: Free Press, 1999, pp. 56–61.

[48] Michael A. Fletcher, 'Ban on Irradiated Ground Beef Lifted in School Lunch Program', *The Washington Post*, 30 May 2003.

[49] Carol Smith, 'Overhaul in Meat Inspection No Small Potatoes', *Seattle Post-Intelligencer*, 29 January 1998.

[50] 'The Need to Improve Antimicrobial Use in Agriculture: Ecological and Human Health Consequences', *Journal of Clinical Infectious Diseases*, The Alliance for Prudent Use of Antibiotics, vol. 34, supplement 3, the FAAIR Report, 1 June 2002.

[51] *Fast Food Nation*, op. cit., p. 202.

[52] 'The Curse of Factory Farms', *The New York Times* editorial, 20 August 2002.

[53] *Fast Food Nation*, op. cit., p. 140.

[54] 'Food without Fear', op. cit.

[55] Benjamin Weiser, 'Big Macs Can Make You Fat? No Kidding, a Judge Rules', *The New York Times*, 23 January 2003.

[56] *From Columbus to ConAgra*, op. cit., p. 139.

[57] Neal D. Barnard and Michele Simon, 'Animal Waste Used as Livestock Feed – Dangers to Human Health', *Preventive Medicine*, September/October 1997.

[58] Jennifer Lee, 'Neighbors of Vast Hog Farms Say Foul Air Endangers Their Health', *The New York Times*, 11 May 2003.

[59] Ibid.

[60] Ibid.

[61] Sheri Venena, 'Growing Pains', *Arkansas Democrat-Gazette*, 18 October 1998.

[62] Felix Rohatyn, 'From New York to Baghdad', *The New York Review of Books*, 21 November 2002.

[63] Michael Broadway, 'Economic Development Programs in the Great Plains: The Example of Nebraska', *Great Plains Research*, vol. 1, no. 2, pp. 324–44.

[64] *From Columbus to ConAgra*, op. cit., p. 138.

[65] *Fast Food Nation*, op. cit., p. 164.

[66] *Nebraska Statistical Handbook*, Lincoln, NE: Nebraska Department of Economic Development, 1991.

[67] USDA Statistics, Summary Report on Structure of Agriculture, 1981, p. 42 and Structural and Financial Characteristics of US Farms, 1994, p. 18, United States Department of Agriculture.

[68] Dean MacCannell, 'Agribusiness and the Small Community', Background Paper to Technology, Public Policy and the Changing Structure of American Agriculture, Washington, DC: Office of Technology Assessment, US Congress, 1983.

[69] Ibid., n. 16, p. 15 and Table 4-7, p. 16.

[70] *Consolidation in U.S. Meatpacking*, op. cit., p. 15.

[71] US General Accounting Office, cited in *Consolidation in U.S. Meatpacking*, op. cit., p. 15.

[72] Duncan Campbell, 'Poultry Pay Puts Fast Food Giant in Dock', *The Guardian*, 8 February 2003.

[73] *From Columbus to ConAgra*, op. cit., p. 142.

[74] Timothy Egan, 'Pastoral Poverty', *The New York Times*, 8 December 2002 for all figures in this section.

[75] Osha Gray Davidson, *Broken Heartland: The Rise of America's Rural Ghetto*, Iowa City, IA: University of Iowa Press, 1996, p. 6.

[76] *Right to Farm Laws: History & Future*, Washington, DC: The US Farm Foundation, November 1998.

[77] Amamdo Toumani Touré (President of Mali) and Blaise Compaoré (President of Burkina Fasso), 'Your Farm Subsidies are Strangling Us', *The New York Times*, 11 July 2003.

[78] Jay Hancock, 'Ending Cotton's Reign in the US to Help World's Poor', *The Irish Times*, 9 August 2004.

[79] Matthew L. Wald and Eric Lichtblau, 'U.S. Discovers Its First Suspected Case of Mad Cow Disease', *The New York Times*, 24 December 2003.

[80] Eric Schlosser, 'The Cow Jumped Over the U.S.D.A.', *The New York Times*, 2 January 2004.

[81] Marian Burros and Donald G. Mcneil, Jr., 'Inspections for Mad Cow Lag Those Done Abroad', *The New York Times*, 24 December 2003.

[82] 'The Cow Jumped Over the U.S.D.A.', op. cit.

[83] Eric Pianin and Guy Guigliotta, 'Banning Sale of "Downer" Meat Represents a Change in Policy', *The Washington Post*, 31 December 2003.

[84] Michel de Pracontal, 'Le mystère américain', *Le Nouvel Observateur*, Paris, no. 2031, 9–15 October 2003.

[85] Adam Smith, *Wealth of Nations*, 1776, bk. 1, ch. 10, pt. 2.

[86] Douglas Jehl, 'Arkansas Rice Farmers Run Dry; Remedy Stirs Debate', *The New York Times*, 11 November 2002.

[87] Larry Roher, 'South America Seeks to Fill the World's Table', *The New York Times*, 12 December 2004.

7 EVILDOERS SUCK!

[1] Pensées, 1699, No. 895.

[2] Max Hastings, 'Save Us from Politicians Who Have god on Their Side', *The Guardian*, 6 December 2004.

[3] Garry Wills, 'The Day the Enlightenment Went Out', *The New York Times*, 4 November 2004.

[4] Matthew Engel, 'Meet the New Zionists', *The Guardian*, 28 October 2002.

[5] Gary Younge, 'God Help America', *The Guardian*, 25 August 2003.

[6] Rupert Cornwell, 'In god He Trusts', *The Independent*, 21 February 2003.

[7] Nicholas D. Kritsof, 'god, Satan and the Media', *The New York Times*, 4 March 2003.

[8] Ibid.

[9] Jack Hitt, 'A Gospel According to the Earth', *Harper's*, vol. 307, no. 1838, July 2003.

[10] 'God Help America', op. cit.

[11] 'Meet the New Zionists', op. cit.

[12] Victoria Clark, 'The Christian Zionists', *Prospect*, July 2003.

[13] 'Meet the New Zionists', op. cit.

[14] From David Frum, *The Right Man: The Surprise Presidency of George W. Bush*, cited in 'Books on Bush', *The New York Review of Books*, 13 February 2003.

[15] Ed Vulliamy, 'The President Rides Out', *The Observer*, 26 January 2003.

[16] Gary Younge, 'Gay is the New Black', *The Guardian*, 16 June 2003.

[17] Martin Amis, 'The Palace of the End – The First War of the Age of Proliferation Will Not Be an Oil-Grab so Much as an Expression of Pure Power', *The Guardian*, 4 March 2003.

[18] Simon Schama, 'Onward Christian Soldiers', *The Guardian*, 5 November 2004.

[19] Quoted in Alex Hannaford, 'Who Can Decide Who is the Worst of the Worst and Who Dies?', *The Guardian*, 22 November 2004.

[20] Editorial, *The New York Times*, 26 June 2004.

[21] James Meek, 'People the Law Forgot', *The Guardian*, 3 December 2003.

[22] Editorial, *The New York Times*, 26 June 2004.

[23] Sylvester J. and Vickie A. Schieber, 'Justice Not Served', *The Washington Post*, 13 June 2004.

[24] US Department of Justice Report, cited in Fox Butterfield, 'Despite a Drop in Crime, an Increase in Inmates', *The New York Times*, 8 November 2004.

[25] Summary Findings, US Department of Justice, Office of Justice Programs, Bureau of Justice Statistics, June 2002.

[26] Will Hutton, *The World We're In*, London: Little, Brown, 2002, p. 33.

[27] Prison Statistics Scotland, Statistical Bulletin CrJ/2001/10, The Scottish Executive, Edinburgh, May 2003, p. 11, Chart 7 Prison Population Rate per 100,000 Population in 2002.

[28] Summary Findings, US Department of Justice, op. cit.

[29] Richard Vedder, Lowell Galloway and David C. Clingman, cited in Michael Moore, *Stupid White Men*, New York: HarperCollins, 2001, p. 62.

[30] Fox Butterfield, 'Despite a Drop in Crime, an Increase in Inmates', *The New York Times*, 8 November 2004.

[31] Summary Findings, US Department of Justice, op. cit.

[32] Adam Liptak, 'State Can Make Inmate Sane Enough to Execute', *The New York Times*, 11 February 2003.

[33] Michael Janofsky, 'Utah Officials Looking for Firing Squad', *The New York Times*, 28 May 2003.

[34] David Rennie, 'Governor's Crusade to End Death Penalty' *The Daily Telegraph*, 12 October 2002.

[35] Jodi Wilgoren, 'Governor Assails System's Errors as He Empties Illinois Death Row', *The New York Times*, 12 January 2003.

[36] Protocol No. 6 to the Convention for the Protection of Human Rights and Fundamental Freedoms concerning the abolition of the death penalty, as amended by Protocol No. 11, Council of Europe, Strasbourg, 28.IV.1983 and Chart of Signatures and Ratifications, Council of Europe (www.coe.int) website, 10 June 2003.

37 Ryan S. King and Marc Mauer, *Aging Behind Bars: "Three Strikes" Seven Years Later*, Washington, DC: The Sentencing Project, August 2001, p. 3.

38 Ibid., p. 3, n.2.

39 S. Turner, P.W. Greenwood, E. Chen and T. Fain, 'The Impact of Truth-in-Sentencing and Three Strikes Legislation: Prison Populations, State Budgets, and Crime Rates', *Stanford Law & Policy Review*, vol. 11, no. 1, Winter 1999, pp. 75–91.

40 California State statistics online: justice.hdcdojnet.state.ca.us/cjsc_stats.

41 *Aging Behind Bars*, op. cit., pp. 5–6.

42 Quoted in Lou Cannon, 'A Dark Side to 3-Strike Laws', *The Washington Post*, 20 June 1994.

43 'Local Election/District Attorney: Three-Strike Cases are a Key Area of Disagreement', *The Los Angeles Times*, 5 November 2000.

44 'Fairness Strikes Out', *The New York Times* editorial, 7 March 2003.

45 P.G. Zimbardo, 'Transforming California's Prisons into Expensive Old Age Homes for Felons: Enormous Hidden Costs and Consequences for California's Taxpayers', San Francisco, CA: Center on Juvenile and Criminal Justice, 1994.

46 Molly Evans, 'Before Texas Spends More on Prisons – Let's Think', *Fort Worth Star-Telegram*, 31 August 2000 commenting on the Justice Policy Institute study 'Texas Tough'.

47 Neely Tucker, 'Study Warns of Rising Tide of Released Inmates', *The Washington Post*, 21 May 2003, reporting on *Invisible Punishment: The Collateral Consequences of Mass Incarceration*, Washington, DC: The Sentencing Project, 2003.

48 Fox Butterfield, 'Inmates Go Free to Help States Reduce Deficits', *The New York Times*, 19 December 2002.

49 *Losing the Vote - The Impact of Felony Disenfranchisement Laws in the United States*, New York: Human Rights Watch and Washington, DC: The Sentencing Project, October 1998, pp. 17–18.

50 Ibid., pp. 4–5.

51 Ibid., p. 7.

52 See Greg Palast, *The Best Democracy Money Can Buy*, London: Pluto Press, 2002.

53 Milly Ivins and Lou Dubose, *Shrub: The Short but Happy Political Life of George W. Bush*, New York: Vintage, 2000, p. 143.

54 Quoted in Ron Suskind, 'Without a Doubt', *The New York Times Magazine*, 17 October 2004.

55 Judy Bachrach, 'John Ashcroft's Patriot Games', *Vanity Fair*, February 2004.

56 'John Ashcroft's Patriot Games', op. cit.

57 *The New York Times* editorial, 20 January 2005.

58 Ann W. O'Neill, 'Miami Federal Court Has "Secret Docket" to Keep Some Cases Hidden from Public', *South Florida Sun-Sentinel*, 9 January 2004.

59 Eric Lichtbau, 'FBI Said to Lag on Translations of Terror Tapes', *The New York Times*, 28 September 2004.

60 Maki Becker and Greg Gittrich, 'Weapons Still Fly at Airports', *New York Daily News*, 4 September 2003.

61 Lewis Lapham, 'Power Points', *Harper's*, August 2002, p. 9.

8 See No Evil, Hear No Evil, Speak No Evil: US Elections, Media and Think Tanks

1 'US Elections 2004 Special Report', *The Guardian*, 18 December 2004.

2 US Federal Election Commission, 'Voter Registration and Turnout 2000', May 2003.

3 Ibid.

4 George Monbiot, 'The Rescue Parties', *The Guardian*, 12 November 2002.

5 US Federal Election Commission, 'International Voter Turnout', May 2003.

6 'The Rescue Parties', op. cit.

7 Edward Walsh, 'Election Turnout Rose Slightly, to 39.3%, GOP Mobilization Credited; Participation Was Down in Some Democratic Areas', *The Washington Post*, 8 November 2002.

8 David Brooks, 'The Bush Democrats', *The New York Times*, 13 January 2004.

9 Francis X. Clines, 'The Graduate Students Search for Signs of Intelligent Campaign Life', *The New York Times*, 4 October 2004.

10 Richard Pérez-Peña, 'As End Nears, New York Race Sets a Record', *The New York Times*, 26 October 2002.

11 US Federal Election Commission figures, released on 14 December 2004.

12 Jeffrey H. Birnbaum, *The Money Men: How the Media Undermine American Democracy*, New York: Crown, 2000, p. 3.

13 Robert Bryce, 'Friends in High Places – Pipe Dreams', extract from his book *Pipe Dreams*, *The Guardian*, 6 November 2002.

14 Greg Palast, *The Best Democracy Money Can Buy*, London: Pluto Press, 2002, p. 119.

15 Thomas B. Edsall and Jonathan Weisman, 'Wall Street Firms Funnel Millions to Bush', *The Washington Post*, 24 May 2004.

16 James V. Grimaldi and Thomas B. Edsall, 'Super Rich Step into Political Vacuum', *The Washington Post*, 17 October 2004.

17 'The Graduate Students Search for Signs of Intelligent Campaign Life', op. cit.

18 Dana Milbank and Jim VandeHei, 'From Bush, Unprecedented Negativity', *The Washington Post*, 31 May 2004.

19 Elizabeth Drew, 'Hung Up in Washington', *The New York Review of Books*, vol. 51, no. 2, 12 February 2004.

20 Michael Moore, *Stupid White Men*, New York: HarperCollins, 2001, pp. 107–108.

21 James V. Risser, 'Endangered Species', *American Journalism Review*, June 1998.

22 Bartholomew H. Sparrow, *Uncertain Guardians: The News Media as a Political Institution*, Baltimore, MA: Johns Hopkins University Press, 1999, cited in Hutton, p. 176.

23 *Stupid White Men*, op. cit., p. 86.

24 Frank Rich, 'Why are We Back in Vietnam?', *The New York Times*, 26 October 2003.

25 Carla Brooks Johnston, *Screened Out: How the Media Control Us and What We Can Do About It*, New York: M.E. Sharpe, 2000.

26 *Stupid White Men*, op. cit., p. 86.

27 Cited in Duncan Campbell, 'Los Angeles Dispatch – Know Thine Enemies', *The Guardian*, 8 April 2003.

28 Frank Ahrens, 'FCC Votes to Ease Media Ownership Rules', *The Washington Post*, 2 June 2003, 'There's No Exit From the Matrix', *The New York Times*, 25 May 2003 and www.grazingsheep.com.

[29] Ted Turner, 'My Beef with Big Media', *The Washington Monthly*, July/August 2004.

[30] Bill Kovach and Tom Rosenstiel, 'All News Media Inc.', *The New York Times*, 7 January 2003.

[31] 'Los Angeles Dispatch – Know Thine Enemies', op. cit.

[32] Amy Goodman and David Goodman, *The Exception to the Rulers*, London: Arrow Books, 2004, p. 194.

[33] 'My Beef with Big Media', op. cit.

[34] Alexandra Marks, 'Media Future; Risk of Monopoly?', *The Christian Science Monitor*, 19 September 2002.

[35] FCC Study No. 4, Brown Williams, 2002, cited in Dean Baker, *Democracy Unhinged: More Media Concentration Means Less Public Discourse, A Critique of the FCC Studies on Media Ownership*, Washington, DC: Department for Professional Employees, AFL-CIO, 2002, p. iv.

[36] *Washington Post* article, 28 March 2003, cited in Bob Edwards, 'The Press and Freedom: Some Disturbing Trends', editorial in *The Courier-Journal*, Louisville, Kentucky, 20 April 2003, adapted from his 8 April 2003 lecture to the University of Kentucky.

[37] 'The Press and Freedom: Some Disturbing Trends', op. cit.

[38] Cited in Will Hutton, *The World We're In*, London: Little, Brown, 2002, p. 174.

[39] 'Formal Comments on Media Ownership', presented by Amy Mitchell, Associate Director of the Project for Excellence in Journalism, at the Forum on Media Ownership, Columbia University, 16 January 2003.

[40] *Washington Post* article, 28 March 2003, quoted by Bob Edwards, 'The Press and Freedom: Some Disturbing Trends', op. cit.

[41] Frank Rich, 'The NASCAR Nightly News: Anchorman Get Your Gun', *The New York Times*, 5 December 2004.

[42] 'Why are We Back in Vietnam?', op. cit.

[43] Ted Turner, 'Monopoly or Democracy?' *The Washington Post*, 30 May 2003.

[44] Quoted in Michael Massing, 'The Unseen War', *The New York Review of Books*, vol. 50, no. 9, 29 May 2003.

[45] Kevin Myers, 'Do I Understand Anything about the US?', *The Irish Times*, 15 June 2004.

[46] Greg Palast, *The Best Democracy Money Can Buy*, UK edition, London: Constable & Robinson, 2003, pp. 11–19.

[47] Paul Harris, 'Vietnam Killing Spree Revelations Shock US, Atrocity to Rival My Lai is Exposed – After 36 Years', *The Observer*, 26 October 2003.

[48] Quoted by Bob Edwards, 'The Press and Freedom: Some Disturbing Trends', op. cit.

[49] See Amy Goodman and David Goodman, *The Exception to the Rulers*, London: Arrow Books, 2004, pp. 14–144.

[50] All comparisons and quotes from 'The Unseen War', op. cit.

[51] Patrick E. Tyler and Janet Elder, 'Poll Finds Most in U.S. Support Delaying a War', *The New York Times*, 14 February 2003.

[52] Gary Younge, 'Now Dissent is Immoral', *The Guardian*, 2 June 2003.

[53] Steve Randall and Tara Broughel, 'Amplifying Officials, Squelching Dissent', quoted in *The Exception to the Rulers*, op. cit.

[54] John Simpson, 'The BBC Has Merely Done Its Duty – That's the Problem', *The Sunday Telegraph*, 6 July 2003.

[55] 'Now Dissent is Immoral', op. cit.

[56] Frank Rich, 'Will We Need a New "All the President's Men"?', *The New York Times*, 14 October 2004.

[57] Cited in 'Monopoly or Democracy?', op. cit.

[58] Mary Maher, 'Searching for Alienated Voters Amid Silent Steel Mills', *The Irish Times*, 11 October 2004.

[59] Barbara Ehrenreich, *Nickel and Dimed*, New York: Henry Holt and Company, 2001, p. 43.

[60] John Simpson, *The Wars against Saddam*, London: Macmillan, 2003, p. 270.

[61] 'Editorial: War and the Press', *The Asahi Shimbun* (Japan), 17 October 2004.

[62] 'Will We Need a New "All the President's Men"?', op. cit.

[63] This has been covered in many pieces – see, for example, Michael Manning, 'Iraq: Now They Tell Us', *The New York Review of Books*, vol. LI, no. 3, 26 February 2004.

[64] Frank Pastore, 'Now the Left in the US Must be Defeated in the Realm of Ideas', *The Irish Times* (*LA Times/Washington Post* Service), 10 November 2004.

[65] Unless otherwise attributed, all historical figures on think tank and related funding from Sally Covington, 'How Conservative Philanthropies and Think Tanks Transform US Policy', mediafiter.org/CAQ/caq63/caq63thintank.html, 27 December 2004.

[66] Michael Dolny, 'Special Report: Think Tank Coverage', June 2004, see www.fair.org/extra/0405/think-tank.html.

[67] Bob Herbert, 'Voting without the Facts', *The New York Times*, 8 November 2004.

[68] Brian Whitaker, 'US Thinktanks Give Lessons in Foreign Policy', *The Guardian*, 19 August 2002.

[69] Paul Gillespie, 'Conservative Group which Sets Bush's Foreign Agenda', *The Irish Times*, 1 March 2003.

[70] See 'US Thinktanks Give Lessons in Foreign Policy' and 'Iraq: Now They Tell Us', op. cit.

[71] 'US Thinktanks Give Lessons in Foreign Policy', op. cit.

[72] American Enterprise Institute (AEI) website, September 2002.

[73] 'US Thinktanks Give Lessons in Foreign Policy', op. cit.

[74] See Sally Covington, 'How Conservative Philanthropies and Think Tanks Transform US Policy', op. cit.

[75] Paul Harris, 'How Bush Tapped into a Well of Faith', *The Observer*, 7 November 2004.

9 THE NEOCONSERVATIVES AND US POWER: WASHINGTON'S REVOLUTIONARIES AND THEIR HYPERPOWER VILLAGE

[1] Rupert Cornwell, 'War is Almost upon Us', *The Independent*, 6 March 2003.

[2] Frances FitzGerald, 'George Bush & The World', *The New York Review of Books*, 26 September 2002.

[3] See Mark Lilla, 'Leo Strauss: The European', *The New York Review of Books*, 21 October 2004. Also Elizabeth Drew, 'The Neocons in Power', *The New York Review of Books*, 12 February 2004.

[4] 'George Bush & The World', op. cit.

[5] Ibid.

[6] 'War is Almost upon Us', op. cit.

[7] 'George Bush & The World', op. cit.

[8] Council for a Livable World, Washington, DC website, 29 October 2002.

[9] Jimmy Carter, 'The Troubling New Face of America', *The Washington Post*, 5 September 2002.

[10] *Rebuilding America's Defenses – Strategy, Forces and Resources for a New Century*, Washington, DC: Project for the New American Century (PNAC), September 2000, p. ii.

[11] Patrick E. Tyler, 'US Strategy Plan Calls for Insuring No Rivals Develop', *The New York Times*, 8 March 1992.

[12] *Statement of Principles*, Washington, DC: Project for the New American Century (PNAC), 3 June 1997.

[13] PNAC letter to President Clinton, 26 January 1998.

[14] *Rebuilding America's Defenses: Strategy, Forces and Resources for a New Century*, op. cit.

[15] Robert Kagan, *Paradise & Power: America and Europe in the New World Order*, London: Atlantic Books, 2003.

[16] Ibid., pp. 16–17.

[17] Ibid., p. 24.

[18] *The National Security Strategy of the United States of America*, Washington, DC: The White House, September 2002, p. 30.

[19] Will Hutton, *The World We're In*, London: Little, Brown, 2002, p. 60.

[20] John Koster, 'Columbian Tragedy', *War Monthly*, Issue 44, 1977, p. 35.

[21] Center for Defense Information, *Military Almanac 2001–2002*, Washington, DC: Center for Defense Information, 2002, p. 21.

[22] Hubert Védrine and Dominique Moïsi, *France in the Age of Globalisation*, Washington, DC: Brookings Institution, 2001.

[23] Professor Janine R. Wedel, 'Flex Power – A Capital Way to Gain Clout, Inside and Out', *The Washington Post*, 12 December 2004.

[24] David Halberstam, *War in a Time of Peace: Bush, Clinton and the Generals*, London: Bloomsbury, 2003.

[25] *The Documentary History of the Truman Presidency*, vol. 23, *The Central Intelligence Agency: Its Founding and the Dispute Over its Mission, 1945–1954*, US National Security Archives.

[26] Stansfield Turner, 'Five Steps to Better Spying', *The New York Times*, 9 February 2004.

[27] 'Intelligence: The United States', *Encyclopaedia Britannica* CD-ROM, 2001.

[28] John Pike, *Intelligence Agencies: Estimates of Budget and Personnel, 1998*, Washington, DC: Federation of American Scientists, July 1998.

[29] *Military Almanac 2001–2002*, op. cit., p. 65.

[30] Thomas Powers, 'War and Its Consequences', *The New York Review of Books*, 27 March 2003, reviewing Dana Priest, *The Mission: Waging War and Keeping Peace with America's Military*, New York: Norton, 2003.

[31] Philip Shenon, 'Establishing New Agency is Expected to Take Years', *The New York Times*, 20 November 2002.

[32] Peter Shaffer, *The Gift of The Gorgon*, London: Viking, 1993, Act II.

[33] Cited in Seumas Milne, 'The Opponents of War on Iraq are Not the Appeasers', *The Guardian*, 13 February 2003.

[34] 'Bush Ready to Use Nuclear Weapons', *The Daily Telegraph*, 31 January 2003.

[35] *Histoire de France*, Paris: Larousse-Bordas, 1998, p. 560.

[36] Speech at Cape Town, South Africa, 3 February 1960, *Pointing the Way*, 1972,

from *The Oxford Dictionary of Quotations*, New York: Oxford University Press, 1999, p. 487, 19.

37 *Histoire de France*, Paris: Larousse-Bordas, 1998, p. 568.

38 Javier Solana, 'Atlantic Drift', *The Guardian*, 10 July 2003.

39 'The Neocons in Power', op. cit.

40 Felipe Gonzalez, 'Les Leçons du chaos irakien', *Le Nouvel Observateur*, (translated from Spanish by Isabelle Gugnon), 7–13 August, 2003, p. 59.

41 *The National Security Strategy of the United States of America*, op. cit., p. 3.

42 Friedrich Nietzsche, *Beyond Good and Evil*, translated by R.J. Hollingdale, London: Penguin Classics, 1973, Section 258.

43 Cited in Bruce Detwiler, *Nietzsche and the Politics of Aristocratic Radicalism*, Chicago, IL: University of Chicago Press, 1990, p. 106.

44 Friedrich Nietzsche, *On the Genealogy of Morals*, translated by Walter Kaufmann and R.J. Hollingdale, London: Random House, 1969, Essay One, Section 13.

45 Friedrich Nietzsche, *Thus Spake Zarathustra*, translated by R.J. Hollingdale, London: Penguin Classics, 1969, Part One.

46 Thomas Hobbes, *Leviathan*, London, 1651, ch. 13, cited in *Humanity – A Moral History of the Twentieth Century*, Jonathan Glover, London: Jonathan Cape, 1999, p. 135.

47 'Flex Power – A Capital Way to Gain Clout, Inside and Out', op. cit.

48 Ron Suskind, 'Without A Doubt!', *The New York Times Magazine*, 17 October 2004.

10 GLOBAL WAR ON TERRORISM (GWOT): DOWN JUNGLE TRAILS OR UP GARDEN PATHS?

1 Andrew Murray, 'Hostages of the Empire', *The Guardian*, 1 July 2003.

2 Eric Mottram, *Blood on the Nash Ambassador: Investigations in American Culture*, London: Hutchinson Radius, 1983, p. 139.

3 Chalmers Johnson, *Blowback*, New York: Henry Holt and Company, Owl Books, 2001 (hardcover Metropolitan Books published 2000), p. 7.

4 Ed Vulliamy, 'The President Rides Out', *The Observer*, 26 January 2003.

5 See George Crile, *Charlie Wilson's War: The Extraordinary Story of the Largest Covert Operation in History*, New York: Atlantic Monthly Press, 2003.

6 Cited in Norman Podhoretz, 'World War IV', *Commentary Magazine*, September 2004.

7 *The 9/11 Commission Report*, Washington, DC: Report of the National Commission on Terrorist Attacks Upon the United States, July 2004, p. 149.

8 US National Security Council Memo: 'The Millennium Terrorist Alert – Next Steps', undated, cited in The *9/11 Commission Report*, op. cit., p. 183.

9 *The 9/11 Commission Report*, op. cit., p. 156.

10 *The 9/11 Commission Report*, op. cit., pp. 160–61.

11 *The War on Terrorism*, Pitcairn Trust Lecture in World Affairs, 10 October 2002, Foreign Policy Research Institute, fpri.org.

12 James Glanz, 'Towers' Strengths Not Tested for a Fire, Inquiry Suggests', *The New York Times*, 8 May 2003.

13 *Blowback*, op. cit., p. 7.

14 Ibid., p. 33.

15 Thomas L. Friedman, 'A Theory of Everything', *The New York Times*, 1 June 2003.

16 David Hirst, 'Arab States Paralysed by Fear of Their People and the US', *The Guardian*, 1 March 2003.

17 Avishai Margalit, 'The Wrong War', *The New York Review of Books*, 13 March 2003.

18 John Simpson, 'Why the US Military is Not About to Go Charging Into Iran', *The Sunday Telegraph*, 1 June 2003.

19 Michael Massing, 'The Unseen War', *The New York Review of Books*, vol. 50, no. 9, 29 May 2003.

20 General Sir Frank Kitson, *Low-intensity Operations: Subversion, Insurgency and Peacekeeping*, London: Faber & Faber, 1971.

21 Malachi O'Doherty, *The Trouble with Guns*, Belfast: Blackstaff Press, 1998, p. 65.

22 Edited extract from Stella Rimington's autobiography *Open Secret*, published in *The Guardian Weekly*, 12–18 September 2002, p. 22.

23 *The War on Terrorism*, op. cit.

24 Seymour Hersh, 'Rumsfeld's Dirty War on Terror', *The Guardian*, 13 September 2004, extract from Seymour M. Hersh, *Chain of Command: The Road from 9/11 to Abu Ghraib*, London: Penguin Press, 2004.

25 Jason Burke, 'Secret World of US Jails', *The Observer*, 13 June 2004.

26 Mark Danner, 'We Are All Torturers Now', *The New York Times*, 6 January 2005.

27 'Rumsfeld's Dirty War on Terror', op. cit.

28 Ibid.

29 Liam Reid, 'Damning Red Cross Report on Abuse of Iraqis', *The Irish Times*, 11 May 2004.

30 Robert Fisk, 'Ariel Sharon has walked into a trap. And we are following him – Osama bin Laden is writing the script in the war against terror', *The Independent on Sunday*, 1 December 2002.

31 Bill Keller, 'The Sunshine Warrior', *The New York Times*, 22 September 2002.

32 Maureen Dowd, 'The Mirror Has Two Faces' *The New York Times*, 1 February 2004.

33 Jason Burke, 'Terror's Myriad Faces – Those Leading the War Against the Bombers Misunderstand the True Nature of al-Qaeda', *The Observer*, 18 May 2003.

34 Josef Joffe, 'Round 1 Goes to Mr. Big', *The New York Times*, 10 February 2003.

35 Richard A. Clarke, *Against All Enemies*, New York: Free Press (Simon & Schuster), 2004, p. 274.

36 Ibid., p. 275.

37 Ibid., p. 245.

38 Seymour M. Hersh, 'The Other War', *The New Yorker*, 12 April 2004.

39 'World War IV', op. cit.

40 Ibid.

41 Gary Younge, 'This is Not a Vote about Ideas', *The Guardian*, 2 November 2004.

42 Cited in Seumas Milne, 'A War that Can't Be Won', *The Guardian*, 21 November 2002.

43 'Abandoned Afghanistan', *The Boston Globe* editorial, 3 November 2002.

44 Cited in 'The Other War', op. cit.

45 Barry Bearak, 'Unreconstructed', *The New York Times Magazine*, 1 June 2003.

46 Warren M. Christopher, 'Iraq Belongs on the Back Burner', *The New York Times*, 31 December 2002.

47 'The Other War', op. cit.

11 BAGHDAD OR BUST

[1] Seymour M. Hersh, 'Selective Intelligence', *The New Yorker*, 12 May 2003.

[2] Nicholas D. Kristof, 'The Man with No Ear', *The New York Times*, 27 June 2003.

[3] George Monbiot, 'Dreamers and Idiots', *The Guardian*, 11 November 2003.

[4] Bob Woodward, *Bush at War*, London: Pocket Books, 2003, pp. 145–6.

[5] On World War One commander Sir Douglas Haig, quoted in Nicholas D. Kristof, 'Al Jazeera: Out-Foxing Fox', *The New York Times*, 3 July 2004.

[6] *Bush at War*, op. cit., p. 27.

[7] Ibid., p. 49.

[8] Ibid., p. 60.

[9] Ibid., p. 83.

[10] Ibid., p. 61.

[11] Ibid.

[12] Ibid., pp, 145–6.

[13] Glenn Kessler, 'US Decision on Iraq Has Puzzling Past', *The Washington Post*, 12 January 2003.

[14] Colin Powell referring to the neoconservatives in a conversation with UK Foreign Secretary Jack Straw, from James Naughtie, *The Accidental American: Tony Blair and the Presidency*, cited in Sidney Blumenthal, 'Colin and the Crazies', *The Guardian*, 18 November 2004.

[15] Cited in *The National Security Strategy of the United States of America*, Washington, DC: The White House, September 2002, p. 13.

[16] Ashton B. Carter and William J. Perry, *Preventive Defence*, Washington, DC: The Brookings Institute, 1999, p. 12.

[17] *Bush at War*, op. cit., pp. 332–5.

[18] From the full text of the speech by Vice-President Dick Cheney to the Veterans of Foreign Wars National Convention, Nashville, Tennessee, 27 August 2002.

[19] *Bush at War*, op. cit., pp. 344–5.

[20] Ibid., pp. 345–8.

[21] 'The Man with No Ear', op. cit.

[22] John Simpson, 'Why I Was Wrong – We're Losing the Battle for Hearts and Minds', *The Sunday Telegraph*, 30 March 2003.

[23] 'Dreamers and Idiots', op. cit.

[24] Ibid.

[25] Daniel Benjamin and Steven Simon, 'The Next Debate: Al Quaeda Link', *The New York Times*, 20 July 2003.

[26] Vincent Jauvert, 'Quand Chirac se préparait à la guerre', *Le Nouvel Observateur*, Paris, no. 2002, 20–26 March 2003, p. 48.

[27] Walter Pincus, 'US Predicts Coup if Iraq is Attacked', *The Washington Post*, 7 October 2002.

[28] Rory McCarthy in Baghdad, Peter Beaumont in London and Ed Vulliamy in New York, 'Saddam Risks War over Arms Dossier', *The Observer*, 8 December 2002.

[29] Steven R. Weisman, 'A Long, Winding Road to a Diplomatic Dead End', *The New York Times*, 17 March 2003.

[30] 'Quand Chirac se préparait à la guerre', op. cit.

[31] James Risen, 'Iraq Said to Have Tried to Reach Last-Minute Deal to Avert War', *The New York Times*, 6 November 2003.

[32] Conor O'Clery, 'Powell Departure a Victory for Conservatives', *The Irish Times*, 16 November 2004.

[33] Bruce. B. Auster, Mark Mazzetti and Edward T. Pound, 'Truth and Consequences', *US News and World Report*, Nation & World, 9 June 2003.

[34] Dan Plesch and Richard Norton-Taylor, 'Straw, Powell had Serious Doubts over Their Iraqi Weapons Claims', *The Guardian*, 31 May 2003.

[35] Kim Sengupta and Anne Penketh, 'Kelly "Should Have Won Nobel Prize" for Work on Iraqi Arms', *The Independent*, 25 July 2003.

[36] Paul Harris and Martin Bright in London, Taji and Ed Helmore in New York, 'US Rivals Turn on Each Other as Weapons Search Draws a Blank', *The Observer*, 11 May 2003.

[37] Jacques Isnard, 'Premier survol de l'Irak par un avion-espion U2', *Le Monde*, 19 February 2003.

[38] 'Selective Intelligence', op. cit.

[39] George Criley, *Charlie Wilson's War*, New York: Atlantic Monthly Press, 2003, p. 14.

[40] Eddie Holt, 'US Minds are Being Poisoned', *The Irish Times*, 5 April 2003.

[41] Paul Krugman, 'Strictly Business', *New York Review of Books*, vol. 50, no. 18, 20 November 2003.

[42] Senator Robert Byrd, 'Why I Weep for My Country', an edited version of his speech, *The Observer*, 23 March 2003.

[43] Sidney Blumenthal, 'Bush and Blair – the Betrayal' *The Guardian*, 14 November 2003.

[44] Andrew Buncombe, 'Carter Savages Blair and Bush', *The Independent*, 22 March 2004.

[45] Normitsu Onishi, 'After 8-Year Trial: Cultist is Sentenced to Death', *The New York Times*, 28 February 2004.

[46] Serge Raffy, 'Madrid Debout', *Le Nouvel Observateur*, Paris, 18–28 March 2004.

[47] John Simpson, 'I Shall be Safe from the Gas but People will be Dying All Around Me', *The Sunday Telegraph*, 19 January 2003.

[48] Owen J. Coté, 'Weapons of Mass Confusion', *The Boston Review*, April/May 2003.

[49] Joby Warrick, 'U.S. Claim on Iraqi Nuclear Program is Called into Question', *The Washington Post*, 24 January 2003.

[50] Robert Novak, 'Mission to Niger', *The Washington Post*, 14 July 2003 and Conor O'Clery, 'CIA Leak Continues to Haunt White House', *The Irish Times*, 4 October 2003.

[51] *The 9/11 Commission Report*, Washington, DC: Report of the National Commission on Terrorist Attacks Upon the United States, July 2004, pp. 228–9 (Atta's Alleged Trip to Prague) and pp. 334–6 (10.3. Phase Two and the Question of Iraq).

[52] Quoted in 'Selective Intelligence', op. cit.

[53] Cited in Deglán de Brádún, 'Elections in Iraq', interview with Koffi Annan, *The Irish Times*, 11 October 2004.

[54] William J. Broad, 'The Impossible Task for America's Spies', *The New York Times Magazine*, 11 May 2003.

[55] Nicholas D. Kristof, 'Missing in Action: Truth', *The New York Times*, 6 May 2003.

[56] Nicholas D. Kristof, 'Iraq War: The First Question', *The New York Times*, 28 January 2003.

[57] Britain, UNSCOM and Iraq, UK Foreign Office: http://special.fco.gov.uk/, 23 July 2003.

[58] James Risen, David E. Sanger and Thom Shanker, 'In Sketchy Data, Trying to Gauge the Iraq Threat', *The New York Times*, 20 July 2003.

[59] Robin Cook, 'Why I Had to Leave the Cabinet', *The Guardian*, 18 March 2003.

[60] *Iraq's Weapons of Mass Destruction: A Net Assessment*, Statement by Dr John Chipman, Director, London: International Institute for Strategic Studies, 9 September 2002, p. 5.

[61] Ibid., p. 6.

[62] Ibid., p. 7.

[63] 'CIA Says Saddam Unlikely to Launch Attack on US', Reuters, on www.ireland.com (*The Irish Times*), 9 October 2002.

[64] 'Selective Intelligence', op. cit.

[65] Ibid.

[66] 'The Impossible Task for America's Spies', op. cit.

[67] Bill Keller, 'The Boys Who Cried Wolfowitz', *The New York Times*, 12 June 2003.

[68] Maureen Dowd, 'The Chicago Way', *The New York Times*, 9 November 2003.

[69] In an interview on NBC's *Meet the Press*, cited in Glenn Kessler, 'U.S. Decision on Iraq Has Puzzling Past', *The Washington Post*, 12 January 2003.

[70] Foreign affairs essay in 1992, quoted in Nicholas D. Kristof, 'Losses, Before Bullets Fly', *The New York Times*, 7 March 2003.

[71] From President George H. Bush, *A World Transformed*, a 1998 book quoted in 'Losses, Before Bullets Fly', op. cit.

[72] Robert Fisk, 'The Case Against War: A Conflict Driven by the Self-Interest of America', *The Independent*, 15 February 2003. See also *A Clean Break: A New Strategy for Securing the Realm* on www.israeleconomy.org/strat1.htm.

[73] Michael Scott Doran, 'Remove The Wedge? Palestine, Iraq, and American Strategy', *Foreign Affairs*, January/February 2003.

[74] Cited in Brian Whitaker, 'Spoils of War' *The Guardian*, 13 October 2003.

[75] 'Thank god for the death of the UN, its abject failure gave us only anarchy. The world needs order', Richard Perle, *The Guardian*, 21 March 2003.

[76] *On War* (1832–4), bk. 8, ch. 6, sect. B. Karl Von Clausewitz, from *The Oxford Dictionary of Quotations*, New York: Oxford University Press, 1999, p. 219, 19.

[77] Cited in Ben Russell, 'So, Mr Straw, Why Did We Go to War?', *The Independent*, 15 May 2003.

[78] Cited in David Usborne, 'WMD Just a Convenient Excuse for War, Admits Wolfowitz', *The Independent*, 30 May 2003.

[79] Cited in Richard Norton-Taylor, 'Tell Us the Truth about the Dossier', *The Guardian*, 15 July 2003.

12 BAGHDAD AND BUST: CATASTROPHIC SUCCESS AND HILLBILLY ARMOUR

[1] In an interview with *Time* magazine, 29 August 2004, cited in Dana Millbank, 'At GOP Convention, Echoes of 9/11', *The Washington Post*, 30 August 2004.

[2] *The New Yorker*, 24 November 2003.

[3] Speaking to the House Budget Committee, 27 February 2003, cited in James Fallows, 'Blind into Baghdad', *The Atlantic Monthly*, January/February 2004.

[4] From Bob Woodward's *Plan of Attack*, cited in Conor O'Clery, 'The Shaming of America', *The Irish Times*, 8 May 2004.

[5] Eric Schmitt, 'Troops' Queries Leave Rumsfeld on Defensive', *The New York*

Times and Reuters, 'Troops Complain to Rumsfeld About Gear', *The Irish Times*, 9 December 2004.

[6] See, amongst others, David Fulghum, 'Info Warfare to Invade Air Defense Networks', *Aviation Week*, 30 November 2003 and Peter Baker, 'Casualties of an Undeclared War', *The Washington Post*, 22 December 2002.

[7] See Lieutenant General T. Michael Mosley, 'Operation Iraqi Freedom – By the Numbers', United States Central Command Air Forces – USCENTAF, Assessment and Analysis Division, 30 April 2003.

[8] Joshua Davis, 'If We Run Out of Batteries, This War is Screwed', *Wired*, www.wired.com/wired/archive/11.06/battlefield_pr.html.

[9] Michael R. Gordon, 'The Strategy to Secure Iraq Did Not Foresee a 2nd War', *The New York Times*, 19 October 2004.

[10] Rick Atkinson, 'The Long, Blinding Road to War', *The Washington Post*, 7 March 2004.

[11] James P. Rubin, 'Stumbling into War', *Foreign Affairs*, September/October 2003.

[12] Michael R. Gordon, 'Poor Intelligence Misled Troops About Risk of Drawn-Out War', *The New York Times*, 20 October 2004.

[13] Rick Atkinson, Peter Baker and Thomas E. Ricks, 'Confused Start, Decisive End', *The Washington Post*, 13 April 2003.

[14] Bill Keller, 'Rumsfeld and the Generals', *The New York Times*, 5 April 2003.

[15] 'Confused Start, Decisive End', op. cit.

[16] 'The Long, Blinding Road to War', op. cit.

[17] George Packer, 'Dreaming of Democracy', *The New York Times Magazine*, 2 March 2003.

[18] John Simpson, 'Why I Was Wrong – We're Losing the Battle for Hearts and Minds', *The Sunday Telegraph*, 30 March 2003.

[19] Rick Atkinson, 'After Chaos in the Capital, Losses Climbed', *The Washington Post*, 9 March 2004.

[20] 'Full List of Casualties', *The Guardian*, 23 April 2003.

[21] CNN, 'Commander in Chief Lands on *USS Lincoln*', 2 May 2003 – www.cnn.com/2003/ALL POLIITCS/05/01/bush.carrier.landing.

[22] Cited in Paul Krugman, 'Man on Horseback', *The New York Times*, 6 May 2003.

[23] From Bob Woodward's *Plan of Attack*, cited in William Safire, 'Politicians Confuse their Metaphors: If you Break It, Don't Fix It', *The New York Times*, 17 October 2004.

[24] 'The Strategy to Secure Iraq Did Not Foresee a 2nd War', op. cit.

[25] Reuters, 'India Says No to US Request for Troops in Iraq', *The Irish Times*, 15 July 2003.

[26] 'The Strategy to Secure Iraq Did Not Foresee a 2nd War', op. cit.

[27] 'Harold Meyerson, Enron-like Unreality', *The Washington Post*, 13 May 2003.

[28] 'Blind into Baghdad', op. cit.

[29] Eric Schmitt and Joel Brinkley, 'State Dept. Study Foresaw Trouble Now Plaguing Iraq', *The New York Times*, 19 October 2003.

[30] 'Blind into Baghdad', op. cit.

[31] 'Army Chief: Force to Occupy Iraq Massive', Associated Press in *USA Today*, 25 February 2003.

[32] Michael R. Gordon, 'How Much Is Enough?', *The New York Times*, 30 May 2003.

[33] 'The Strategy to Secure Iraq Did Not Foresee a 2nd War', op. cit.

34 'State Dept. Study Foresaw Trouble Now Plaguing Iraq', op. cit.

35 Paul Martin in Kuwait, Ed Vulliamy in Washington and Gaby Hinsliff, 'US Army Was Told to Protect Looted Museum', *The Observer*, 20 April 2003.

36 Michael R. Gordon, 'U.S. Planning to Regroup Armed Forces in Baghdad, Adding to Military Police', *The New York Times*, 30 April 2003.

37 David Rieff, 'Blueprint for a Mess', *The New York Times Magazine*, 2 November 2003.

38 Michael R. Gordon, 'Debate Lingering on Decision to Dissolve the Iraqi Military', *The New York Times*, 21 October 2004.

39 'Blueprint for a Mess', op. cit.

40 Ariana Eunjung Cha, 'Iraqi Experts Tossed with the Water – Workers Ineligible to Fix Polluted Systems', *The Washington Post*, 27 February 2004.

41 Edmund L. Andrews and Susan Sachs, 'Iraq's Slide into Lawlessness Squanders Good Will for U.S.', *The New York Times*, 18 May 2003.

42 Con Coughlin, 'This is No Way to Run an Occupation', *The Daily Telegraph*, 18 May 2003.

43 'Iraqi Experts Tossed with the Water', op. cit.

44 Rajiv Chandrasekaran, 'As Handover Nears, U.S. Mistakes Loom Large', *The Washington Post*, 20 June 2004.

45 George Packer, 'War after the War', *The New Yorker*, 24 November 2003.

46 'As Handover Nears, U.S. Mistakes Loom Large', op. cit.

47 Paul Krugman, 'Accounting and Accountability', *The New York Times*, 23 July 2004.

48 Quoted in 'As Handover Nears, U.S. Mistakes Loom Large', op. cit.

49 Kanan Makiya, 'Our Hopes Betrayed', *The Observer*, 16 February 2003.

50 General Anthony Zinni, 'Eye on Iraq', remarks at CDI Board of Directors Dinner, 12 May 2004, Washington, DC: Center for Defense Information, 14 May 2004.

51 Lawrence J. Korb, 'Fixing the Mix', *Foreign Affairs*, vol. 83, no. 2, March/April 2004.

52 *Soviet Military Power: An Assessment of the Threat*, Washington, DC: US Department of Defense, 1988, pp. 24–5.

53 See Anthony H. Cordesman, *The Developing Iraq Insurgency: Status at End 2004*, Washington, DC: Center for Strategic and International Studies, working draft, 22 December 2004, in particular from p. 346 for comments on US approach (www.csis.org).

54 Tom Clonan, 'Sophisticated Command Structure Behind Attacks on US Troops in Iraq', *The Irish Times*, 18 July 2003.

55 'Fixing the Mix', op. cit.

56 Thomas E. Ricks, 'General Reported Shortages in Iraq', *The Washington Post*, 18 October 2004.

57 Cited in Thom Shanker and Eric Schmitt, 'Armor Scarce for Big Trucks Transporting Cargo in Iraq', *The New York Times*, 10 December 2004.

58 Eric Schmitt, 'Force Protection – Cargo Flights Added to Cut Risky Land Trips', *The New York Times*, 15 December 2004.

59 Jonathan Weisman, 'Army Posts Scramble to Keep the Troops Equipped', *The Washington Post*, 13 December 2004.

60 Thom Shanker, 'Rumsfeld Doubles Estimate for Cost of Troops in Iraq', *The New York Times*, 10 July 2003.

61 'Sophisticated Command Structure Behind Attacks on US Troops in Iraq', op. cit.

[62] *The Lancet*, 29 October 2004, http://image.thelancet.com/extras/04art10342web.pdf, Baltimore, MD: Center for International Emergency Disaster and Refugee Studies, Johns Hopkins Bloomberg School of Public Health (L. Roberts, PhD and G. Burnham, MD); Baghdad: Department of Community Medicine, College of Medicine, Al-Mustansiriya University (R. Lafta, MD and J. Khudhairi, MD); and New York: School of Nursing, Columbia University (Prof R. Gareld, DrPH).

[63] Seymour M. Hersh, 'The Coming Wars', *The New Yorker*, 24 January 2005.

13 A POST WASHINGTON WORLD

[1] Thomas L. Friedman, 'Two Nations under God', *The New York Times*, 4 November 2004.

[2] *Julius Caesar* (1599), Act V, sc. i.

[3] Letter to his son, 1648, in J.F. af Lundlblad *Svensk Plutark*, 1826, pt. 2.

[4] Speech in London reported in *The Times*, 17 December 1970.

[5] See 'Central Banks Shift Reserves Away from US', *The Financial Times*, 24 January 2005.

[6] 'Scientific Challenge', *The Irish Times* editorial, 15 January 2005.

[7] Bob Herbert, 'Fiddling as Iraq Burns', *The New York Times*, 17 December 2004.

[8] Referring to the 1983 US invasion of Grenada, cited in Jonathan Steele, 'Regime Change, the Prequel', *The Guardian*, 11 October 2003.

[9] See Armand Van Dormael, *Bretton Woods: Birth of a Monetary System*, London: Macmillan, 1978.

[10] See *Report of the Independent Inquiry into the Action of the United Nations During the 1994 Genocide in Rwanda*, New York: UN, December 1999.

[11] Ian Black, 'NATO Chief Scorns Europe Forces', *The Guardian*, 9 November 2002.

[12] UK Ministry of Defence press notice, A400M contract signed, 27 May 2003.

[13] See Sophie Boukhari, Ethirajan Anbarasan and John Kohut, 'James Tobin: Reining in the Markets', *The UNESCO Courier*, 1 February 1999.

[14] David Firestone and Richard Pérez-Peña, 'Power Failure Reveals a Creaky System', *The New York Times*, 15 August 2003.

[15] Larry Elliott, 'In 1973 Rising Oil Prices Meant Recession: Not Now', *The Guardian*, 3 June 2004.

[16] Philip Longman, 'The Global Baby Bust', *Foreign Affairs*, May/June 2004.

[17] Mike Townsend and Paul Harris, 'Now Pentagon Tells Bush Climate Change Will Destroy US', *The Observer*, 22 February 2004.

[18] *A Human Security Doctrine for Europe – The Barcelona Report of the Study Group on Europe's Security Capabilities*, Barcelona: 15 September 2004, p. 7. www.lse.ac.uk/depts/global/studygroup/studygroup.htm.

[19] Ibid.

[20] Ibid.

[21] See David Rohde, *Endgame: The Betrayal and Fall of Srebrenica*, New York: Farrar, Strauss and Giroux, 1997.

[22] Quoted in *The Responsibility to Protect*, Report of the International Commission on Intervention and State Sovereignty, December 2001, p. vii.

[23] See George Monbiot, *The Age of Consent*, Harper Perennial, London 2004.

INDEX

Support **tasc** – a think tank for action on social change

'The limited development of think tanks is a striking feature [of Ireland] for such bodies could do much to focus new thinking about the country's future democratic and political development'

(Report to the Joseph Rowntree Charitable Trust, 2002)

Ireland, almost uniquely in Europe, has relatively few think tanks of any kind and, prior to the establishment of tasc, none whose sole agenda is to foster new thinking on ways to create a more progressive and equal society. Such an independent public policy think tank is long overdue and urgently needed in Ireland.

Your support is essential. If you would like to make a contribution to tasc – a think tank for action on social change – please send your donation to the address below.

tasc – a think tank for action on social change
26 South Frederick St
Dublin 2
tasc

Phone: + 353 1 6169050
E-mail: contact@tascnet.ie
www.tascnet.ie